Applied Econometrics

Applied Econometrics

Potluri Rao   Roger LeRoy Miller

University of Washington

Wadsworth Publishing Company, Inc., Belmont, California

L. C. Cat. Card No.: 71-
147193
ISBN-0-534-00031-2
Printed in the United States
of America

5 6 7 8 9 10—80 79 78

Preface

Econometric theory has progressed a great deal during the last decade. With the availability of computer facilities and the infusion of new concepts, econometrics is becoming increasingly sophisticated. Sophistication, in turn, obscures the fundamental difference between theoretical statistics and econometrics. An econometrician can no longer be content with the distributional properties of an estimator. His objective now is to venture into real life and apply the tools to it. It is not surprising that he encounters numerous problems often ignored by the profession, since ideal textbook-style examples seldom occur in real life.

Even though one estimation procedure may be better than another on paper, the distinction may not be clear in practice. In this book we present some of the questions frequently asked by applied econometricians, and we suggest some answers. We emphasize the relevance of a tool to a practical situation rather than its theoretical properties under appropriate sets of assumptions.

We are grateful to Professor Zvi Griliches for stimulating our interest in applied econometrics. His insistence on applying econometric tools to real life examples made us realize the wide gulf between theory and practice in econometrics. Our indebtedness for his help in the preparation of this book cannot be expressed in mere words. We also express our thanks to Professors Yoram Barzel and C. Mike Rahm for commenting on various aspects of the manuscript.

We acknowledge the assistance received from the Institute for Economic Research, University of Washington, in preparing the manuscript. We thank Sharyl Weber for her speedy typing and also Mrs. Marion Dunsmore and Catherine McDole for their expert editorial assistance. Of course, we alone are responsible for any possible errors or omissions.

We are indebted to the Literary Executor of the late Sir Ronald A. Fisher, F.R.S., and to Oliver & Boyd, Edinburgh for their permission to reprint tables from their book *Statistical Methods for Research Workers.*

Contents

Applied Econometrics

1

Introduction to the
Linear Regression Model

The starting point for econometric research is a regression equation model which postulates a causal relationship between a dependent variable and one or more independent variables. A variable is called dependent because it is supposed to be functionally dependent on other variables. The regression model attempts to explain observed changes in a dependent variable as being caused by changes in the independent variables (or explanatory variables). Conceptually, the changes in the independent variables are observed independently of the causal relation expressed by the model.

The causal relation between the dependent variable (Y) and the independent variables ($X_1, X_2, \ldots, X_N$) may be of any implicit functional form. Consider for example the relation†

$$Y = f(X_1, X_2, \ldots, X_N), \tag{1.1}$$

where $f(\ )$ is an implicit functional form. But the available techniques of estimation require that the function $f(\ )$ be an explicit function. Given the

---

† All equations are numbered with the chapter first and then the equation; for example, (4.11) is equation 11 in the fourth chapter. All lower-case letters in equations denote variables measured from their means. For example, $x = X - \bar{X}$ where $\bar{X}$ is merely the sample mean of the X's. All Greek letters *without* hats or tildes ($\hat{\ }$ $\tilde{\ }$) are unknown parameters. All Greek letters with hats, tildes, or a combination of the two are estimates of the unknown parameters.

state of the art of estimation, not all explicit functional forms are estimable. When the explicit functional form is unknown, or the functional form is known but not estimable, the researcher of necessity may approximate the functional form $f(\ \ )$ by a familiar estimable one.

An explicit functional form widely used to express the causal relation between a dependent variable and independent variables is the linear form. Even if the relation is not linear, when the relevant range of operation is small the linear form may adequately represent the true functional form. The linear relation between the dependent and independent variables may be expressed as

$$Y = \beta_1 X_1 + \beta_2 X_2 + \cdots + \beta_N X_N + \Psi, \tag{1.2}$$

where Ψ is the error due to the linear approximation of some other implicit functional form. When the true relation is linear then, of course, the error term Ψ is zero. The β's are the parameters of the function.

When the list of X's exhausts the sources of variation in Y, then all observed sets of (Y, X) satisfy the relation (1.2). When there are several observations, distinguished by the subscript t, we may rewrite equation (1.2) as

$$Y_t = \beta_1 X_{1t} + \beta_2 X_{2t} + \cdots + \beta_N X_{Nt} + \Psi_t. \tag{1.3}$$

In a real-life situation, however, this equation does not strictly hold because of the randomness of the observed phenomena. Even when we completely control all independent variables and the functional form, we still observe some "unaccounted for" variation in the dependent variable. All biological and natural data exhibit this characteristic, some of it inherent in the phenomena and some of it due to errors of measurement. Since this random variation in the dependent variable has no systematic explanation or reason, it may be called "pure noise," and it is denoted as η. For all real situations the causal relation (1.3) may be expressed as

$$Y_t = \beta_1 X_{1t} + \beta_2 X_{2t} + \cdots + \beta_N X_{Nt} + \Psi_t + \eta_t. \tag{1.4}$$

Equation (1.4) specifies the causal relation between the dependent variable and all conceivable variables that could have caused change in it. In a practical situation, however, not all such variables are observable or quantifiable. In empirical research only the measured independent variables may be used in estimating the causal relation. For example, let us suppose that only the first two independent variables are measured and that the rest are not. Equation (1.4), expressed in terms of the two measured variables alone, may be written as

$$Y_t = \beta_1 X_{1t} + \beta_2 X_{2t} + Z_t + \Psi_t + \eta_t, \tag{1.5}$$

where Z stands for the combined influence of all the nonmeasurable variables. The value of Z depends on the values of X_3 to X_N, so a change in the values of these variables results in a change in Z.

For convenience of presentation we may express the variable Z and the error of approximation Ψ as deviations from their respective means and rewrite equation (1.5) as

$$Y_t = \beta_1 X_{1t} + \beta_2 X_{2t} + (\bar{Z} + z_t) + (\bar{\Psi} + \psi_t) + \eta_t \tag{1.6}$$

with

$$Z_t = \bar{Z} + z_t \tag{1.7}$$

and

$$\Psi_t = \bar{\Psi} + \psi_t. \tag{1.8}$$

In this case z and ψ are deviations of Z and Ψ from their respective means. Since the pure noise term η does not have any systematic fluctuations, its mean is zero. By rearrangement of terms we may write equation (1.6) as

$$Y_t = \beta_0 + \beta_1 X_{1t} + \beta_2 X_{2t} + \varepsilon_t, \tag{1.9}$$

where

$$\beta_0 = \bar{Z} + \bar{\Psi} \quad \text{and} \quad \varepsilon_t = z_t + \psi_t + \eta_t. \tag{1.10}$$

The reader will readily recognize equation (1.9) as the standard linear regression equation with two independent variables. The β's are the regression parameters, and the ε's are the so-called error terms.

In applied econometrics the researcher has data on the dependent and independent variables and wants to find the values of the parameters (β's). When no errors are present (that is, when ε's are zero) then, of course, the problem of finding the values of parameters is easy. For example, to find the values of the parameters (β's) in equation (1.9) when ε's are zero the researcher needs only three observations. Since all these satisfy (1.9), he has three linear equations in three unknowns (β's). By solving these three equations for the three unknowns, the values of the β's can be obtained. But the case is rarely so simple in econometrics because error terms are always present. Since the values of these error terms are generally unknown, we have to look for alternative ways of solving for the unknowns (β's). An exact mathematical solution is unattainable, and any values of the parameters that are obtained from statistical estimation procedures depend on the sample data; therefore we shall refer to the values of the parameters obtained from any data as *estimates of the parameters.*

What is the best procedure for obtaining these estimates? This is a difficult question, and its answer depends on what the researcher wants to do with the estimates of the parameters. There are three major reasons why a researcher may be interested in obtaining the values of the parameters of equation (1.9): (1) to verify empirically a theoretical proposition; (2) to make a decision upon which profits and losses will depend; and (3) to predict values of a specified variable for planning purposes. His primary objective will dictate the best way of estimating the parameters, depending on how the error terms are distributed. If the researcher can specify, at least in some minimum way, the nature of the behavior of the error terms in (1.9), then he can derive the best method of estimating the parameters according to a given criterion. The subject of econometrics deals, *inter alia*, with these decisions.

The error terms could have been generated in many different ways. As a starting point in research we shall treat them as having come from a simple situation and assume that they were randomly generated; that is, the error term corresponding to one observation does not depend on the error term corresponding to another. We shall also assume that the value of the error term does not depend on the value of the X's in a particular observation. These assumptions imply that the researcher cannot infer the value of the error term within a given observation on the basis of available information on that or any other observation, but this need not always be true in econometric research. The problems of estimating the parameters when these assumptions are relaxed is the subject of later chapters of this book.

1.1 Regression Coefficients

Equation (1.9) contains three parameters, namely β_0, β_1, and β_2. Let us consider the interpretation of β_1 and β_2, ignoring for the moment the problems of estimation. Parameters β_1 and β_2 can be interpreted as the partial derivatives of Y with respect to X_1 and X_2 respectively: $\partial Y/\partial X_1 = \beta_1$; $\partial Y/\partial X_2 = \beta_2$. Thus β_1 tells us by what amount Y will change in response to a unit change in X_1 when X_2 is maintained at a given level, with no other information; β_2 can be interpreted similarly.

Consider now the following two equations:

$$Y_t = \beta_0 + \beta_1 X_{1t} + \beta_2 X_{2t} + \varepsilon_{1t} \tag{1.11}$$

$$Y_t = \gamma_0 + \gamma_1 X_{1t} + \gamma_3 X_{3t} + \varepsilon_{2t}, \tag{1.12}$$

one containing X_1 and X_2, the other containing X_1 and X_3.

In each of these equations, (1.11) and (1.12), the same independent variable (X_1) appears; but unless X_2 is identical to X_3 the interpretation of X_1's coefficient differs in the two equations. β_1 is the partial derivative of Y with respect to X_1 holding X_2 constant, whereas γ_1 is the partial derivative of Y with respect to X_1 holding X_3 constant.

Consider also a set of two equations that differ in the number of their independent variables:

$$Y_t = \beta_0 + \beta_1 X_{1t} + \beta_2 X_{2t} + \beta_3 X_{3t} + \varepsilon_{1t} \tag{1.13}$$

$$Y_t = \gamma_0 + \gamma_1 X_{1t} + \gamma_2 X_{2t} + \varepsilon_{2t}. \tag{1.14}$$

The interpretation of partial derivatives of Y with respect to X_1 in the above two equations is not the same, because in the first equation (1.13) the partial derivative is defined holding X_2 and X_3 constant, whereas in the second equation (1.14) it is defined holding only X_2 constant.

1.2 The Constant Term

Now we turn to interpretation of the parameter β_0, the so-called constant term. To understand the problems of its interpretation the reader must fully distinguish between a mathematical model and an econometric *interpretation* of a mathematical model. In a mathematical model the interpretation of the constant term is obvious: it is the intercept, the value that Y takes on when all independent variables are set to zero. But such is not always the case in an econometric model.

In a mathematical model, the case with $X_1 = 0$ and $X_2 = 0$ can have a legitimate interpretation, but in econometric work this is not necessarily so.

Consider, for example, an equation in which Y is the number of fish caught by a fisherman and X is the number of nets he operates. The regression equation attempts to explain the number of fish caught by nets during a specified time period. A person who does not have any nets is not considered as a fisherman for the study. The regression equation is used to explain the number of fish caught by fishermen and not, say, by a lawyer who has no nets and never attempted to catch fish. In this case people are separated into two categories, namely fishermen and nonfishermen, distinguished on the basis of whether the independent variables are zero or nonzero. One should not try to explain the behavior of a nonfisherman by a regression equation relating to a fisherman.

An econometric model (regression equation) is used to explain the behavior of a subpopulation that contains at least one nonzero independent variable. When all the independent variables are zero then the observation does not belong to the subpopulation under investigation, and the regression equation has no valid interpretation. In this context the constant term should not be interpreted as the equation's intercept in the mathematical sense. Rather, it is to be interpreted as the mean effect on Y of all the excluded variables for the relevant subpopulation. When the mean value of the omitted variables (Z) changes for some reason, then the constant term will change.

There are some circumstances in which the constant term can be interpreted as the intercept in the mathematical sense of the word. For example, consider the case of a railroad company whose total costs are a linear function of the volume of traffic. When this volume is zero, which sometimes happens during off-season periods, then the constant term in the relation represents the fixed costs to the railroad company.

Consider, though, the case when $\bar{Z}$ is zero because we have included all the independent variables but have used a linear approximation to what may be a nonlinear world. Our study relates to data within which the linear approximation is valid. Take, for example, the functional relationship between Y and X represented by the curved line in Figure 1.1. Even though the functional relation between the two variables is curvilinear, the data correspond to the values of X between X^* and X^{**}. The linear approximation, $Y_t = \beta_0 + \beta_1 X_{1t}$, is used to explain the movements of Y within the region over which the linear approximation is assumed to be valid, but not outside this region. In this case the constant β_0 has no operational interpretation.

1.3 Least Squares Estimation

So far we have discussed problems associated with the interpretation of parameters. But we do not have the values for these parameters, and they must be estimated from available data. The problems of estimation may be said to concern the properties of the estimates. We want the " best " possible

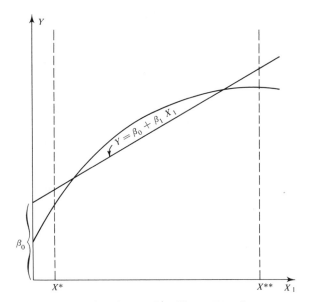

Figure 1.1. Linear Approximation to Curvilinear Function

estimates for our parameters. Unfortunately there is no unique "best" estimation procedure, and each of several may excel in certain cases. This book deals, in part, with the choice of the appropriate estimation procedure for a given situation. We will begin with the most widely known method. Consider the linear regression equation

$$Y_t = \beta_0 + \beta_1 X_{1t} + \beta_2 X_{2t} + \cdots + \beta_K X_{Kt} + \varepsilon_t. \qquad (1.15)$$

Suppose we find an estimation procedure that gives $\hat{\beta}_i$ as an estimate corresponding to the parameter β_i. Then we define the residual, e_t, as the difference between the observed value Y_t and the so-called predicted value of Y_t on the basis of the estimated values of the parameters.

$$e_t = Y_t - \hat{\beta}_0 - \hat{\beta}_1 X_{1t} - \hat{\beta}_2 X_{2t} - \cdots - \hat{\beta}_K X_{Kt}. \qquad (1.16)$$

Note that different values of $\hat{\beta}_i$ would generate different sets of e_t. Just as $\hat{\beta}_i$ corresponds to β_i, e_t corresponds to ε_t. In some sense an ideal estimator $\hat{\beta}_i$ will generate a set of e's having the same properties as those of the ε's.

The error term ε consists of three components: η, the pure noise term; z, the influence of excluded variables; and ψ, the error of approximation of the functional form. Since we assume that there is no systematic component in the η's, we expect them to have a zero mean. The influence of the excluded variables and of ψ enter the error term as deviations from their means; they always have zero mean. Accordingly, the error term ε is expected to have a zero mean.

For the analysis of linear regression we are assuming that the error term ε is not correlated with any of the independent variables. When we cannot make this assumption, we have to use a simultaneous-equations estimation procedure, as discussed in Chapter 8. When the ε's are uncorrelated with the X's then the single-equation estimation procedure can be used.

In the specification of the linear regression equation we therefore now assume that the error terms (ε's) have zero mean and are not correlated with the independent variables.

Since the residuals, e, "correspond" to ε, we require them to have the same properties, namely that their mean be zero and that they be uncorrelated with the independent variables. Since different values of $\hat{\beta}$'s produce different sets of e's, we choose that set of $\hat{\beta}$'s that produces residuals having these required properties. This problem can be solved by imposing the following conditions on the residuals: mean of e is zero; correlation between e and X_1 is zero; correlation between e and X_2 is zero; ... ; correlation between e and X_K is zero. These conditions can alternatively be expressed as: $\sum e = 0$; $\sum X_1 e = 0$; $\sum X_2 e = 0$; ...; $\sum X_K e = 0$.

When the regression equation includes a constant term, the solution to this problem is identical to the solution of minimizing the sum of squares of the residuals, $\sum e^2$. This procedure is called the Ordinary Least Squares (OLS) estimation.[1] On the other hand, if the regression equation does not include a constant term we cannot simultaneously minimize the residual sum of squares and satisfy the required properties of the residuals.

Since an ideal estimator should produce a set of residuals having the same properties as the unknown disturbance terms in the original equation, it is advisable to include the constant term in all the regression equations unless the researcher has strong theoretical reasons for doing otherwise. Of course, if all the variables are measured as deviations from their corresponding means, then the constant term is implicit and does not appear in the regression equation. Whether one estimates a linear regression on the original data with a constant term, or a regression without a constant on the deviations from their respective means, the same regression coefficients and corresponding statistics result.[2]

---

[1] Conventionally these estimates are derived by minimization of the $\sum e^2$. Since all textbooks (see Specific References, p. 221) present this procedure, we shall not tax the reader with these derivations.

[2] The researcher may verify this point by considering the constraints imposed on the residuals in these two cases. See Johnston, *Econometric Methods*, McGraw-Hill Book Company, Inc. (New York), 1963, 11–12.

This estimation procedure (OLS) imposes on the residuals constraints that are equal to the number of parameters estimated in the regression equation. For a nontrivial solution the number of observations must be larger than the number of parameters being estimated. The excess of the number of observations over the number of parameters estimated is called the *number of degrees of freedom*.

1.4 An Illustration: A Consumption Function

To illustrate the ordinary least squares estimation procedure, let us consider the estimation of a consumption function for the United States. It is postulated that aggregate consumption in a given quarter depends on the disposable income during that quarter and on the aggregate consumption during the previous quarter. The causal relation between the dependent variable (consumption in the current quarter) and the independent variables (disposable income in the current quarter and consumption in the previous quarter) may be expressed by a linear functional form as

$$C_t = \beta_0 + \beta_1 Y_t + \beta_2 C_{t-1} + \varepsilon_t, \tag{1.17}$$

where C is consumption, Y is income, and ε is the error term.

The parameters (β's) are unknown and are to be estimated from data corresponding to the time period 1956–60. The data compiled by Griliches et al. are presented in Table 1.1. Corresponding to the first quarter of 1956 the data for C_{t-1} are missing, hence we shall delete this observation for our study. Thus the total number of observations in the study, that is, the sample size (T), is 19.

Let $\hat{\beta}_0$, $\hat{\beta}_1$, and $\hat{\beta}_2$ be estimates of β_0, β_1, and β_2 respectively. The residuals corresponding to these estimates are

$$e_t = C_t - \hat{\beta}_0 - \hat{\beta}_1 Y_t - \hat{\beta}_2 C_{t-1}. \tag{1.18}$$

We want the estimates ($\hat{\beta}$'s) to be such that the residuals given by equation (1.18) satisfy the same properties as those of the true error terms (ε's) in (1.17). These conditions are

$$\sum e_t = 0, \tag{1.19}$$

$$\sum Y_t e_t = 0, \tag{1.20}$$

$$\sum C_{t-1} e_t = 0. \tag{1.21}$$

Table 1.1. Quarterly Data on Consumption and Income for the United States, 1956–60

(1) Year and Quarter	(2) Consumption C_t ($\$10^{11}$)	(3) Disposable Income Y_t ($\$10^{11}$)
1956 I	2.632	2.820
II	2.637	2.862
III	2.634	2.877
IV	2.669	2.910
1957 I	2.689	2.911
II	2.704	2.946
III	2.734	2.961
IV	2.721	2.933
1958 I	2.689	2.913
II	2.709	2.926
III	2.744	2.999
IV	2.787	3.021
1959 I	2.838	3.059
II	2.897	3.125
III	2.908	3.113
IV	2.928	3.132
1960 I	2.954	3.154
II	2.995	3.203
III	2.986	3.210
IV	2.996	3.201

Source: Griliches, Z., et al., "Notes on Estimated Aggregate Quarterly Consumption Functions," *Econometrica*, Vol. 30, No. 5, July 1962, pp. 499–500.

By the substitution of equation (1.18) for e, equations (1.19), (1.20), and (1.21) may be rewritten as

$$\sum \hat{\beta}_0 + \hat{\beta}_1 \sum Y_t + \hat{\beta}_2 \sum C_{t-1} = \sum C_t, \tag{1.22}$$

$$\hat{\beta}_0 \sum Y_t + \hat{\beta}_1 \sum Y_t^2 + \hat{\beta}_2 \sum Y_t C_{t-1} = \sum Y_t C_t, \tag{1.23}$$

$$\hat{\beta}_0 \sum C_{t-1} + \hat{\beta}_1 \sum Y_t C_{t-1} + \hat{\beta}_2 \sum C_{t-1}^2 = \sum C_t C_{t-1}. \tag{1.24}$$

Except for the three $\hat{\beta}$'s, all the terms in these equations are known, as computed from the data:

$$\sum C_t = 53.220 \qquad \sum Y_t = 57.456 \qquad \sum C_{t-1} = 52.856$$

$$\sum C_t^2 = 149.37 \qquad \sum Y_t^2 = 174.01 \qquad \sum C_{t-1}^2 = 147.32$$

$$\sum Y_t C_t = 161.21 \qquad \sum Y_t C_{t-1} = 160.10 \qquad \sum C_t C_{t-1} = 148.33.$$

By substitution of these values, equations (1.22), (1.23), and (1.24) may be written as

$$19\hat{\beta}_0 + 57.456\hat{\beta}_1 + 52.856\hat{\beta}_2 = 53.220, \tag{1.25}$$

$$57.456\hat{\beta}_0 + 174.01\hat{\beta}_1 + 160.10\hat{\beta}_2 = 161.21, \tag{1.26}$$

$$52.856\hat{\beta}_0 + 160.10\hat{\beta}_1 + 147.32\hat{\beta}_2 = 148.33. \tag{1.27}$$

The three linear equations involve three unknowns, hence the values of the unknowns are uniquely determined. The technique of solving n simultaneous linear equations for n unknowns may be found in any algebra textbook. By solving for the three unknowns in equations (1.25), (1.26), and (1.27) we obtain

$$\hat{\beta}_0 = -0.34, \tag{1.28}$$

$$\hat{\beta}_1 = 0.76, \tag{1.29}$$

$$\hat{\beta}_2 = 0.30. \tag{1.30}$$

The regression equation that yields residuals satisfying the conditions imposed on the residuals is

$$C_t = -0.34 + 0.76 Y_t + 0.30 C_{t-1}. \tag{1.31}$$

This regression equation may be interpreted as follows: Holding the consumption during the previous quarter constant, if disposable income in the current quarter increases by one dollar, then aggregate consumption increases by 0.76 dollars. Similarly, holding income in the current quarter constant, if consumption in the previous quarter is increased by a dollar, then consumption in the current quarter will increase by 0.30 dollars.

This estimation procedure may be used for any number of parameters, although the computational burden of solving for the unknowns increases with their number. Currently, most research centers are equipped with computer facilities that can easily handle ordinary least squares computations. When a researcher has no access to computer facilities he may follow the computational procedures suggested in Klein or Ezekiel and Fox.[3]

A general treatment of the problems of linear regression is usually presented in matrix notation. We will avoid using such notation whenever possible; although its compact notation simplifies the algebra, it may cost the researcher insight into his problem. In applied econometric research, intuitive feel and insight are more rewarding than mere simplicity of notation.

---

[3] L. R. Klein, *A Textbook of Econometrics*, Row, Peterson (Evanston), 1953. M. Ezekiel and K. A. Fox, *Methods of Correlation and Regression Analysis*, John Wiley & Sons Inc. (New York), 3rd edition, 1959.

2

Uses of Summary
Statistics in Linear Regression

After having obtained estimates of the parameters in a linear regression equation, the researcher usually computes summary statistics to assess the usefulness of the estimates. The meaning and use of these statistics is especially valuable in applied econometrics, where their role is not always to provide cut-and-dried answers. Instead they are the basic tools of the applied econometrician in working his way through an empirical problem. The typical "textbook" econometric problem in which the model is clearly specified is seldom encountered in empirical research. Applied econometricians use a great deal of judgment at various stages of research by utilizing summary statistics to "feel the data."

It is difficult to set up definite rules concerning the uses and abuses of these summary statistics as econometric tools, since their proper selection requires skill and intuition on the part of the researcher. He should be aware of when to use a tool and also of when *not* to use it. It should be kept in mind throughout this book that applied econometrics is an art.

2.1 Multiple Correlation Coefficient

In linear regression estimation, the residuals indicate the extent of the movement in the dependent variable that is not explained by the independent variables. If the residuals are small relative to the total movement in the dependent variable, then it follows that a major part of the movement has been accounted for. Accordingly, the summary statistic known as the *multiple correlation coefficient* is defined to measure the extent of movement in the dependent variable that is explained by the independent variables. Conventionally, instead of the multiple correlation coefficient, its square (R^2) is reported with all the regression equations.

The square of the multiple correlation coefficient is defined as

$$R^2 = \frac{\text{variation explained by the regression equation}}{\text{total variation of the dependent variable}}. \tag{2.1}$$

Since the residuals represent the movement in the dependent variable that is unexplained by the independent variables, the R^2 may also be expressed as

$$R^2 = \frac{\sum (Y - \bar{Y})^2 - \sum e^2}{\sum (Y - \bar{Y})^2} \tag{2.2}$$

where $\sum (Y - \bar{Y})^2$ and $\sum e^2$ are variations of the dependent variable and of the residual respectively.

The summary statistic so defined measures the proportion of variation in the dependent variable that is explained by the independent variables. This particular definition has a valid interpretation as a summary statistic only when the regression equation contains the constant term either explicitly or implicitly.

In ordinary least squares estimation, when the researcher includes an additional variable in the regression equation the sum of squares of the residuals ($\sum e^2$) necessarily decreases. This is a mathematical property and does not depend on the "relevance" of the additional variable in the causal relation. Therefore, whenever a variable is added to the regression the R^2 necessarily increases.

The researcher should note that even though R^2 is used as a measure of the proportion of variation in the dependent variable that is explained by the regression equation, it should not always be interpreted as a determinant of "goodness of fit" of the causal relation. We will treat this point in more detail later on.

As an illustration, consider the consumption function estimated for the United States by using data from Table 1.1:

$$C_t = -0.34 + 0.76 Y_t + 0.30 C_{t-1}. \tag{2.3}$$

The sum of squares of residuals $(\sum e^2)$ corresponding to this equation is 0.0015, and the variation in the dependent variable $(\sum (C_t - \bar{C})^2)$ is 0.3010. Using definition (2.2), the R^2 may be computed as

$$R^2 = \frac{0.3010 - 0.0015}{0.3010} = 0.99. \tag{2.4}$$

When presenting his results, the researcher customarily gives the statistic R^2 as a part of the estimated regression equation, usually in the following manner:

$$C_t = -0.34 + 0.76 Y_t + 0.30 C_{t-1} \qquad R^2 = 0.99. \tag{2.5}$$

Regression equation (2.5) explains 99 percent of the variation in the dependent variable C.

Suppose that instead of estimating the consumption function the researcher is trying to explain aggregate savings, and suppose that he has postulated the causal relation

$$S_t = \alpha_0 + \alpha_1 Y_t + \alpha_2 C_{t-1} + \varepsilon_t, \tag{2.6}$$

where S_t is aggregate savings in a given quarter defined as

$$S_t = Y_t - C_t. \tag{2.7}$$

For the data presented in Table 1.1 (page 10) the researcher would obtain the following estimated equation:

$$S_t = 0.34 + 0.24 Y_t - 0.30 C_{t-1} \qquad R^2 = 0.64. \tag{2.8}$$

Whereas the consumption function explains 99 percent of the variation in the dependent variable, the savings function explains only 64 percent. The researcher, concluding that the consumption function is a "better causal relation " than the savings function, may be tempted to retain the consumption function for policy purposes and never to mention the savings function again. He should cultivate resistance to such temptations, for reasons that will become clear.

Let us turn now to an interpretation of the consumption and savings functions. If while holding the previous quarter's consumption constant the income of the economy (Y) is increased by one dollar, then according to the consumption function the consumption in the current quarter increases by 0.76 dollars, and according to the savings function savings increase by 0.24 dollars—which is, in fact, that part of the additional dollar that was not spent $(1 - 0.76)$ according to the consumption function. *Both the consumption function and the savings function are providing identical information on the consumption behavior of the United States.* Similarly, holding current income constant, if we increase the previous quarter's consumption by one dollar we get identical answers from both equation (2.5) and equation (2.8).

Even though the two regression equations corresponding to the same data are providing identical information on the economy, one has a larger value for the summary statistic R^2 than the other. To use R^2 as a measure of the appropriateness of the regression equation for explaining the movements in the dependent variable would, in this situation, be a misuse of the statistic. A high R^2 may imply the appropriateness of a regression equation for explaining the movements of a dependent variable, *but a low R^2 does not necessarily imply that the regression equation is inappropriate.* The source of this possible misuse of R^2 lies in its definition.

In estimating the two equations (2.5) and (2.8) the researcher is imposing certain conditions on the residuals of each. Close examination reveals that these conditions are the same for both estimations. Since the same set of residuals satisfies the conditions imposed by the two equations, the implicit regression estimates and the variation in the residuals must be the same. The implicit correspondence between the regression coefficients may readily be seen by inserting the identity (2.7) into the savings function (2.8) to produce

$$Y_t - C_t = 0.34 + 0.24 \ Y_t - 0.30 \ C_{t-1}, \tag{2.9}$$

which is nothing but the consumption equation (2.5) expressed in a different form. This can be seen by taking Y_t to the right-hand side of (2.9) and then multiplying through by -1. The result is (2.5).

Even though the residual sum of squares for the two regression equations is the same, the variation in the dependent variables is different because in one case we have C and in the other case S as the dependent variable: $[\sum (C_t - \bar{C})^2]$ is not equal to $[\sum (S_t - \bar{S})^2]$. By using definition (2.2) we obtain different values for R^2 for the two equations even though the implicit regression coefficients and the variation in the residuals are identical.

In general, if instead of using the dependent variable one uses any linear combination of dependent and independent variables, he is bound to get the same residual sum of squares and implicit parameter coefficients, but different R^2's. Numerous examples can be found in current empirical studies. The most common case occurs in demand functions, in which the quantity demanded is specified as a function of certain independent variables. Given a change in some independent variable, a new value of the dependent variable is obtained, but this "desired" quantity cannot be attained instantaneously. Therefore, the partial-adjustment mechanism is posited.[1] A typical resulting equation might then be

$$Y_t = \beta_0 + \beta_1 X_{1t} + \beta_2 Y_{t-1} + \varepsilon_t. \qquad (2.10)$$

(handwritten annotations: "quantity" above Y_t; "Δ'r in demand" above Y_{t-1})

Suppose that instead of the *level of quantity demanded*, Y_t, the researcher wants *changes in demand* to be predicted by his regression equation. He then substracts Y_{t-1} from both sides of the equation, obtaining

$$(Y_t - Y_{t-1}) = \beta_0 + \beta_1 X_{1t} + \beta_3 Y_{t-1} + \varepsilon_t. \qquad (2.11)$$

(handwritten annotation: $\beta_3 = \beta_2 - 1$)

The R^2 from this equation will usually be smaller than the R^2 from the equation (2.10), but a relatively low R^2 does not necessarily mean a poor fit. Note that we are explaining the variance of changes in Y_t in one equation and the variance of Y_t in the other.[2]

This result occurs because the dependent variable is not the same in both equations. Another situation arises when the dependent variables are different

---

[1] See for example, A. S. Goldberger, *Econometric Theory*, John Wiley & Sons, Inc. (New York), 1964, 275–6.

[2] In some empirical work the dependent variable is the percentage change of a variable. The standard procedure to compute the percentage change is to use the formula $(y_t - y_{t-1})/y_{t-1}$. This formula is appropriate in empirical studies only when the variable y is increasing at the point y_{t-1}. When y is decreasing at the point y_{t-1}, that is, when $y_t - y_{t-1}$ is negative, then the formula for percentage change is $(y_t - y_{t-1})/y_t$. Note that the denominators in the computations are not the same for increases as for decreases in y. An arithmetic example may clarify the inappropriateness of using the same formula for increasing and decreasing values. In demand analysis, suppose at a price of \$1 a unit the quantity demanded is 10 units and total revenue is \$10. When the price is reduced to 50 cents, let the quantity demanded be 20, so that the total revenue remains the same. In such a case the elasticity is unity, which implies that the percentage change in price and quantity are the same. Only when we use different formulae for the cases of increase and of decrease do we get meaningful answers. The reader may do the same exercise by taking the price as \$2 with 5 units demanded.

functional forms of the same variable. In these cases, also, the R^2 cannot be used for comparison of the two equations. Consider, for example, the following:

$$Y_t = \beta_0 + \beta_1 X_{1t} + \beta_2 X_{2t} + \varepsilon_{1t} \tag{2.12}$$

$$\log Y_t = \gamma_0 + \gamma_1 X_{1t} + \gamma_2 X_{2t} + \varepsilon_{2t}. \tag{2.13}$$

The specification of the model, the error terms, and the computation of R^2 for these two equations are entirely different and provide no common ground for comparison of the relative performance of these equations[3] on the basis of computations of R^2.

It is clear from the above discussion that R^2 can be legitimately used for comparison of the relative performance of two competing regression equations only when the dependent variables are the same. And since R^2 always increases when independent variables are added, we need the further restriction that the number of X's be the same in each equation being compared.

It may seem now that R^2 has little, if any, value; but this is not the case. For example, we may use it to determine which of several competing definitions of an independent variable is most appropriate *empirically*. Consider a simple Cobb-Douglas production function:

$$\log Q = \beta_0 + \beta_1 \log K + \beta_2 \log L + \varepsilon. \tag{2.14}$$

The variable K, capital, in this example is assumed to be well defined, but suppose the researcher is faced with several competing definitions of the variable L, labor. Suppose also that on theoretical grounds it is not obvious which of the several definitions is most appropriate. One way to proceed is to estimate a separate production function for each of the definitions of labor; the definition that produces the highest R^2 when used in the equation may be considered *empirically* preferable. "The argument for this procedure is that the precise empirical definition of variables should be selected so as to put the theory in question in its best light."[4]

This procedure should not be misused. It applies only to the choice among a well-selected and theoretically acceptable set of alternative definitions of a given variable. It may happen that a nonsensical definition of the variable will give the highest R^2; this, of course, does not mean that it is the appropriate

---

[3] But see p. 107 for a way around this problem.

[4] M. Friedman and David Meiselman, "The Relative Stability of Monetary Velocity and the Investment Multiplier in the United States, 1897–1958," *Stabilization Policies*, Commission on Money and Credit (New York), 1963, p. 181.

one to use. Basing the choice of appropriate definition of an independent variable on a maximum R^2 is justified only when the model has been fully specified and all the other variables of the model are well defined. This procedure is a guide in empirical research, and not a theoretical rule.

Consider the case of a researcher who is working on the same regression equation for several sets of data—for example, the production function for each state separately. It may be that no definition of a particular variable, say labor, will give the highest R^2 in every case. Suppose the theoretically valid definition is efficiency units of labor, and suppose that data are available on variables such as the number of workers, wages paid, education of workers, industrial concentration, etc. The efficiency of workers may depend in one state on the level of education, in another state on the concentration of minority groups, etc. In these cases selection according to the highest R^2 will yield different empirically appropriate definitions of labor. When use of the highest R^2 suggests the use of different definitions for different states then, of course, the researcher should investigate the reasons underlying such behavior of the data. When a theoretical justification for the anomaly is not forthcoming and when he has strong reasons to believe that the efficiency units of labor in all the states should have the same definition, then he may select the definition that gives the highest R^2 most of the time, using his own judgment in weighing empirical and theoretical considerations underlying the problem. Whenever he uses R^2 as a criterion the researcher should guard against inadvertently selecting a possible candidate which is actually some disguised form of the dependent variable. For example, suppose that the researcher is estimating the relation between output and man-hours. The published monthly and quarterly output data may have been interpolated by the data-collecting agency from information on man-hours. Thus the researcher should expect to obtain a high R^2 when he regresses output on man-hours or man-hours on output. A high R^2 in this case gives little, if any, information.

When the R^2 values from different definitions of a variable do not differ substantially from each other, then the use of the highest R^2 as a guide has little significance, and one definition is as good as the other.

Another example of the meaningful use of highest R^2 concerns the choice of the appropriate lag for an independent variable. Suppose that we wish to explain the level of interest rates, i_t, and suppose we have theoretically considered the lagged money supply to be a relevant independent variable along with many others. That is, a change in the money supply is considered to have a once-for-all effect on the level of the "interest rate" after τ time periods. (This is not to be confused with the distributed lag effect to be discussed in Chapter 7.) Then our regression equation would be specified as

$$i_t = \beta_0 + \beta_1 M_{t-\tau} + \beta_2 X_{2t} + \beta_3 X_{3t} + \varepsilon_t, \qquad (2.15)$$

where τ is the lag period in the money supply (M).

The empirically appropriate lag in the supply of money in explaining the interest rate may be obtained by fitting equation (2.15) for various values of τ and considering as empirically appropriate that value which gives the highest R^2. This procedure is, of course, valid only when the rest of the specification is correct.

In empirical research one comes across many such occasions where R^2 can be used as a guide rather than as a summary statistic.

2.2   Residual Variance

Consider the case in which the dependent variable is the same in all regressions, but the list of independent variables is different. For example, examine the following two regression equations:

$$Y_t = \beta_0 + \beta_1 X_{1t} + \varepsilon_{1t}, \tag{2.16}$$

$$Y_t = \beta_0 + \beta_1 X_{1t} + \beta_2 X_{2t} + \varepsilon_{2t}. \tag{2.17}$$

Even though the dependent variables are the same, the R^2 for the two equations are not comparable because the *number* of independent variables is not the same. As mentioned before, the second equation (2.17) necessarily gives a higher R^2. The sum of squares of the residuals will be smaller, but estimation of the second equation imposes an extra condition on the residuals. Is the reduction in the residual sum of squares worth the "price" of the extra constraint? To answer this, a summary statistic—residual variance—is computed:

$$V(e) = \frac{\sum e^2}{v}, \tag{2.18}$$

where v is the degrees of freedom (that is, the total number of observations less the number of constraints imposed on the residuals in estimating the parameters). Even though the residual sum of squares $(\sum e^2)$ necessarily decreases with the addition of a variable, the residual variance, $V(e)$, need not, because the denominator in (2.18) is also changing. The residual variance takes into consideration information about the degrees of freedom, whereas the R^2 does not. Note that $V(e)$ as defined in equation (2.18) is meaningful only when the regression equation has a constant term.

A summary statistic analogous to R^2 is defined on the basis of the residual variance by[5]

$$\bar{R}^2 = 1 - V(e)/V(Y), \tag{2.19}$$

where $V(Y)$ is the variance of Y defined as $V(Y) = \sum (Y - \bar{Y})^2/(T - 1)$. So defined, the statistic $\bar{R}^2$ can decrease when a new variable is added to a regression equation even though R^2 necessarily increases. Since $V(Y)$ does not depend on the independent variables, there is one-to-one correspondence between the $\bar{R}^2$ and the variance of the residual $V(e)$.

One should not jump to the conclusion that the equation which yields least residual variance (the largest $\bar{R}^2$) is necessarily always desirable. In a regression equation, the decision on including or excluding a variable is based on theoretical considerations and the use to which the regression is put, rather than on mere maximization of the summary statistics R^2 and $\bar{R}^2$.

However, as an example of an occasion when the equation with the least residual variance is desirable, consider the case in which a researcher is interested in predicting the values of a dependent variable to a yet-unknown period. The predicted value need not be the same as the value of the dependent variable actually observed for that period, because of the error of prediction. Given two predictors, one would choose that one which has the smallest variance of the error of prediction. A regression equation with smaller residual variance also has smaller variance of the error of prediction.

When adding an independent variable increases the $\bar{R}^2$, the prediction power can be increased by including that variable, because the variance of the error of prediction is thereby decreased. When adding an independent variable decreases the $\bar{R}^2$, then the researcher, of course, is losing reliability in prediction by including that variable in the regression.

When the objective is testing of a null hypothesis based on the regression estimates and not prediction of a future value of the dependent variable, then the researcher is interested in unbiased estimates of his parameters. Unbiased estimates may be obtained only by including all the theoretically specified variables in a regression equation irrespective of what they do to the summary statistic $\bar{R}^2$. Discarding a theoretically relevant variable may increase $\bar{R}^2$, but it may result in biased estimates of the parameters.

The problem of prediction is an integral part of econometric research. When a researcher is interested primarily in predicting values of a specific variable rather than in testing a theory, he will choose his variables in such a way as to obtain the regression equation with the least residual variance.

---

[5] Also $\bar{R}^2 = 1 - (1 - R^2)(T - 1)/(T - K)$, $T =$ total observations; $K =$ total number of parameters, including the constant term.

2.3 Standard Errors

Having obtained the regression coefficients by using the ordinary least squares procedure, the researcher is interested in assessing the "precision" of the estimation procedure. To this end, he computes standard errors of the regression coefficients.

These computed standard errors do not necessarily reflect the true precision of the estimates, which is measured by the theoretical variance of the distribution of an estimate, not by the standard errors. The theoretical variance, however, is an unknown. To bring out the distinction let us first consider the theoretical variance.

When several estimation procedures exist for the same parameters from the same data, the researcher would like to use the one offering maximum precision. Even when no choice in estimation procedures is available, he may still be interested in discovering the precision of his estimates for the purpose of testing a null hypothesis.

Consider a situation in which the truth is

$$y_t = \beta_1 x_{1t} + \beta_2 x_{2t} + \varepsilon_t, \tag{2.20}$$

where lower-case letters indicate deviations from the mean; hence the constant is implicit. Let us suppose that the values of the parameters (β's) and the independent variables (x's) are known. Then the value of the dependent variable depends on the values of the error terms in equation (2.20). Since in this example all the terms on the right-hand side of the equation are known except for the error terms, the values of y vary with the error terms alone. For different sets of y's (which depend on the ε's), and of given x's, we obtain different estimates of the parameters by using the ordinary least squares estimation procedure. The question then is: how sensitive are the estimates going to be to the particular values of the error terms?

We are assuming that the error terms are distributed independently of each other and that they are uncorrelated with the independent variables (x's). Many sets of error terms may satisfy these conditions. Suppose the errors are a particular set, say ε^*. Corresponding to these error terms is a set of y values given by equation (2.20). When these values of y are regressed on the independent variables we obtain one set of estimates for the parameters, say $\hat{\beta}^*$. These estimates need not be equal to the parameters, because the ordinary least squares estimates are chosen to minimize the residual sum of squares, and the true parameter values need not correspond to the minimum residual sum of squares in any given sample. If, instead of ε^*, the errors were a different set, say ε^{**}, then we would have obtained a different set of estimates for the parameters, say $\hat{\beta}^{**}$. Since we do not know which set of errors corresponds to the given data on the y's, we cannot say anything about the extent of deviation of these estimates from the true parameters. We can, however, study how much dispersion the estimates would exhibit if the errors were in fact drawn at random from a population with known variance. In such a situation any combination of error terms has an equal chance of corresponding to the given data on the y's. When the errors are drawn at random from a population with zero mean and constant variance σ_ε^2, then the regression coefficients have a distribution which can be established analytically, as will be shown in Chapter 3.

In defining the precision of the estimates in this way, we are using information on the distribution of error terms when the values of independent variables and parameters are known. Since the precision is defined conditionally upon these values, we expect precision to depend on these values as well. In a linear regression equation the precision depends only on the values of the x's, and not on the values of the parameters.

The conventional way of measuring precision when the statistical distribution of an estimate is known is by its variance. The smaller the variance of an estimate the greater its precision—that is, the less sensitive the estimates will be to different sets of error terms that could have occurred in the y's.

The theoretical variance of the distribution of $\hat{\beta}_1$ in equation (2.20) may be derived as (see p. 57)

$$V(\hat{\beta}_1) = \frac{\sigma_\varepsilon^2}{\sum x_1^2(1 - r_{x_1x_2}^2)} \tag{2.21}$$

where σ_ε^2 is the variance of the population that generated the error terms and $r_{x_1x_2}$ is the correlation between x_1 and x_2.[6] It can be seen from equation (2.21) that the larger the variation of the independent variable x_1 relative to the variance of the error term, the smaller the variance of the estimate $\hat{\beta}_1$. That is, the precision of the regression coefficient corresponding to an independent variable increases with the variation of that variable. Precision also depends on the comovements of the independent variables. The smaller the correlation between the independent variables, the higher the precision of the regression estimates.

These are theoretical results, and they involve σ_ε^2, which is generally unknown. The researcher can, however, estimate the variance of the error term from the residuals of the regression equation. And, since the variance of the

---

[6] See p. 157 for the definition of the correlation coefficient.

estimate of $\hat{\beta}_1$ is unknown, we may estimate it by replacing σ_ε^2 by its sample estimate. Thus, an estimate of the variance of $\hat{\beta}_1$ is

$$\hat{V}(\hat{\beta}_1) = \frac{V(e)}{\sum x_1^2 (1 - r_{x_1 x_2}^2)}, \tag{2.22}$$

where $\hat{V}(\hat{\beta}_1)$ stands for an estimate of $V(\hat{\beta}_1)$, and $V(e)$ is the sample variance of the residual (e):

$$V(e) = \frac{\sum e^2}{v} \qquad \text{where } v = \text{degree of freedom.} \tag{2.23}$$

The variance is in square units of the regression coefficient. To convert them to comparable units, the standard deviation of the regression coefficient is defined as the square root of the variance of the regression coefficient. The true standard deviation is a theoretical quantity. When computation of the standard deviation is based on the *estimate of variance* rather than on the *variance itself*, it is called the *standard error* to distinguish it from its theoretical value.

Whenever the researcher reports the standard error of his estimate he is explicitly stating that the result is an estimate of the standard deviation of the coefficient and is not the standard deviation itself. Despite the distinction in labels, researchers often overlook this point and use standard errors as if they were standard deviations; such misuse of the results should be discouraged. When the estimate of variance of the regression coefficient is biased (see p. 137), the estimated variance does not reflect the precision of the regression coefficients. In such cases the theoretical standard deviation reflects the precision, but the standard error does not.

When the researcher has a choice between two alternative estimation procedures, he may wish to choose the one having the greater precision. Since the precision of estimates is reflected only in the standard deviations and not in the standard errors, he should not conclude that the estimation procedure which yields smaller standard errors is necessarily preferable. A thorough investigation into the theoretical properties and standard deviations must precede such decisions.

Computational precision as evidenced by small standard errors of regression coefficients does not necessarily indicate that the most theoretically precise estimation procedure has been used.

To illustrate the above points, consider the consumption function example:

$$C_t = \hat{\beta}_0 + \hat{\beta}_1 Y_t + \hat{\beta}_2 C_{t-1} + e_t, \qquad (2.24)$$

where the $\hat{\beta}$'s are the least squares estimates. The standard errors of $\hat{\beta}_1$ and $\hat{\beta}_2$ may be computed from the following summary information derived from Table 1.1:

$$V(e) = \frac{\sum e^2}{v} = \frac{0.001512}{19 - 3} = 0.0000945, \qquad (2.25)$$

$$\sum y_t^2 = \sum (Y_t - \bar{Y})^2 = \sum Y_t^2 - \frac{\sum Y_t}{T} \cdot \sum Y_t = 0.2604, \qquad (2.26)$$

$$\sum c_{t-1}^2 = \sum (C_{t-1} - \bar{C})^2 = \sum C_{t-1}^2 - \frac{\sum C_{t-1}}{T} \cdot \sum C_{t-1} = 0.2845, \qquad (2.27)$$

$$r_{y_t c_{t-1}} = \frac{\sum y_t c_{t-1}}{\sqrt{\sum y_t^2 \cdot \sum c_{t-1}^2}} = \frac{\sum Y_t C_{t-1} - \frac{\sum Y_t}{T} \cdot \sum C_{t-1}}{\sqrt{\sum y_t^2 \cdot \sum c_{t-1}^2}} = 0.9728. \qquad (2.28)$$

To obtain a measure of precision, we should use the formulae for theoretical variance:

$$V(\hat{\beta}_1) = \frac{\sigma_\varepsilon^2}{\sum y_t^2(1 - r_{y_t c_{t-1}}^2)}, \qquad (2.29)$$

$$V(\hat{\beta}_2) = \frac{\sigma_\varepsilon^2}{\sum c_{t-1}^2(1 - r_{y_t c_{t-1}}^2)}. \qquad (2.30)$$

Since σ_ε^2 is unknown, we shall estimate the variances by replacing σ_ε^2 by $V(e)$:

$$\hat{V}(\hat{\beta}_1) = \frac{V(e)}{\sum y_t^2(1 - r_{y_t c_{t-1}}^2)} = \frac{0.0000945}{0.2604(0.0272)} = 0.00676, \qquad (2.31)$$

$$\hat{V}(\hat{\beta}_2) = \frac{V(e)}{\sum c_{t-1}^2(1 - r_{y_t c_{t-1}}^2)} = \frac{0.0000945}{0.2845(0.0272)} = 0.00619. \qquad (2.32)$$

The *standard errors* of $\hat{\beta}_1$ and $\hat{\beta}_2$ are therefore

$$\text{St. error } (\hat{\beta}_1) = \sqrt{\hat{V}(\hat{\beta}_1)} = 0.082, \qquad (2.33)$$

$$\text{St. error } (\hat{\beta}_2) = \sqrt{\hat{V}(\hat{\beta}_2)} = 0.079. \qquad (2.34)$$

It is conventional to report the standard errors of the coefficient estimates as a part of the regression equation by enclosing them in parentheses below the respective estimates. In its final form of presentation the consumption function would be

$$C_t = -0.34 + 0.76\ Y_t + 0.30\ C_{t-1} \qquad R^2 = 0.99. \qquad (2.35)$$
$$(0.082)\quad (0.079)$$

In the case of more than two variables, computation of standard errors by using explicit formulae as above would be computationally burdensome. Standard computer programs provide the standard errors of the estimates, together with the estimates, at an insignificant marginal cost. When the researcher has only one or two independent variables and wants to figure the regression coefficients and their standard errors, he will find it convenient to use a slide rule and the formulae given in this section. (See p. 56 for the formula for the theoretical variance of a least squares estimate with one independent variable.)

2.4 Bias in the Estimates

For any given set of independent variables the regression estimates of a parameter depend on the error terms actually present in the data. When the errors are not known but are assumed to have been drawn randomly from a population with known distributional properties, then the regression estimates have a statistical distribution. We studied the interpretation of the variance of this distribution in the preceding section. Now we concentrate on the *mean* of this distribution.

The statistical distribution of a regression estimate may or may not center around its corresponding parameter. Consider, for example, a case in which there are three different alternative ways of estimating a parameter, β, and in which the distributions of these estimates ($\hat{\beta}$, $\tilde{\beta}$, and $\hat{\beta}^*$), are as presented in Figure 2.1. The distribution of $\tilde{\beta}$ is centered around its parameter value β.

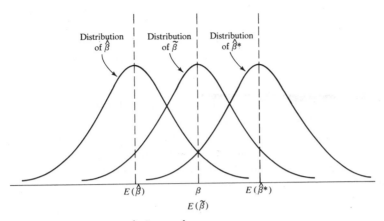

Figure 2.1. Distribution of $\hat{\beta}$, $\tilde{\beta}$, and β^*

Such estimates are called *unbiased*. The estimates $\tilde{\beta}$ and β^* are not centered around their parameter values and are called *biased*. The bias of an estimate is measured as the difference between the mean value of the distribution of an estimate and its true parameter value. When the bias is positive—that is, when the mean value of the distribution is larger than its parameter, as in the case of β^*—then the estimator is said to be upward biased. Conversely, when the bias is negative, as in the case of $\tilde{\beta}$, the estimator is negatively biased.

The use to which an estimate is to be put determines which one is chosen as "appropriate." When the researcher is interested in testing a null hypothesis, for example, he may prefer an unbiased estimate because many test procedures are based only on unbiased estimators of a parameter. When his objective is not the elimination of bias but maximum precision, then, of course, he will look for the minimum variance estimator even though it may be biased. When the researcher is faced with a situation in which he has to choose between an unbiased estimate with large variance and a biased estimate with small variance, he cannot use either the bias or the variance as the sole criterion but must give some weight to each aspect. One criterion that gives equal importance to these two measures is the *mean square error*. Since the variance is in the square units of bias, the giving of equal importance to bias and to variance implies that equal importance is attached to variance and to the *square* of bias. Thus the mean square error is defined as the sum of variance and of the square of bias. If one of these two components gets smaller at the expense of the other, then the net "benefit" is reflected by the mean square error. The mean square error (MSE) of an estimate $\hat{\beta}$ may be written as

$$\text{MSE}(\hat{\beta}) = V(\hat{\beta}) + [\text{Bias}(\hat{\beta})]^2. \tag{2.36}$$

The mean square error of an estimate is a theoretical property based on the two unknown quantities, variance $[V(\hat{\beta})]$ and bias [Bias $(\hat{\beta})$]. A researcher using an estimate in a decision-making process will probably want the estimate to have the smallest mean square error rather than the smallest of one of its two components.

The choice of estimation procedure depends crucially on the prospective use of an estimate. In some cases the researcher looks for unbiased estimates at any cost, in other cases he wants maximum precision even though the estimate may be biased, in yet other cases he wants the minimum mean square error. The point is that in applied econometrics the researcher should be alert to all aspects of his estimation procedure and should not rely on only one of them.

2.5   Best Linear Unbiased Estimates

In a typical textbook example of a regression equation, the causal relationship between the dependent and independent variables is linear and the specified relation is the truth. In this case the independent variables are clearly defined and exhaust the sources of variation in the dependent variable. We may express the true specification as

$$y_t = \beta_1 x_{1t} + \beta_2 x_{2t} + \cdots + \beta_k x_{kt} + \varepsilon_t, \qquad (2.37)$$

where lower-case letters represent the deviations of the variables from their respective means. In this case the constant term is implicit.

Suppose the researcher conducts a hypothetical experiment in which he draws a set of error terms (ε's) at random from a known distribution and computes y on the basis of these errors and of the independent variables (x's). Corresponding to a set of errors he obtains a set of least squares estimates for the β's. If he repeats the experiment, drawing a new set of errors every time but keeping the same values for the x's, then the least squares estimates of the β's obtained in each trial will exhibit a statistical distribution.

The Gauss-Markov theorem[7] states that when the estimated equation is the truth, the distribution of the ordinary least squares estimate of any of the parameters in the above experiment is centered around the true values; that is, all the estimates are unbiased. Further, the ordinary least squares estimates are the least variance estimates in the family of linear unbiased estimates.

When an estimate is unbiased and has minimum variance in the family of

---

[7] Since the proof of the Gauss-Markov theorem is well known and can be found in many textbooks (See specific References, p. 221) we shall not reproduce it here.

linear unbiased estimates, then it is called the Best Linear Unbiased Estimate (BLUE), or the minimum variance unbiased estimate. This is a theoretical property of the estimation procedure because the bias and variance are based on the theoretical statistical distribution of the least squares estimate in the above experiment.

In applied econometric research, the theoretical properties of an estimate are unattainable goals and serve only as points of reference. Researchers seldom know the truth which would let them take advantage of any of these theoretical properties.

When an applied econometrician deviates from the truth—for example, by estimating a regression equation which is not the truth or by using a definition of a variable that is not the truth—he commits a "sin." That is, his estimates may not have the same theoretical properties as though he had used the truth. In all real situations the alternatives open to an applied econometrician involve certain amounts of such sin, and the best he can hope for in estimating a parameter is to follow the least sinful procedure of them all.

2.6 Left-Out Variables

The true regression specification can be estimated only when the researcher knows the truth and has data on all the variables to estimate it. A common situation is one in which the researcher has "left out" variables either because he is unaware of their presence in the true specification or because he does not have data for including them in the estimated equation.

The use of ordinary least squares when some variables are left out may introduce bias into the estimates. Bias that originates in this way is called *specification bias*. For instance, let the truth be

$$y_t = \beta_1 x_{1t} + \beta_2 x_{2t} + \varepsilon_t. \tag{2.38}$$

Here the lower-case letters are again deviations from the mean, hence the constant is implicit. We assume that no data are forthcoming for the variable x_2, which is therefore operationally unobservable, so the following regression equation is estimated:

$$y_t = \hat{\beta}_1 x_{1t} + e_t. \tag{2.39}$$

The ordinary least squares estimate $\hat{\beta}_1$ is obtained by imposing restrictions on the residuals (e's) (see page 8). Since the constant term is implicit in the estimation, $\sum e = 0$. The second constraint ($\sum x_1 e = 0$) yields

$$\sum x_1 y = \hat{\beta}_1 \sum x_1^2. \tag{2.40}$$

The estimate $\hat{\beta}_1$ that satisfies the constraints on the residuals is

$$\hat{\beta}_1 = \sum x_1 y / \sum x_1^2. \tag{2.41}$$

Since the truth is given by (2.38), equation (2.41) can be rewritten as

$$\hat{\beta}_1 = (\beta_1 \sum x_1^2 + \beta_2 \sum x_1 x_2 + \sum x_1 \varepsilon) / \sum x_1^2. \tag{2.42}$$

Since the x's are held constant in repeated trials and the distribution of ε is assumed to have zero mean, the mean value of the theoretical distribution of $\hat{\beta}_1$ is[8]

$$E(\hat{\beta}_1) = \beta_1 + \beta_2 \cdot \sum x_1 x_2 / \sum x_1^2. \tag{2.43}$$

The estimate of β_1 from the ordinary least squares estimation of (2.40) when the truth is (2.38) is a biased estimate of the parameter β_1. The bias $(\beta_2 \cdot \sum x_1 x_2 / \sum x_1^2)$ depends on two terms, namely the regression coefficient of the left-out variable in the true relation (β_2), and the comovements of the left-out variable with the included variable $(\sum x_1 x_2 / \sum x_1^2)$.

The expression in equation (2.43) can be generalized into a case with K variables by using the Yule notation.[9] A linear regression equation in Yule notation may be written as

$$y = b_{y1, 23 \cdots K} x_1 + b_{y2, 13 \cdots K} x_2 + \cdots + b_{yK, 123 \cdots (K-1)} x_K + e. \tag{2.44}$$

---

[8] A more rigorous treatment of this topic is presented in Chapter 3.

[9] G. U. Yule and M. G. Kendall, *An Introduction to the Theory of Statistics*, Griffen & Co. (London), 14th ed., 1958, p. 284.

The coefficients (*b*'s) are given subscripts in a systematic way. The first subscript denotes the dependent variable, the second denotes the corresponding independent variable. The list after the comma (,) indicates other independent variables included in the regression. Since the estimates of the regression coefficients depend on which other independent variables are present in a regression, these subscripts are explicitly stated in each case.

In the case with x_2 as the dependent variable and x_1 as the independent variable, the regression equation in the Yule notation may be written as

$$x_2 = b_{21}x_1 + e. \tag{2.45}$$

Where b_{21} is the ordinary least squares estimate from equation (2.45):

$$b_{21} = \sum x_1 x_2 / \sum x_1^2. \tag{2.46}$$

Using the Yule notation we may rewrite expression (2.43) as

$$E(\hat{\beta}_1) = \beta_1 + \beta_2 \cdot b_{21}, \tag{2.47}$$

where b_{21} is computationally equivalent to the regression coefficient when x_2 is the dependent variable, x_1 is the independent variable, and no other variables are present in the regression equation. This term is used in simplifying the algebraic expressions and does not have any causal or economic interpretation.

The expression for bias in the general case where the truth is

$$y_t = \beta_1 x_{1t} + \beta_2 x_{2t} + \beta_3 x_{3t} + \cdots + \beta_K x_{Kt} + \varepsilon_t, \tag{2.48}$$

and where the following regression equation, without x_2, is estimated,

$$y_t = \hat{\beta}_1 x_{1t} + \hat{\beta}_3 x_{3t} + \cdots + \hat{\beta}_K x_{Kt} + e_t, \tag{2.49}$$

the expected value of the estimate $\hat{\beta}_1$ is given by

$$E(\hat{\beta}_1) = \beta_1 + \beta_2 \cdot b_{21, 3 \cdots K}, \tag{2.50}$$

where $b_{21,3\ldots K}$ is computationally equivalent to the regression coefficient of x_1 when x_2 is the dependent variable and all the variables $x_1, x_3, \ldots, x_K$ are included in the regression equation.[10]

When an independent variable in the true relation is omitted, the regression coefficients from the OLS estimation procedure are biased. The extent of bias in each coefficient can be obtained from equation (2.50). When a variable from the true relation is left out, a part of its influence in explaining the movements of the dependent variable is captured by the other independent variables. The relative share of each included variable in capturing the influence of the left-out variable is given by the b's (also called the auxiliary regression coefficients). If one independent variable has a larger partial relation to the left-out variable than another, then the extent of bias in its coefficient will be larger.

When the left-out variable is not correlated with any of the independent variables then, of course, none of the coefficients is biased. In any sample the researcher rarely observes zero correlation; hence some bias always exists, however small it may be. The applied econometrician is not worried about the mere existence of bias, but about its extent. When the bias is of second order in magnitude (smaller than the rounding error in truncating decimals), or even smaller, it causes no concern in most practical situations.

2.7   An Example of Bias

Consider the linear regression equation (2.51) which attempts to explain the quantity of rice produced in the Guntur district of India for the period 1941–61. (The data are presented in Table 2.1.)

$$\text{Rice}_t = 993.633 + 0.046\, I_t + 0.706\, D_t + 48.219\, R_t \qquad R^2 = 0.56 \qquad (2.51)$$
$$\phantom{\text{Rice}_t =\ } (1368.440) \quad (0.273) \quad\;\; (0.945) \qquad (11.282)$$

where I, D, and R are acres of irrigated area, acres of dry area, and inches of rainfall respectively.

The estimates of the regression parameters are disturbing, because it is well known that dry land does not produce .706 tons at the margin whereas irrigated land produces only .046 tons at the margin, keeping all other independent variables constant. This strange result is a consequence of misspecification of the estimated regression equation. The true specification of the rice production function includes many variables in addition to those included in (2.51).

---

[10] $x_2 = b_{21,34\ldots K}\, x_1 + b_{23,14\ldots K}\, x_3 + \cdots + b_{2K,134\ldots K-1}\, x_K + e^*$.

Table 2.1. Data for the Rice Production Function for Guntur District (India)

Year	Rice Produced (100 tons)	Irrigated Area (100 acres)	Dry Area (100 acres)	Rainfall (inches)
1941–42	3325	3910	414	30
–43	2948	4047	484	25
–44	3146	4188	267	34
–45	3341	4177	329	38
–46	3372	4254	263	32
–47	2796	4201	312	37
–48	3250	4252	384	36
–49	3260	4266	385	31
–50	3313	4280	494	42
–51	2180	4315	359	27
1951–52	2120	4378	274	27
–53	2203	4311	246	21
–54	3038	4441	212	31
–55	3038	4439	227	39
–56	2991	4680	328	34
–57	2779	4732	176	33
–58	3130	4910	249	28
–59	3523	5073	136	50
–60	2911	4992	314	31
–61	3845	5356	153	46
1961–62	3650	4624	125	46

Source: *Indian Agricultural Statistics*, Ministry of Food and Agriculture (New Delhi); and *Statistical Abstract of Andhra Pradesh*, Government of Andhra Pradesh (Hyderabad).

When the nature and data of these other variables are known, then we will include them in the regression equation to correct for the bias in (2.51)

In this particular example, let us assume that data on the other variables are not available. We may conjecture that the combined influence of the variables left out in the true equation is a smooth function of time. This influence could comprise any systematic factors that affect the production function, whose movements may be changing with time in a smooth linear form. (Discussion of the interpretation of such variables may be found in Chapter 4.)

The regression equation, with "t," time, as an explicit independent variable for our example, is

$$\text{Rice}_t = -739.9 + 0.578\, I_t + 0.218\, D_t + 46.6\, R_t - 40.4\, t \qquad R^2 = 0.61.$$
$$(1755.4)\ (0.442)\quad (0.959)\quad (10.9)\quad (26.9)$$

$$(2.52)$$

Equation (2.52) is consistent with our a priori experience. Comparison of (2.51) with (2.52) reveals that the omission of a crucial variable from equation (2.51) has caused the independent variables, I and D, to capture a part of the omitted variable's influence on the dependent variable. In the case of I the bias is negative, and in the case of D it is positive. Apparently the left-out variable has not substantially biased the coefficient of the rainfall variable.

In this particular example, equation (2.51) indicates the presence of specification bias, and equation (2.52) sheds some light on the nature of the problem. The variable "t" here helps us by pointing out the presence of specification bias but does not explain what variables caused it. When the researcher has knowledge of the variables left out, inclusion of them will improve the situation. In our example, one has to explore for the factors causing the specification bias by using the signals provided by the variable "t." In many practical problems the bias in the estimates may not be so conspicuous.

2.8   Irrelevant Variables

A case inverse to that of left-out variables is the case in which a variable not specified in the true equation is added. Such variables are called *irrelevant*.
Consider the true equation

$$y_t = \beta_1 x_{1t} + \varepsilon_t. \tag{2.53}$$

Instead, the following equation is estimated:

$$y_t = \hat{\beta}_1 x_{1t} + \hat{\beta}_2 x_{2t} + e_t. \tag{2.54}$$

The OLS estimate $\hat{\beta}_1$ is given by[11]

$$\hat{\beta}_1 = \frac{\sum x_2^2 \cdot \sum x_1 y - \sum x_2 x_1 \cdot \sum x_2 y}{\sum x_1^2 \cdot \sum x_2^2 - \sum x_1 x_2 \cdot \sum x_1 x_2}. \tag{2.55}$$

---

[11] The ordinary least squares estimation of (2.54) imposes three constraints on the error term (e). They are $\sum e = 0$, $\sum x_1 e = 0$ and $\sum x_2 e = 0$. Since the constant term is implicit $\sum e = 0$, the other two constraints yield

$$\sum x_1 y = \beta_1 \sum x_1^2 + \beta_2 \sum x_1 x_2,$$
$$\sum x_2 y = \beta_1 \sum x_1 x_2 + \beta_2 \sum x_2^2.$$

Eliminating $\hat{\beta}_2$ from these two equations we obtain (2.55).

The true relation is given by the equation (2.53). By substituting this expression in (2.55) we obtain

$$\hat{\beta}_1 = \beta_1 + \frac{\sum x_2^2 \sum x_1 \varepsilon - \sum x_1 x_2 \sum x_2 \varepsilon}{\sum x_1^2 \sum x_2^2 - \sum x_1 x_2 \sum x_1 x_2}. \qquad (2.56)$$

When expected values are taken on both the sides of (2.56), it may be seen that the OLS estimate of β_1 from equation (2.54) is nonetheless an unbiased estimate: $E(\hat{\beta}_1) = \beta_1$.

The addition of an irrelevant variable to a true specification does not cause bias in the estimates of the other independent variables. However, such an addition does necessarily increase the variance of the estimates of all the coefficients. This result is shown on page 57. Thus, even though the irrelevant variable does not introduce bias in the regression coefficients, it will reduce the precision of the estimates. This result can be generalized to a K-variable model.

The researcher may verify that the ordinary least squares estimate of β_2 is also an unbiased estimate. The mean value of the theoretical distribution of $\hat{\beta}_2$ is centered around its true value, namely zero. For analytical convenience the true equation (2.53) may also be written as

$$y_t = \beta_1 x_{1t} + 0 \cdot x_{2t} + \varepsilon_t. \qquad (2.57)$$

Obviously, in an empirical situation the addition of an irrelevant variable will typically yield a nonzero coefficient value for $\hat{\beta}_2$. This should not be interpreted as indicating that its distribution has a nonzero mean, for such is not the case when the true equation is (2.53).

2.9 Superfluous Variables

Up to this point we have been dealing with cases in which the truth is known. In applied econometrics the expressions for bias and variance offer only cold comfort, for in many practical situations it is neither simple nor unambiguous to state which is a left-out variable or an irrelevant variable. The theoretical results previously cited are useful only when we can "stick our necks out" and categorically state what we believe to be the truth. When the choice between competing alternatives will not make serious operational difference, a practicing econometrician should follow guidelines that involve a certain amount of judgment; he should not rely solely on knowledge of theoretical derivations.

When a new independent variable is added to a regression equation, the regression coefficients either (1) change substantially or (2) do not change substantially. When the coefficients change, it can be either because specification bias was present in the regression coefficients before the variable was added or because the added variable is irrelevant and the estimates after inclusion of the new variable are coming from a different distribution with larger variance but with the same mean.

When the true equation is known we can distinguish between these possible situations, but when the researcher has only the computed regressions the problem requires a less straightforward assessment. Whenever the regression coefficients in the two situations are obviously different, our decision as to which equation to use may be extremely crucial for the interpretation of the parameter estimates. In this case we must rely purely on the theoretical underpinnings of the regression equation to tell us which to choose.

On the other hand, we may have the following situation, in which the researcher fits the two regressions

$$Y_t = \beta_0 + \beta_1 X_{1t} + \varepsilon_{1t}, \tag{2.58}$$

$$Y_t = \beta_0 + \beta_1 X_{1t} + \beta_2 X_{2t} + \varepsilon_{2t}. \tag{2.59}$$

Assume that no unambiguous theory exists that specifies which of the two equations is the truth. If equation (2.58) is true, estimation of equation (2.59) yields an unbiased estimate of β_1 but with a larger variance than to the corresponding estimate from equation (2.58). If equation (2.59) is true and (2.58) is estimated, then $\hat{\beta}_1$ is biased but has a smaller variance than the corresponding estimate from (2.59). A full discussion of this point is postponed until Chapter 3 (p. 60). Which equation should be chosen for empirically estimating the parameters is not easily answered, and the distribution properties of the estimates help us very little.

In some situations, the variable X_2 may be such that, if (2.58) is true, adding it as an independent variable and estimating equation (2.59) will yield less precise estimates, but the loss in precision may be minor. It may also happen the other way—that is, if equation (2.59) is the true specification, leaving out the variable X_2 and estimating (2.58), will yield biased estimates, but the bias may be minor. If X_2 displays these two traits when included and excluded respectively, then we label it as a *superfluous variable*. A superfluous variable's exclusion or inclusion in a regression equation does not alter the other coefficient estimates or their standard errors "significantly." That is, when such a variable is added or deleted in a regression, the "damage" to the regression coefficients of the other variables is not operationally significant. Since we do not know the truth, we use or discard the superfluous variables to suit our convenience.

Some standard guidelines in the use of superfluous variables are given here, but a word of warning is needed. These rules are applicable only to variables whose legitimacy in the regression under study is dubious. When the theory unambiguously states that a variable is a specified explanatory variable then, of course, it should not be omitted even though it might appear superfluous.

As one guideline, then, when X_2 is a superfluous variable and its inclusion does not increase R^2 sufficiently to increase the $\bar{R}^2$, then the variable is deleted from the regression. When inclusion of a superfluous variable increases R^2 sufficiently to increase $\bar{R}^2$, then it is included because it reduces the residual variance but does not affect the other regression coefficients. When its inclusion reduces the residual variance, this implies that the residuals have some systematic component which is being captured by the included variable, and error terms are thereby better specified.

What we mean by "better specification of the errors" may be seen in the following example. Suppose the two possible truths are (2.58) and (2.59). When both are estimated, it is seen that the estimate of β_1 does not change when (2.59) is estimated but that $\bar{R}^2$ goes up. Here X_2 is superfluous, but ε_1 contains $\beta_2 X_2$ which is systematic, so that ε_2 is better specified in (2.59) as a random variable because the systematic part, $\beta_2 X_2$, was purged from ε_1. So we say that in this particular case we may choose (2.59) as the appropriate regression equation because (1) we can still correctly interpret the estimated results and (2) we have significantly taken account of a systematic part of the error term.

A common practice among many researchers is to compute the *t*-ratios of the regression coefficients defined as

$$t(\hat{\beta}_i) = \hat{\beta}_i/\text{st. error}(\hat{\beta}_i) \tag{2.60}$$

and to discard the variables with *t*-ratios below a certain small value. This is not recommended as a common research method, for it is not possible to recognize a superfluous variable solely on the basis of the magnitude of its *t*-ratio. It is true that when a variable with a *t*-ratio smaller than unity is discarded from a regression equation the $\bar{R}^2$ increases,[12] but this increase does

---

[12] A proof of this statement may be found in Y. Haitovsky, "A Note on the Maximization of $\bar{R}^2$," *American Statistician*, **23** (No. 1), Feb. 1969, pp. 20–21. This statement is valid only when one variable alone is being discarded; it should not be used for successive selection of variables or for discarding several variables from the same equation. See P. Rao, "Letter to the Editor," *American Statistician*, **24** (No. 3), June 1970, p. 27.

not imply that the variable is superfluous. It may or may not be. *If the discarding of a variable changes the regression coefficients of other variables, then it cannot be superfluous even if its deletion increases R^2.* In such cases even if the variables in question have very small t-ratios their continued presence in the regression equation is dictated by theoretical considerations and not by the summary statistics.

2.10 Example of Misuse of Criteria for Identification of Superfluous Variables

If the researcher starts out with conceptual errors, the standard criteria for identification of superfluous variables can no longer be used. For example, suppose theory has indicated that the demand for Ceylonese tea (TEA) in the United States is a function of disposable income (Y^d), the price of Ceylonese tea (P_{CY}), and the price of a close substitute—Brazilian coffee (P_{BZ})—all relative to the price of food commodities in the United States. In the log-linear form the estimated demand function for the period 1947–68 (data are presented in Table 2.2) is

$$\log \text{TEA} = 3.95 + 0.14 \log P_{BZ} + 0.75 \log Y^d + 0.05 \log P_{CY} \qquad \bar{R}^2 = 0.52.$$
$$\quad\ (1.99)\ \ (0.14) \qquad\qquad (0.24) \qquad\quad (0.41)$$

$$(2.61)$$

Here the t-ratio of the price variable (P_{CY}) is very "low" and the coefficient has the "wrong" sign. If the researcher concludes that the demand for Ceylonese tea is price inelastic and discards (P_{CY}) while reestimating the demand function, he gets

$$\log \text{TEA} = 3.73 + 0.14 \log P_{BZ} + 0.73 \log Y^d \qquad \bar{R}^2 = 0.54.$$
$$\quad\ (0.71)\ \ (0.13) \qquad\qquad (0.14)$$

$$(2.62)$$

By comparing (2.61) and (2.62) he may jump to the conclusion that the price variable (P_{CY}) is superfluous and might interpret it as evidence that the demand for Ceylonese tea is, in fact, price inelastic.

He will be misguided, though, because he has forgotten one salient aspect of the demand for Ceylonese tea in the United States: the strong competition

Table 2.2. Quantity and Prices of Tea and Substitutes

	Quantity of Tea Imported TEA	Import Price of Ceylonese Tea P_{CY}	Import Price of Brazilian Coffee P_{BZ}	U.S. Disposable Income (Billions \$) Y^d	Consumer Price Index (Food Commodities)	Import Price of Indian Tea P_I
1947	19.89	0.453	0.225	169.8	81.3	0.389
48	45.08	0.514	0.230	189.1	88.2	0.528
49	31.70	0.522	0.254	188.6	84.7	0.514
50	44.56	0.484	0.450	206.9	85.8	0.490
51	31.12	0.480	0.494	226.6	95.4	0.491
52	41.37	0.444	0.501	238.3	97.1	0.420
53	45.94	0.473	0.529	252.6	95.6	0.424
54	39.80	0.576	0.648	257.4	95.4	0.565
55	38.89	0.580	0.478	275.3	94.0	0.678
56	41.90	0.523	0.461	293.2	94.7	0.532
57	46.04	0.492	0.449	308.5	97.8	0.556
58	39.43	0.480	0.412	381.8	101.9	0.517
59	43.54	0.496	0.322	337.3	100.3	0.536
60	48.32	0.513	0.326	350.0	101.4	0.563
61	44.31	0.507	0.322	364.4	102.6	0.575
62	51.50	0.471	0.301	385.3	103.6	0.547
63	53.49	0.463	0.297	404.6	105.1	0.553
64	58.94	0.453	0.396	438.1	106.4	0.542
65	53.29	0.468	0.399	473.2	108.8	0.543
66	53.54	0.450	0.368	511.6	114.2	0.530
67	56.05	0.439	0.347	546.3	115.2	0.510
1968	49.91	0.417	0.336	589.0	119.2	0.471

Source: U.S. Department of Commerce, *United States Imports of Merchandise for Consumption, Commodity by Country of Origin*, Bureau of the Census. Disposable income and price of food commodities are taken from the *Economic Report of the President*.

from other tea-growing countries of the world. He should be reluctant to accept the implication that the price of other close substitutes does not influence the demand for Ceylonese tea.

One must, therefore, always search the theory for any conceptual errors. In this case the error can be readily recognized, since Ceylonese tea and Indian tea are such close substitutes in consumption that as the price of Indian tea changes, so does the demand schedule for Ceylonese tea. The latter can be properly interpreted only when the price of Indian tea is held constant.

Multiple regression analysis allows us to hold other specified variables constant only when they are included in the regression equation. Clearly, the demand for tea equation (2.61) did not include the price of Indian tea, and therefore the coefficient of log P_{CY} was including two effects: changes in the price of Ceylonese tea (movements along a given demand schedule) and changes in the price of Indian tea (shifts in the demand schedule).

Even if our coefficient estimate for $\log P_{CY}$ were of the correct sign, we would still be observing the combined effect, and as a result the variable might seem superfluous according to our usual criteria.

Inclusion of the price of Indian tea (P_I) in the regression equation gives the following estimates:

$$\log \text{TEA} = 2.84 + 0.19 \log P_{BZ} + 0.26 \log Y^d - 1.48 \log P_{CY} + 1.18 \log P_I$$
$$\quad (2.00) \ (0.13) \qquad\quad (0.37) \qquad\quad (0.98) \qquad\quad (0.69)$$

$$\bar{R}^2 = 0.56.$$

$$(2.63)$$

The empirical results now confirm our theoretical expectations. *A general rule, then, is not to throw out automatically a variable which seems superfluous by standard criteria. Rather, one must first fully eliminate all possible conceptual errors that could have led to these results.* When there is a conceptual error one must *not* look to his data to tell him whether a superfluous variable is present in his regression equation.

2.11 Dominant Variables

In many empirical studies theory tells us unambiguously that a particular independent variable is relevant in explaining the movements of the dependent variable, but it cannot be included in the regression equation because it is a *dominant* variable. Such a variable dominates all the other variables in the regression and attempts to account for all variation in the dependent variable, leaving nothing to be explained by other variables. This situation frequently occurs in empirical research where the dependent variable is somehow functionally related to an independent variable in "fixed proportions." For example, in a production function of wheat a relation is fixed between the output and the amount of seed used. This relation is fairly constant for all observations, and when the amount of seed is used as an independent variable it explains all the variation in the dependent variable despite the presence of other variables such as capital, labor, etc.

Dominant variables present a problem of estimation techniques rather than a theoretical issue as to the relevance of an independent variable. As E. D. Domar puts it:

I wonder what has happened in all these [production function] studies to material inputs. If they are omitted because of the lack of required data, we have an answer, even if, to my mind, a regrettable one .... It seems to me that a production function is supposed to explain a productive process, such as the making of potato chips from potatoes (and other ingredients), labor and capital. It must take some ingenuity to make potato chips without potatoes.[13]

Domar's statement cannot be contested on theoretical grounds. Empirical work, however, may require the deletion of primary material inputs in a production function simply because these inputs are so "dominant" as to cause all other included variables to become superfluous. An example will serve to demonstrate this point.

Consider the problem of estimating the production function for Indian woolen textile industries. Let the production function, relating the output (Q) with the inputs—capital (K), labor(L), and raw materials (M)—be

$$Q = AK^{\beta_1}L^{\beta_2}M^{\beta_3}e^{\varepsilon}, \qquad (2.64)$$

where the error terms are specified as exponential to the natural base (e). When the prices of all the inputs and of output are constant for all observations the production function may also be expressed as

$$q = ak^{\beta_1}l^{\beta_2}m^{\beta_3}e^{\varepsilon}, \qquad (2.65)$$

where the lower-case letters now stand for the values of output and of inputs. The parameters (β's) in equations (2.64) and (2.65) are the same.

The production function for woolen textiles estimated from the data presented in Table 2.3 is

$$\log q = -0.408 - 0.059 \log k - 0.002 \log l + 1.094 \log m \qquad \bar{R}^2 = 0.997.$$
$$\quad (0.256) \quad (0.043) \qquad (0.051) \qquad (0.065)$$

$$(2.66)$$

---

[13] Murray Brown, ed., *The Theory and Empirical Analysis of Production*, NBER by Columbia Univ. Press (N.Y.), 1967. pp. 471–72.

Table 2.3.   Inputs and Output of Indian Woolen Textiles

	Value of Output (1,000 Rs.) q	Wage Bill (1,000 Rs.) l	Book Value of Fixed Capital (1,000 Rs.) k	Value of Raw Material (1,000 Rs.) m
1956 Bombay	49224	9506	17088	37108
U.P.	27074	8666	2246	18283
Mysore	1355	439	716	1269
Punjab	60035	12295	9256	47306
Bengal	18036	2521	1802	13235
1957 Bombay	76359	7790	19395	55676
U.P.	28562	4871	3259	19656
Mysore	1045	196	637	1005
Punjab	68134	7144	10461	51132
Bengal	17221	1379	2878	12556
1958 Bombay	74356	8365	20421	50242
U.P.	30752	5015	2707	22269
Mysore	1270	176	614	973
Punjab	72225	8227	11989	53165
Bengal	16794	1353	2749	13069

Source: *Census of Indian Manufactures*, Central Statistical Organization (Calcutta).

In a production function we expect all the β's to be positive, but the regression equation (2.66) yields negative values for the estimates of β_1 and β_2. By discarding the variables (log k) and (log l) and re-estimating the production function we obtain

$$\log q = -0.531 + 1.049 \log m \qquad \bar{R}^2 = 0.998. \qquad (2.67)$$
$$(0.232) \quad (0.014)$$

A comparison of equations (2.66) and (2.67) leads to the conclusion that capital and labor are superfluous variables in the production of woolen textiles. This, however, is a misinterpretation of the regression equation. In this example the raw materials variable is *dominant*, and is being transformed into output at a more or less fixed conversion ratio. The inclusion of log m as an independent variable leaves no room for other inputs. By deleting this variable (log m) from regression equation (2.66) and re-estimating the function, we obtain

$$\log q = -0.026 + 0.413 \log k + 0.708 \log l \qquad \bar{R}^2 = 0.938. \qquad (2.68)$$
$$(1.255) \quad (0.161) \qquad (0.138)$$

Estimates of β_1 and β_2 in equation (2.68) have proper signs and reasonable magnitudes.

Even though, theoretically speaking, the production function is given by equation (2.65), its parameters are not empirically estimable, because of the dominant role played by the input (raw materials). The production functions given by (2.66) and (2.68) may not have the same theoretical interpretation. However, the regression equation (2.68) can legitimately be interpreted as describing a production process that uses capital and labor in transforming raw materials into output. The output may be viewed either as the product (textiles) or the amount of raw material (wool) processed by the industry. As long as there is one-to-one correspondence between the raw materials and the product, the production function given by the regression equation (2.68) is operationally useful—for example, in hiring and firing labor—and has not been harmed by the exclusion of raw materials as an input.

Some researchers have overcome the conceptual problems presented by raw materials by deleting them and specifying the dependent variable in a production function as *value added by manufacturing* instead of total real output or as the total value of output.

The presence of dominant variables cannot be ascertained on a priori grounds. There may always be a possibility of substitution between the dominant variable and the other independent variables. For example, consider the production of wheat. It might appear that a farmer must always plant the same proportion of seed to wheat. Yet some farmers may be able to obtain the same yield by planting less seed while employing extra workers to scare the crows away so that none of the seed will be eaten before germination. Other farmers may find it more economical to let the crows have their way, not to hire extra workers, and instead to plant more seeds. Here labor can be substituted for raw materials. We cannot know that the substitution took place until we attempt to estimate our wheat production function. Only in the case in which some farmers substitute labor for seed and others do not, can seed be treated as a nondominant variable in the regression equation. That is, if the sample shows a sufficient amount of substitution between the raw material and other variables, then the raw material will not show up as dominant.

A similar example occurs in the production of sugar, in which substitution is possible between capital used and sugar cane. With more capital, one can extract a larger percentage of sucrose from the cane.

Whether a variable is truly superfluous or is a consequence of the presence of dominant variables must be determined by investigation, and no rule of thumb can be given to solve this problem. If conceptual errors exist in the specification, these guidelines are not valid. It is to be kept in mind that *no statistical tool or econometric guide is a good substitute for theory*. Guidelines indicate where to look in case of trouble, but not necessarily how to solve the problem.

2.12 Regression Coefficients with Wrong Signs

Often when regression coefficients are estimated the sign is opposite to that which the researcher believes to be true. When this happens, many researchers unfortunately drop the guilty variable from the regression equation with no further mention. In many cases, however, this is not an acceptable procedure, for a wrong sign may be a warning, *inter alia*, of incorrect definitions, specifications, or interpretations.

We frequently interpret coefficients in such a way that the estimated sign or magnitude appears to be different from what is expected. This may be due to an incorrect interpretation, which in turn may have resulted from treating an implicit form of the equation as the explicit form. That is, our estimating equation may be derived from another equation; and thus some of our explicit coefficients may be equivalent to a function of some unrecognized implicit coefficients.

Consider, for example, the following income determination equation for India for the period 1951–63, from data presented in Table 2.4:

$$Y_t = 11.20 + 0.406 \, I_t + 0.887 \, Y_{t-1} \qquad \bar{R}^2 = 0.96, \qquad (2.69)$$
$$(11.42) \quad (0.455) \quad (0.147)$$

Table 2.4. National Income and Investment in India at Constant Prices

Year	National Income at '48–49 Prices (Billions of Rs.)	Investment at '48–49 Prices (Billions of Rs.)
1951	88.5	4.96
52	99.0	6.88
53	94.6	3.77
54	100.3	5.38
55	102.8	8.67
56	104.8	10.86
57	110.0	14.15
58	108.9	12.30
59	116.5	12.30
60	118.6	12.46
1961	127.3	16.83
62	130.6	15.49
63	133.1	16.94

Source: *Reserve Bank of India Bulletin*, March 1965.

where Y is the national income in constant prices and I is investment in constant prices defined as the sum of savings and net capital inflow (Reserve Bank of India estimates).

If the researcher interprets the coefficient of I as the investment multiplier, he will immediately conclude that there is a misspecification of some sort. If he recomputes the regression by discarding the variable Y_{t-1}, he obtains the following equation:

$$Y_t = 77.27 + 2.997\ I_t \qquad \bar{R}^2 = 0.84. \qquad (2.70)$$
$$(4.40)\quad (0.377)$$

The coefficient of I in (2.70) is consistent with the a priori notions of the investment multiplier.

If comparison of (2.69) and (2.70) then leads to the conclusion that Y_{t-1} does not belong in the equation, the deduction is wrong. In the first place, the coefficient of I_t in (2.69) should not be interpreted as the long-run investment multiplier; rather, it is the *impact* investment multiplier. The coefficient of I_t in (2.70) also cannot be interpreted as the long-run investment multiplier, for equation (2.70) violates economic theory: it implies that investment has a once-and-for-all one-shot effect on income.[14]

If the researcher desires the true long-run multiplier, he must look at the steady-state solution of (2.69), where Y_t is assumed to be equal to Y_{t-1}. He then obtains an implicit long-run investment multiplier of

$$\left[\frac{0.406}{1 - 0.887} \right] \simeq 3.6.$$

Had the researcher understood the implications of (2.69), his remarking of a "small" coefficient of I_t would not have induced him to throw Y_{t-1} out of the equation.

Often the estimated results need not be conspicuous to warn of the presence of conceptual errors. When a signal is given in the form of a wrong sign or magnitude, the researcher should not ignore the warning, but rather should try to improve his specification of the regression equation.

A common cause of wrong signs in empirical research occurs when the

---

[14] Economic theory tells us that the effect of investment on income is felt over a long period of time, and not during the current period alone. Estimation of problems of this nature are discussed in Chapter 7.

variables are not appropriately defined. Consider, for example, the demand for a commodity (Q) as a function of disposable income (Y), the price of the commodity (P), and the price of all other commodities represented by the wholesale price index (W):

$$\log Q_t = \beta_0 + \beta_1 \log Y_t + \beta_2 \log P_t + \beta_3 \log W_t + \varepsilon_t. \tag{2.71}$$

Suppose the variable Y is measured in current prices, whereas the true relation is in constant prices. If disposable income in constant prices is (Y/W), then the true relation is

$$\log Q_t = \alpha_0 + \alpha_1 \log (Y/W)_t + \alpha_2 \log P_t + \alpha_3 \log W_t + \varepsilon_t, \tag{2.72}$$

which simplifies to

$$\log Q_t = \alpha_0 + \alpha_1 \log Y_t + \alpha_2 \log P_t + (\alpha_3 - \alpha_1) \log W_t + \varepsilon_t. \tag{2.73}$$

The estimated coefficient of $\log W$ in equation (2.73) is actually a function of several parameters, and interpretation as if it were $\hat{\alpha}_3$ leads to wrong conclusions.

If specification and interpretation of the coefficients are correct, a coefficient can still attain a wrong sign because of the sampling distribution of the estimates. If this is the case, we generally observe the coefficient to be not significantly different from zero statistically; deletion of the variable because of its wrong sign may still lead to misspecification. When the coefficient is significantly different from zero statistically and has the wrong sign, then some aspect of the problem has not been unveiled. Instead of throwing away the variable, it is better to retain it in the equation so that other researchers may be able to explain the apparent inconsistency. When the variable with a wrong sign is superfluous, in the sense that its deletion does not affect the other coefficients and does not decrease $\bar{R}^2$, then this problem is not serious.

2.13 Multicollinearity

In some cases, even though a theory clearly indicates the independent variables in explaining movements in a dependent variable, it may not be possible to interpret some of the parameters of the regression equation.

Consider the following example:

$$S_t = \beta_0 + \beta_1 L_t + \beta_2 R_t + \beta_3 X_{3t} + \beta_4 X_{4t} + \varepsilon_t, \qquad (2.74)$$

where S is sales revenue, L is the number of left shoes sold, R is the number of right shoes sold, and X_3 and X_4 are other products. The revenue comes from selling *both* the right and the left shoes, therefore each has legal claim in explaining the movements in sales revenue; but then some of the parameters in equation (2.74) have no meaningful interpretation.

The parameter β_1, for example, is the partial derivative of S with respect to left shoes, keeping all the other variables, including right shoes, constant. Such a situation is never observed because shoes are always sold in pairs. Even if the parameter values β_1 and β_2 in (2.74) were somehow obtained, they could not be interpreted. This problem arises whenever there is a fixed relationship between independent variables.

In many empirical problems the basis of interconnection may not be so conspicuous, but even in the absence of any theoretical reason the data may be such that a one-to-one relation between the variables is present. Whatever the source of the fixed relation, the problem can be averted by redefining the variables in such a way as to make the parameters subject to interpretation. For example, in the above case instead of specifying the independent variables as left and right shoes separately, a new variable defined as "a pair of shoes" may be used. The equation then becomes

$$S_t = \beta_0 + \beta P_t + \beta_3 X_{3t} + \beta_4 X_{4t} + \varepsilon_t, \qquad (2.75)$$

where P is the number of pairs of shoes sold.

Now consider the reverse case. In many situations, even though theoretically a technical relation exists between independent variables, the observed data may not exhibit any such relation. Consider, for example, the following hypothetical equation to explain long-run price levels:

$$P_t = \beta_0 + \beta_1 C_t + \beta_2 DD_t + \beta_3 X_{3t} + \beta_4 X_{4t} + \varepsilon_t, \qquad (2.76)$$

where P, C, and DD are price levels, currency, and demand deposits, respectively. Suppose a law requires a minimum currency reserve ratio (C/DD). The researcher may expect a technical relation between C and DD; but if the banks in fact maintain free reserves he does not observe any such technical relation in his data. In such cases the parameters of equation (2.76) do have a valid interpretation. Regardless of what might have been expected a priori, the technical relation between independent variables poses problems of interpretation only when it appears in the data.

The presence of any fixed relation between independent variables presents a problem called *multicollinearity*.

Although researchers show a growing tendency to blame all econometric problems on this demon, we suggest that it may often be largely a theoretical nightmare rather than an empirical reality.

The applied econometrician does need some guidelines in order to detect the presence of multicollinearity in his data, however, and a few indicators are available. A standard rule that some investigators have been using calls for inspection of the simple correlations among the independent variables. One should realize that simple correlations are only elements of the entire correlation matrix and, hence, may or may not contribute to problems of multicollinearity. *One should not, a priori, rule out estimation of any regression equation because of high simple correlations between any two independent variables.*

Consider, for example, the following regression, which attempts to explain heartbeat (Y) among cardiac patients in a given hospital by the length of the right leg (X_1) and the length of the left leg (X_2):

$$Y_t = \beta_0 + \beta_1 X_{1t} + \beta_2 X_{2t} + \varepsilon_t. \tag{2.77}$$

If the researcher computes the simple correlation between X_1 and X_2 he will observe "high" correlation; he therefore suspects multicollinearity and hesitates to estimate the equation. If another researcher were to look at the same equation with X_1 and $X_2^*(=X_2 - X_1)$ he would see a "low" correlation between X_1 and X_2^* and conclude that multicollinearity was not a problem. But the implicit estimates of β_1 and β_2 from (2.77) will be identical whether the second independent variable is X_2 or X_2^*. This is so because the conditions imposed on the residuals for estimation in either case are implicitly the same.

The researcher would get a meaningful regression equation by including X_1 and X_2. If one of the variables were deleted, he would obtain nonsensical results. Because of the asymmetry of the heart, its beat is a function of *difference* in the length of the legs and not of the length of either. By including both variables, the researcher is implicitly allowing the difference in the two variables to enter the regression equation as an independent variable. This example (due to Professor Maurice G. Kendall) serves to show that the inspection of simple correlations for an indication of multicollinearity is not an adequate rule.

When one independent variable is a linear function of the other, then the ordinary least squares estimation procedure fails. For example, in equation (2.77) the estimates of the three parameters β_0, β_1, and β_2 are obtained by solving the three constraints on the residuals:

$$\sum e = 0, \tag{2.78}$$

$$\sum x_1 e = 0, \tag{2.79}$$

$$\sum x_2 e = 0. \tag{2.80}$$

A nontrivial solution exists only when the above three constraints are independent. When a linear relation exists between X_1 and X_2, the second and the third equations are not independent. Hence, when X_2 is a linear function of X_1 the ordinary least squares solution of $\hat{\beta}$'s cannot be obtained. This property may be used in detecting the existence of fixed relations between independent variables.

When a regression equation has several parameters to be estimated, the least squares algorithm for $\hat{\beta}$ is usually expressed in matrix notation as

$$\hat{\beta} = (X'X)^{-1}X'Y. \tag{2.81}$$

When a linear relation exists between independent variables, then the matrix $(X'X)$ is singular and has no inverse. The applied econometrician rarely inverts the matrix in one step. All algorithms obtain the inverse by "pivoting-in" (including) one variable at a time. When a variable being pivoted-in is a linear function of already pivoted-in variables, the diagonal element of the matrix becomes zero, or nearly zero, when computational errors are present. Such variables can be detected and skipped with no difficulty. Most computer programs check for zero elements along the diagonal at each step and notify the researcher of the presence of any linear relation. These problems can easily be remedied by appropriately redefining the independent variables.

Sometimes the computational errors and errors of measurement can be large enough to cause a nonzero diagonal element in the matrix. In such cases the regression coefficients will remain fairly stable before and after the variable is introduced, but the standard errors of all the coefficients will increase beyond reasonable limits following its introduction. When X_1 and X_2 are collinear, X_2 will turn out to be superfluous when X_1 is already in the regression, and vice versa. The $\bar{R}^2$ invariably goes down when the second variable is added to the equation.

Some researchers attribute even a slight change in standard errors to multi-collinearity. This practice should be discouraged. Consider, for example, the two estimated equations

$$y_t = \hat{\beta}_1 x_{1t} + e_{1t}, \tag{2.82}$$

$$y_t = \tilde{\beta}_1 x_{1t} + \tilde{\beta}_2 x_{2t} + e_{2t}, \tag{2.83}$$

where both were estimated by ordinary least squares.

The estimates $\hat{\beta}_1$ and $\tilde{\beta}_1$ have two different theoretical distributions with different variances (see p. 56):

$$V(\hat{\beta}_1) = \sigma_\varepsilon^2 / \sum x_1^2, \tag{2.84}$$

$$V(\tilde{\beta}_1) = \sigma_\varepsilon^2 / \left[\sum x_1^2 (1 - r_{x_1 x_2}^2) \right]. \tag{2.85}$$

When correlation between the two independent variables ($r_{x_1 x_2}$) differs from zero, then the variance of $\tilde{\beta}_1$ is larger than that of $\hat{\beta}_1$.

In some situations the correlation between the independent variables may be close enough to unity to make the variance of the estimate extremely large. In such cases the estimate is not "reliable." When the (unknown) standard deviation of the estimate is very large relative to the mean of the distribution, the researcher may discard the variable to improve the mean square error of the other estimates (see p. 66). He should remember that the theoretical variance of an estimate depends not only on the correlation between the independent variables but also on the variation of the independent variables; for example, the variances of both the estimates $\hat{\beta}_1$ and $\tilde{\beta}_1$ decrease with $\sum x_1^2$.

Even though the correlation between the independent variables is "nearly" unity, the variation in the independent variable $\sum x_1^2$ may offset the term $(1 - r_{x_1 x_2}^2)$ and make the theoretical variance very small.[15] Since the value of $\sum x_1^2$ increases with the sample size, the problem of multicollinearity, except in the sense of a fixed relation between the independent variables as in the example of right and left shoes, does not usually arise in large samples.

When multicollinearity is present, the exclusion of one of the variables

---

[15] This is precisely what was happening in the heart beat example.

from the regression equation does not decrease the explanation of the dependent variable. Consider the equation

$$Y_t = \beta_0 + \beta_1 X_{1t} + \beta_2 X_{2t} + \beta_3 X_{3t} + \varepsilon_t. \tag{2.86}$$

Let there be a linear functional relationship between X_1 and X_3,

$$X_{3t} = a + b X_{1t}. \tag{2.87}$$

Suppose that instead of (2.86) the following regression equation is estimated:

$$Y_t = \hat{\beta}_0 + \hat{\beta}_1 X_{1t} + \hat{\beta}_2 X_{2t} + e_t. \tag{2.88}$$

By using equation (2.50), we have

$$E(\hat{\beta}_1) = \beta_1 + \beta_3 \cdot b, \tag{2.89}$$

$$E(\hat{\beta}_2) = \beta_2. \tag{2.90}$$

Since X_3 can be defined in any arbitrary units, we define the units such that $b = 1$, and we have equation (2.89) as

$$E(\hat{\beta}_1) = \beta_1 + \beta_3. \tag{2.91}$$

The entire influence of the variable X_3 is captured by the included variable, and the other coefficients are totally unaffected.

When the researcher is interested in explaining the movements of the dependent variable, or in predicting the values of Y, then it makes no difference whether the variable X_3 is in the regression or not. When his objective is to estimate the coefficients of the other independent variables, for example β_2, then again exclusion of the variable X_3 will not damage the estimate. To isolate the influences of X_1 and X_3, however, becomes a computationally impossible task. This is a fortuitous situation, for even if the researcher were given the empirical estimates he would have no way of interpreting them.

The problem of which variables are to be included in a regression equation is a major problem in applied econometrics. Rules are helpful, but they cannot make decisions for the applied econometrician.

> The capacity to judge that these are or are not to be disregarded, that they should or should not affect what observable phenomena are to be identified with what entities in the model, is something that cannot be taught; it can be learned but only by experience and exposure in the "right" scientific atmosphere, not by rote. It is at this point that the "amateur" is separated from the "professional" in all sciences and that the thin line is drawn which distinguishes the "crackpot" from the "scientist."[16]

---

[16] M. Friedman, *Essays in Positive Economics*, University of Chicago Press (Chicago), 1953, p. 25.

3

Bias and Precision of
the Regression Estimates

In the previous chapter we presented an intuitive feel for a number of problems of estimation in applied econometrics. We shall now turn to a more rigorous treatment of some of these problems. In many empirical situations the researcher leaves out some independent variables or includes others that do not belong in the true specification of a causal relation between the dependent and the independent variables. In this chapter we shall study the nature of the bias and of the precision of ordinary least squares estimates when the estimated equation is not the truth. Since bias and precision depend crucially on the theoretical distribution of the error terms, we shall analyze the distributional properties of regression estimates under different specifications of the error terms.

To set the stage, let us consider a case in which the truth is given by

$$y_t = \beta_1 x_{1t} + \varepsilon_t, \tag{3.1}$$

where the lower-case letters refer to variables measured as deviations from their respective means.

The ordinary least squares estimate of β_1 from a set of given values of y and x is obtained as

$$\hat{\beta}_1 = \sum x_{1t} y_t / \sum x_{1t}^2. \tag{3.2}$$

The estimate given by (3.2) may not be equal to the parameter value β_1, because

$$\hat{\beta}_1 = \sum x_{1t}(\beta_1 x_{1t} + \varepsilon_t)/\sum x_{1t}^2, \qquad (3.3)$$

$$\hat{\beta}_1 = \beta_1 + \sum x_{1t}\varepsilon_t/\sum x_{1t}^2, \qquad (3.4)$$

and the term $\sum x_{1t}\varepsilon_t/\sum x_{1t}^2$ is not always equal to zero. Different sets of ε's will give different values for the estimate $\hat{\beta}_1$ even though the values of x_1 are the same. Since the values of the ε's are unknown, the researcher has no way of discovering the seriousness of the deviation of the estimate $\hat{\beta}_1$ from the parameter, or in which direction this deviation lies. The best he can do is to establish the theoretical distribution of the estimate $\hat{\beta}_1$ when he knows the properties of the error terms. The statistical distribution of $\hat{\beta}_1$ for various specifications of the error term constitutes the problem of precision of the estimates.

There are several ways of approaching this problem. A convenient specification that serves the needs of applied econometricians is to treat the x's as constants (fixed in repeated samples) and to study the statistical properties of $\hat{\beta}_1$ given by equation (3.4). When the error terms are assumed to have been generated by a specified statistical process, the distributional properties of $\hat{\beta}_1$ can be theoretically established.

A simple case is one in which the error terms are assumed to have been generated by a random selection from a statistical distribution with a mean of zero and a constant variance, σ_ε^2. In this specification the error term corresponding to any time period t, is generated by the same statistical distribution, and the error term corresponding to one time period does not depend in any systematic way on the error terms of the other time periods. This specification of the error generating process may be stated as

$$E(\varepsilon_t) = 0, \qquad (3.5)$$

$$E(\varepsilon_t^2) = \sigma_\varepsilon^2, \qquad (3.6)$$

$$E(\varepsilon_t \varepsilon_{t'}) = 0 \quad \text{for} \quad t \neq t'. \qquad (3.7)$$

The first two equations, (3.5) and (3.6), specify that the error terms are generated by a statistical distribution with mean zero and variance σ_ε^2 for all time periods, and the last equation, (3.7), specifies that they are generated by a random selection.

Since the error terms have a statistical distribution, the estimate $\hat{\beta}_1$ which depends on these error terms also has a statistical distribution. The mean of the distribution of $\hat{\beta}_1$ may be obtained by taking the expected value of the estimate

$$E(\hat{\beta}_1) = \beta_1 + E(\sum x_{1t}\varepsilon_t / \sum x_{1t}^2). \tag{3.8}$$

Since the distribution of $\hat{\beta}_1$ is defined for our purposes under the assumption that the x_1's are fixed in repeated samples, we obtain under assumption (3.5)

$$E(\hat{\beta}_1) = \beta_1 + \frac{\sum x_{1t}E(\varepsilon_t)}{\sum x_{1t}^2} = \beta_1, \tag{3.9}$$

since $E(\varepsilon_t) = 0$ for all t.

The ordinary least squares estimate $\hat{\beta}_1$ has a statistical distribution with mean β_1, the parameter value itself. Thus $\hat{\beta}_1$ is an unbiased estimate of β_1 in the true equation.

Let us now turn to the variance of the theoretical distribution of $\hat{\beta}_1$. When $\hat{\beta}_1$ is an estimate with a statistical distribution, its variance is defined as

$$V(\hat{\beta}_1) = E[\hat{\beta}_1 - E(\hat{\beta}_1)]^2 \tag{3.10}$$

$$= E[\sum x_{1t}\varepsilon_t / \sum x_{1t}^2]^2 \tag{3.11}$$

$$= (1/\sum x_{1t}^2)^2 \cdot E[\sum x_{1t}\varepsilon_t]^2. \tag{3.12}$$

Using the relation

$$E[\sum x_{1t}\varepsilon_t]^2 = E[x_{11}^2\varepsilon_1^2 + x_{12}^2\varepsilon_2^2 + \cdots + 2x_{11}x_{12}\varepsilon_1\varepsilon_2 + \cdots]$$
$$= x_{11}^2 E(\varepsilon_1^2) + x_{12}^2 E(\varepsilon_2^2) + \cdots + 2x_{11}x_{12}E(\varepsilon_1\varepsilon_2) + \cdots \tag{3.13}$$

and substituting the specifications (3.6) and (3.7) in equation (3.13) we obtain

$$E[\sum x_{1t}\varepsilon_t]^2 = \sigma_\varepsilon^2 \cdot \sum x_{1t}^2. \tag{3.14}$$

The variance of the estimate $\hat{\beta}_1$ may be obtained by substituting equation (3.14) in equation (3.12) to obtain

$$V(\hat{\beta}_1) = \sigma_\varepsilon^2 / \sum x_{1t}^2 . \tag{3.15}$$

The variance of the estimate $\hat{\beta}_1$ depends on the variance of ε and on the values of the independent variable. The variance of $\hat{\beta}_1$ increases with the variance of the error term and decreases with $\sum x_{1t}^2$.

The variance of the estimate $\hat{\beta}_1$ provides a measure of the precision of the estimate. The larger the variance of the estimate, the more widespread the distribution and the smaller the precision of the estimate.

When the error terms are generated randomly by a statistical distribution with mean zero and variance σ_ε^2, the ordinary least squares estimate $\hat{\beta}_1$ has a theoretical distribution with mean β_1 and variance $\sigma_\varepsilon^2 / \sum x_{1t}^2$. The variance of the estimate involves the variance of the error term from the regression equation, which is generally unknown. We can still use these results for comparison of alternative estimation procedures if all procedures involve the same unknowns.

3.1 Irrelevant Variables

Consider a situation in which the researcher could have estimated the parameter β_1 by estimating the regression equation

$$y_t = \tilde{\beta}_1 x_{1t} + \tilde{\beta}_2 x_{2t} + e_t. \tag{3.16}$$

When equation (3.1) is the truth, estimated equation (3.16) is a misspecification of the model, because it includes an irrelevant variable, (x_2).

In the ordinary least squares estimation procedure the estimate $\tilde{\beta}_1$ is obtained (see p. 34) as

$$\tilde{\beta}_1 = \frac{\sum x_2^2 \cdot \sum x_1 y - \sum x_1 x_2 \cdot \sum x_2 y}{\sum x_1^2 \cdot \sum x_2^2 - \sum x_1 x_2 \cdot \sum x_1 x_2} . \tag{3.17}$$

By substituting the true relation (3.1) for y in equation (3.17) we obtain

$$\tilde{\beta}_1 = \beta_1 + \frac{\sum x_2^2 \sum x_1 \varepsilon - \sum x_1 x_2 \sum x_2 \varepsilon}{\sum x_1^2 \sum x_2^2 - \sum x_1 x_2 \cdot \sum x_1 x_2} . \tag{3.18}$$

Using the specification of the error terms (3.5) and assuming that the x's are fixed in repeated samples (nonstochastic), we can show that

$$E(\tilde{\beta}_1) = \beta_1. \tag{3.19}$$

The distribution of $\tilde{\beta}_1$, the estimate of β_1 obtained from the misspecified model (3.16), has a mean of β_1. Even though x_2 is an irrelevant variable (does not appear in the true equation) the estimate $\tilde{\beta}_1$ is an unbiased estimate.

Now the researcher has two different ways of estimating β_1, both of which yield unbiased estimates, and he can base his choice on the precision of each. The variance of estimate $\hat{\beta}_1$ is given by (3.15), so we turn to the variance of estimate $\tilde{\beta}_1$:

$$V(\tilde{\beta}_1) = E[\tilde{\beta}_1 - E(\tilde{\beta}_1)]^2 \tag{3.20}$$

$$= E\left[\frac{\sum x_2^2 \sum x_1\varepsilon - \sum x_1 x_2 \sum x_2 \varepsilon}{\sum x_1^2 \sum x_2^2 - \sum x_1 x_2 \cdot \sum x_1 x_2}\right]^2 \tag{3.21}$$

$$= \frac{(\sum x_2^2)^2 \cdot E(\sum x_1\varepsilon)^2 + (\sum x_1 x_2)^2 \cdot E(\sum x_2 \varepsilon)^2 - 2 \cdot \sum x_2^2 \cdot \sum x_1 x_2 \, E(\sum x_1\varepsilon \cdot \sum x_2 \varepsilon)}{[\sum x_1^2 \cdot \sum x_2^2 - \sum x_1 x_2 \cdot \sum x_1 x_2]^2}. \tag{3.22}$$

Using the specification of errors (3.6) and (3.7), and evaluating the terms as in (3.10) through (3.15), equation (3.22) can be simplified to

$$V(\tilde{\beta}_1) = \sigma_\varepsilon^2 \cdot \sum x_2^2 \cdot \frac{\sum x_1^2 \cdot \sum x_2^2 - \sum x_1 x_2 \cdot \sum x_1 x_2}{[\sum x_1^2 \cdot \sum x_2^2 - \sum x_1 x_2 \cdot \sum x_1 x_2]^2} \tag{3.23}$$

$$= \sigma_\varepsilon^2 \cdot \sum x_2^2 / [\sum x_1^2 \cdot \sum x_2^2 - \sum x_1 x_2 \cdot \sum x_1 x_2] \tag{3.24}$$

$$= \sigma_\varepsilon^2 / [\sum x_1^2 (1 - r_{x_1 x_2}^2)]. \tag{3.25}$$

The variance of the estimate $\tilde{\beta}_1$ depends on $\sum x_1^2$ as well as on the correlation between variables x_1 and x_2. The variance of the estimate $\hat{\beta}_1$ does not depend on the correlation between the two variables. Since the square of the correlation coefficient is always a positive fraction (non-zero), the variance of $\tilde{\beta}_1$ is usually larger than the variance of $\hat{\beta}_1$.

However, when the correlation between the two independent variables $(r_{x_1x_2})$ is zero, both $\hat{\beta}_1$ and $\tilde{\beta}_1$ have the same variance. In this case both the estimates are identical, because zero correlation implies $(\sum x_1x_2 = 0)$. When the term $(\sum x_1x_2)$ is zero, equation (3.17) reduces to

$$\tilde{\beta}_1 = \sum x_1y / \sum x_1^2, \tag{3.26}$$

which is the same as the estimate $\hat{\beta}_1$ given by equation (3.2).

Now let us turn to the distributional properties of $\tilde{\beta}_2$, the regression coefficient of the irrelevant variable. The ordinary least squares estimate $\tilde{\beta}_2$ is obtained as

$$\tilde{\beta}_2 = \frac{\sum x_1^2 \sum x_2y - \sum x_1x_2 \sum x_1y}{\sum x_1^2 \sum x_2^2 - \sum x_1x_2 \sum x_1x_2}. \tag{3.27}$$

By substitution of the true relation (3.1) for y,

$$\tilde{\beta}_2 = \frac{\sum x_1^2 \sum x_2\varepsilon - \sum x_1x_2 \sum x_1\varepsilon}{\sum x_1^2 \sum x_2^2 - \sum x_1x_2 \sum x_1x_2}. \tag{3.28}$$

The value of $\tilde{\beta}_2$ also depends on the error terms (ε's). Since the error terms follow a statistical distribution, so does $\tilde{\beta}_2$. The mean value of the theoretical distribution of $\tilde{\beta}_2$ is

$$E(\tilde{\beta}_2) = 0. \tag{3.29}$$

The true value of the parameter β_2 is, however, zero, because for analytical purposes the true relation (3.1) may also be written as

$$y_t = \beta_1x_{1t} + 0 \cdot x_{2t} + \varepsilon_t. \tag{3.30}$$

The regression coefficient of the irrelevant variable has a statistical distribution with mean zero which is its true parameter value; $\tilde{\beta}_2$ is, therefore, an unbiased estimate.

This result may be generalized to a case of several irrelevant variables by rewriting the truth as

$$y_t = \beta_1 x_{1t} + 0 \cdot x_{2t} + \cdots + 0 \cdot x_{kt} + \varepsilon_t, \qquad (3.31)$$

where the independent variables x_2 through x_k are irrelevant variables. The estimates of regression coefficients of all the irrelevant variables (x_2 through x_k) have theoretical distributions with zero mean, which is their true value. The estimate of the regression coefficient of x_1 is still unbiased.[1]

The variance of the distribution of $\tilde{\beta}_2$ is

$$V(\tilde{\beta}_2) = E[\tilde{\beta}_2 - E(\tilde{\beta}_2)]^2. \qquad (3.32)$$

Following the derivations in equations (3.21) through (3.25), we may derive the variance of $\tilde{\beta}_2$ in equation (3.16) as

$$V(\tilde{\beta}_2) = \sigma_\varepsilon^2 / \left[\sum x_2^2 (1 - r_{x_1 x_2}^2) \right]. \qquad (3.33)$$

Even though x_2 is an irrelevant variable according to the specification of the truth, its regression coefficient has nonzero variance. That is, when the regression is estimated the researcher may observe a nonzero value for $\tilde{\beta}_2$.

In the general case of a regression equation with k independent variables, whether they are relevant or not, the variance of $\tilde{\beta}_i$ is given by the ith diagonal element, and the covariance between $\tilde{\beta}_i$ and $\tilde{\beta}_j$ by the element in the ith column and jth row, in the following matrix:

$$\sigma_\varepsilon^2 \begin{bmatrix} \sum x_1^2 & \sum x_1 x_2 & \cdots & \sum x_1 x_k \\ \sum x_2 x_1 & \sum x_2^2 & \cdots & \sum x_2 x_k \\ \vdots & \vdots & \cdots & \vdots \\ \sum x_k x_1 & \sum x_k x_2 & \cdots & \sum x_k^2 \end{bmatrix}^{-1}$$

---

[1] The variance of the estimate $\tilde{\beta}_1$, however, increases with the number of irrelevant variables present in the equation. The unbiasedness of $\tilde{\beta}_1$ in the presence of irrelevant variables is not "free of charge."

3.2 Left-Out Variables

A similar situation frequently found in empirical research is one in which a parameter can be estimated from two different regression equations, one of which has a left-out variable. To analyze this case let us consider that the true relation is

$$y_t = \beta_1 x_{1t} + \beta_2 x_{2t} + \varepsilon_t, \tag{3.34}$$

where the error term (ε) follows the specification given by equations (3.5), (3.6), and (3.7).

When the researcher estimates the true relation (3.34), the estimate of β_1 by ordinary least squares is obtained as

$$\hat{\beta}_1 = \frac{\sum x_2^2 \sum x_1 y - \sum x_1 x_2 \sum x_2 y}{\sum x_1^2 \sum x_2^2 - \sum x_1 x_2 \sum x_1 x_2}. \tag{3.35}$$

By substituting the true relation (3.34) for y in equation (3.35) we obtain

$$\hat{\beta}_1 = \beta_1 + \frac{\sum x_2^2 \sum x_1 \varepsilon - \sum x_1 x_2 \sum x_2 \varepsilon}{\sum x_1^2 \sum x_2^2 - \sum x_1 x_2 \sum x_1 x_2}. \tag{3.36}$$

Since the error terms follow specification (3.5), it is easily seen that

$$E(\hat{\beta}_1) = \beta_1. \tag{3.37}$$

The theoretical distribution of $\hat{\beta}_1$ has the mean β_1, the true parameter value. The variance of the estimate $\hat{\beta}_1$ is

$$V(\hat{\beta}_1) = E[\hat{\beta}_1 - E(\hat{\beta}_1)]^2. \tag{3.38}$$

The algebra involved in evaluating expression (3.38) is similar to that used in evaluating equation (3.20), hence

$$V(\hat{\beta}_1) = \sigma_\varepsilon^2 / [\sum x_1^2 (1 - r_{x_1 x_2}^2)]. \tag{3.39}$$

The estimate $\hat{\beta}_1$ obtained by estimating the true relation (3.34) has a statistical distribution with mean β_1 and variance (3.39) when the error terms follow specifications (3.5), (3.6), and (3.7). Suppose the researcher, by misspecification, estimates the following regression equation:

$$y_t = \tilde{\beta}_1 x_{1t} + e_t. \tag{3.40}$$

The ordinary least squares estimate of β_1 in the misspecified model is obtained as

$$\tilde{\beta}_1 = \sum x_1 y / \sum x_1^2. \tag{3.41}$$

By substituting the true relation (3.34) for y in equation (3.41) we obtain

$$\tilde{\beta}_1 = \beta_1 + \beta_2 \sum x_1 x_2 / \sum x_1^2 + \sum x_1 \varepsilon / \sum x_1^2. \tag{3.42}$$

The mean value of the statistical distribution of $\tilde{\beta}_1$ when the errors follow specification (3.5) is

$$E(\tilde{\beta}_1) = \beta_1 + \beta_2 \frac{\sum x_1 x_2}{\sum x_1^2}. \tag{3.43}$$

Using the Yule notation, we may rewrite (3.43) as[2]

$$E(\tilde{\beta}_1) = \beta_1 + \beta_2 b_{21}. \qquad (3.43a)$$

When the true relation is (3.34) and the errors are generated by specification (3.5), the researcher has two alternative estimators, namely $\hat{\beta}_1$ and $\tilde{\beta}_1$. The first is unbiased, whereas $\tilde{\beta}_1$ is biased as a result of the misspecification

---

[2] This result may be generalized to a case in which several variables are left out. Consider, for example, the truth

$$y_t = \beta_1 x_{1t} + \beta_2 x_{2t} + \cdots + \beta_k x_{kt} + \varepsilon_t,$$

where the researcher has estimated (3.40) instead. The ordinary least squares estimate $\tilde{\beta}_1$ obtained by equation (3.41) may be expressed as

$$\tilde{\beta}_1 = \beta_1 + \beta_2 \Sigma x_2 x_1 / \Sigma x_1^2 + \cdots + \beta_k \Sigma x_k x_1 / \Sigma x_1^2 + \Sigma x_1 \varepsilon / \Sigma x_1^2.$$

The expected value of $\tilde{\beta}_1$ in the Yule notation is

$$E(\tilde{\beta}_1) = \beta_1 + \beta_2 b_{21} + \cdots + \beta_k b_{k1}.$$

A general expression for the bias of an estimate may be obtained by using the Yule notation. When the truth is

$$y_t = \beta_1 x_{1t} + \beta_2 x_{2t} + \beta_3 x_{3t} + \beta_4 x_{4t} + \beta_5 x_{5t} + \varepsilon_t,$$

and the estimated equation is

$$y_t = \tilde{\beta}_1 x_{1t} + \tilde{\beta}_2 x_{2t} + e_t,$$

by use of equation (3.35) it may be shown that

$$E(\tilde{\beta}_1) = \beta_1 + \beta_3 b_{31,2} + \beta_4 b_{41,2} + \beta_5 b_{51,2},$$
$$E(\tilde{\beta}_2) = \beta_2 + \beta_3 b_{32,1} + \beta_4 b_{42,1} + \beta_5 b_{52,1}.$$

In the b's the second primary subscript corresponds to the variable associated with the estimate, and the secondary subscripts correspond to all other independent variables present in the estimated equation. The number of terms contributing to bias is equal to the number of left-out variables.

of the model. If the researcher is interested only in unbiased estimators, his choice is obvious. But if he wants to consider the precision of the estimates as well, then he needs the variance of the distribution of the estimate.

The variance of $\tilde{\beta}_1$ is

$$
\begin{aligned}
V(\tilde{\beta}_1) &= E[\tilde{\beta}_1 - E(\tilde{\beta}_1)]^2 \\
&= E\left[\beta_1 + \beta_2 b_{21} + \frac{\sum x_1 \varepsilon}{\sum x_2^2} - \beta_1 - \beta_2 b_{21}\right]^2 \\
&= E\left[\frac{\sum x_1 \varepsilon}{\sum x_1^2}\right]^2.
\end{aligned}
\tag{3.44}
$$

The algebra involved in evaluating the expression $E[\sum x_1 \varepsilon / \sum x_1^2]^2$ is the same as in equations (3.10) through (3.15); hence[3]

$$
V(\tilde{\beta}_1) = \sigma_\varepsilon^2 / \sum x_1^2.
\tag{3.45}
$$

The variance of $\tilde{\beta}_1$ in equation (3.45) is therefore smaller than the variance of $\hat{\beta}_1$ in equation (3.39), even though the estimate $\tilde{\beta}_1$ corresponds to a mis-specified model, (3.40).[4] If the researcher can live with bias in the estimates and wants only estimates with smaller variance, then he will chose $\tilde{\beta}_1$ instead of $\hat{\beta}_1$ as an estimate of β_1.

In this case he has the option of choosing between a less efficient estimate of the true parameter β_1 and a more efficient estimate of a wrong (biased) value $(\beta_1 + \beta_2 \cdot b_{21})$. If lack of bias is the prime criterion, he will choose one estimate; he will choose the other if precision takes precedence. The better choice is not obvious unless he has some additional criterion of selection.

Since there is a trade-off between bias and precision of the estimates, separate consideration of either may not be desirable. One rule that weighs both these aspects is the concept of "quadratic loss." Whenever an estimate of a parameter differs from its true value, a loss proportional to the square of the difference between the estimate value and the parameter value

---

[3] Notice that even with several left-out variables the variance of $\tilde{\beta}_1$ is still given by equation (3.45).

[4] The variances are the same when $r_{x1x2} = 0$, in which case both the true and misspecified model yield the same estimate value.

is associated with that value of the estimate. Since the loss is assessed proportional to the square of the difference, it is called the "quadratic loss." Thus defined, the quadratic loss has a statistical distribution because its value depends on the value of the estimate, which has a statistical distribution. The expected value of the distribution of quadratic loss is called the *mean quadratic loss*, or the *mean square error*. The estimator having the least mean quadratic loss tends to minimize the quadratic loss to a decision maker if he uses the same estimator in repeated trials.

The mean square error, or the mean quadratic loss, may be formally defined as

$$\text{MSE}(\hat{\theta}) = E(\hat{\theta} - \theta)^2, \tag{3.46}$$

where θ is the parameter and $\hat{\theta}$ is an estimate of that parameter.

Mean square error can be expressed in terms of the variance and the bias of the estimate by first adding and then subtracting $E(\hat{\theta})$ in (3.46),

$$\text{MSE}(\hat{\theta}) = E[\hat{\theta} - E(\hat{\theta}) + E(\hat{\theta}) - \theta]^2 \tag{3.47}$$

$$= E[\hat{\theta} - E(\hat{\theta})]^2 + [E(\hat{\theta}) - \theta]^2 \tag{3.48}$$

because the cross-product term has a zero expected value. Hence, the mean square error may be written as

$$\text{MSE}(\hat{\theta}) = \text{Variance } (\hat{\theta}) + [\text{Bias } (\hat{\theta})]^2. \tag{3.49}$$

Using the concept of mean square error, we can compare the two previous estimates of β_1, namely $\hat{\beta}_1$ and $\tilde{\beta}_1$. Since $\hat{\beta}_1$ is an unbiased estimate of β_1, the mean square error of $\hat{\beta}_1$ is merely the variance of the estimate itself:

$$\text{MSE}(\hat{\beta}_1) = \sigma_\varepsilon^2 / [\sum x_1^2 (1 - r_{x_1 x_2}^2)]. \tag{3.50}$$

However, $\tilde{\beta}_1$ is biased, hence the mean square error is

$$\text{MSE}(\tilde{\beta}_1) = \sigma_\varepsilon^2 / \sum x_1^2 + \beta_2^2 \cdot b_{21}^2. \tag{3.51}$$

Although $\tilde{\beta}_1$ is obtained from a misspecified model, its mean square error can be smaller than that of $\hat{\beta}_1$. The condition under which this may occur may be obtained as

$$\text{MSE}(\hat{\beta}_1) > \text{MSE}(\tilde{\beta}_1). \tag{3.52}$$

By using the corresponding expressions for the mean square errors,

$$\sigma_\varepsilon^2 / \left[\sum x_1^2 (1 - r_{x_1 x_2}^2) \right] > \sigma_\varepsilon^2 / \sum x_1^2 + \beta_2^2 \left(\sum x_1 x_2 / \sum x_1^2 \right)^2, \tag{3.53}$$

$$\sigma_\varepsilon^2 / (1 - r_{x_1 x_2}^2) > \sigma_\varepsilon^2 + \beta_2^2 \sum x_2^2 \cdot r_{x_1 x_2}^2, \tag{3.54}$$

$$\sigma_\varepsilon^2 \left(\frac{1}{1 - r_{x_1 x_2}^2} - 1 \right) > \beta_2^2 \sum x_2^2 \cdot r_{x_1 x_2}^2, \tag{3.55}$$

$$1 > \beta_2^2 / \left[\frac{\sigma_\varepsilon^2}{\sum x_2^2 (1 - r_{x_1 x_2}^2)} \right]. \tag{3.56}$$

The expression

$$\frac{\sigma_\varepsilon^2}{\sum x_2^2 (1 - r_{x_1 x_2}^2)}$$

is the theoretical variance of the estimate $\hat{\beta}_2$ in the true equation (3.34). By using this relationship we can rewrite the condition (3.56) for smaller $\text{MSE}(\tilde{\beta}_1)$ compared to $\text{MSE}(\hat{\beta}_1)$ as

$$1 > \beta_2^2 / V(\hat{\beta}_2) \tag{3.57}$$

or

$$1 > |\tau|, \tag{3.58}$$

where

$$\tau = \beta_2/\sqrt{V(\hat{\beta}_2)} = \beta_2 \cdot \sqrt{\frac{\sum x_2^2(1 - r_{x_1 x_2}^2)}{\sigma_\varepsilon^2}}. \tag{3.59}$$

The researcher should note that τ is not the same as the t-ratio corresponding to $\hat{\beta}_2$. The t-ratio has estimates of the parameter and variance in the numerator and denominator, whereas τ has the theoretical values.

When τ is less than unity in magnitude the researcher can obtain a smaller mean square error for the estimate of β_1 by misspecifying the model rather than estimating the true regression equation.[5] The value of τ is, however, based on the true values of the parameter and of the variance of the estimate, both of which are generally unknown. This result can be successfully employed only when the researcher has reason to believe that the parameter value cannot take on certain prespecified values. For example, it is usually assumed that the marginal propensity to consume is always a positive fraction, and so is elasticity of output with respect to labor in a production function. If the researcher believes that even the extreme value of this parameter cannot make τ exceed unity, then he can discard the variable *if the only objective is to minimize the mean square error of the estimate of β_1*.

Note that as the sample size increases the quantity $\sum x_2^2$ also increases. Since this quantity appears in the numerator of equation (3.59), τ is an increasing function of sample size. With a large enough sample size the value of τ will exceed unity, therefore rule (3.58) will dictate that no variable should be deleted from the true equation.[6] Thus we may state that the gain in the mean square error of an estimate is essentially a small sample property of the ordinary least squares estimates due to deletion of a variable for which $|\tau| < 1$.

The choice of an estimator in applied econometrics is necessarily dictated by many considerations beyond the textbook properties of best linear unbiased estimates. The researcher seldom, if ever, knows the true specification and frequently cannot afford to include all variables that might seem relevant in explaining the movements of a dependent variable. When he includes a variable which does not belong in the true specification, he is increasing the

---

[5] In a regression equation with several independent variables, discarding an independent variable whose τ is less than unity in magnitude decreases the mean square error of *all* the other regression coefficients. The proof for a two variable case is due to T. D. Wallace, "Efficiencies for Stepwise Regressions," *Journal of the American Statistical Association*, Vol. 59, 1964, 1179–82. A proof for a K variable case is presented by P. Rao, "Some Notes on Misspecification in Multiple Regressions," *The American Statistician*, forthcoming.

[6] Note that irrelevant variables have $\tau = 0$; hence they always increase the mean square error of other estimates irrespective of the sample size.

variance of the estimates without biasing them. When he discards a variable he may be biasing the estimates but gaining in precision. The net effect of precision and bias can be more, or less, than with estimating the true relation. How much bias a researcher is willing to accept or how much precision he can forego depends on the specific situation and on the seriousness of the consequences of the results; no general guidelines can be set up.

3.3 Serial Correlation in the Errors

In some econometric studies the specification that the error terms in each observation are drawn independently of other error terms may be inappropriate. For example, in cases of expectation models and distributed lag specifications, even though the errors in the theoretical model may be independent of each other, those in the estimated equation may not be. A frequent case of dependence in error terms occurs in the context of time series studies where the errors in one time period are dependent on errors in previous periods.

When error terms are serially dependent, ordinary least squares estimation does not yield the best linear unbiased estimates, even if the estimated equation is the truth. In order to study the distributional properties of ordinary least squares estimates in such a case, let us consider a simple specification in which the error terms are generated by a first order Markov scheme:

$$\varepsilon_t = \rho\varepsilon_{t-1} + v_t, \tag{3.60}$$

where v is assumed to be drawn at random from a distribution with mean zero and variance σ_v^2 and is distributed independently of past values of the ε's.

By squaring equation (3.60) and taking the expected value we see that

$$V(\varepsilon) = \rho^2 V(\varepsilon) + V(v), \tag{3.61}$$

or

$$\sigma_\varepsilon^2 = \rho^2\sigma_\varepsilon^2 + \sigma_v^2 \tag{3.62}$$

$$\sigma_\varepsilon^2 = \sigma_v^2/(1 - \rho^2). \tag{3.63}$$

Given the value of the parameter ρ, the variance of ε is related to the variance of v.

The specification of error terms in the case of a first order Markov scheme may be written as

$$E(\varepsilon_t) = 0, \tag{3.64}$$

$$E(\varepsilon_t \varepsilon_{t-s}) = \rho^s \sigma_\varepsilon^2. \tag{3.65}$$

Let us consider the simple case in which the truth is

$$y_t = \beta x_t + \varepsilon_t. \tag{3.66}$$

The ordinary least squares estimation yields (see p. 55)

$$E(\hat{\beta}) = \beta + E(\sum x_t \varepsilon_t / \sum x_t^2). \tag{3.67}$$

Since $E(\varepsilon_t) = 0$ and the x's are assumed to be fixed in repeated samples, the estimate $\hat{\beta}$ is still unbiased. The serial correlation in the error terms does not introduce any bias in the regression estimates as long as we retain specification (3.64).

However, when the error terms are serially correlated the precision of the estimate $\hat{\beta}$ depends on the serial correlation parameter as well as on the process generating the independent variable. Consider the variance of $\hat{\beta}$:

$$V(\hat{\beta}) = E[\hat{\beta} - E(\hat{\beta})]^2 \tag{3.68}$$

$$= E[\sum x_t \varepsilon_t / \sum x_t^2]^2 \tag{3.69}$$

$$= (1/\sum x_t^2)^2 \cdot E[x_1^2 \varepsilon_1^2 + x_2^2 \varepsilon_2^2 + \cdots$$
$$+ 2 \cdot x_1 x_2 \varepsilon_1 \varepsilon_2 + 2 \cdot x_2 x_3 \varepsilon_2 \varepsilon_3 + \cdots$$
$$+ 2 \cdot x_1 x_3 \varepsilon_1 \varepsilon_3 + 2 \cdot x_2 x_4 \varepsilon_2 \varepsilon_4 + \cdots$$
$$+ \cdots]. \tag{3.70}$$

Since the x's are assumed to be fixed, using the specifications of the error terms (3.64) and (3.65) we obtain

$$V(\hat{\beta}) = \left(1/\sum x_t^2\right)^2 \cdot \sigma_\varepsilon^2 \cdot \left[\sum x_t^2 + 2 \sum \rho^s \sum x_t \cdot x_{t+s}\right]. \qquad (3.71)$$

When the error terms are serially independent ($\rho = 0$), then the variance of the estimate depends only on $\sum x^2$ and σ_ε^2; but when the errors are serially correlated the variance of $\hat{\beta}$ depends also on the terms $\sum x_t \cdot x_{t+s}$.

To incorporate the information on the independent variable as well as the error term, let us consider a simple case in which the independent variable is also generated by a first order Markov scheme:

$$x_t = \lambda x_{t-1} + w_t, \qquad (3.72)$$

where w_t is serially independent and has a statistical distribution with mean zero and variance σ_w^2. By assuming that the w's are independent of past values of the x's, we can use the following approximation to simplify the algebra:[7]

$$\sum x_t x_{t+s} \simeq \lambda^s \sum x_t^2. \qquad (3.73)$$

When the x's are generated by a first order Markov scheme with parameter λ, expression (3.71) may be written as

$$\begin{aligned} V(\hat{\beta}) &= \left(1/\sum x_t^2\right)^2 \cdot \sigma_\varepsilon^2 \cdot \left[\sum x_t^2 (1 + 2 \sum \rho^s \lambda^s)\right] \\ &= \left(\sigma_\varepsilon^2 / \sum x_t^2\right)[1 + 2\rho\lambda(1 + \rho\lambda + \rho^2\lambda^2 + \cdots)] \\ &= \left(\sigma_\varepsilon^2 / \sum x_t^2\right)[1 + 2\rho\lambda/(1 - \rho\lambda)] \\ &= \left(\sigma_\varepsilon^2 / \sum x_t^2\right)(1 + \rho\lambda)/(1 - \rho\lambda). \end{aligned} \qquad (3.74)$$

In this example the precision of the least squares estimate depends also on how the independent variable and the error terms are generated. The precision increases with the magnitude of ρ and λ when they are of the opposite sign and decreases when they are of the same sign.

When the error terms are serially correlated, the ordinary least squares estimate, though unbiased, does not have minimum variance. According to the well known Gauss-Markov theorem, the ordinary least squares estimate is the minimum-variance unbiased estimate only when the error terms are

---

[7] Since λ is a fraction, λ^s converges to zero as s increases.

serially independent and have the same variance for all observations. If the researcher knows the value of the parameter, ρ, then, by a suitable linear transformation of the variables, he can reduce equation (3.66) to a form in which the ordinary least squares estimation provides such minimum-variance estimates.

To explain this procedure: when the parameter ρ is known, the following transformation on the error terms generates a new error term which is serially independent:

$$\varepsilon_t^* = \varepsilon_t - \rho\varepsilon_{t-1}. \tag{3.75}$$

Since ε^* is nothing but v in equation (3.60), which is by specification serially independent and has the same variance for all observations, it satisfies all requirements for ordinary least squares estimation to yield the minimum-variance estimate. Consider equation (3.66) corresponding to time periods t and $t-1$:

$$y_t = \beta x_t + \varepsilon_t, \tag{3.76}$$

$$y_{t-1} = \beta x_{t-1} + \varepsilon_{t-1}. \tag{3.77}$$

By multiplying equation (3.77) by ρ and then subtracting it from equation (3.76) we obtain

$$(y_t - \rho y_{t-1}) = \beta(x_t - \rho x_{t-1}) + (\varepsilon_t - \rho\varepsilon_{t-1}). \tag{3.78}$$

By defining variables y^* and x^* as $(y_t - \rho y_{t-1})$ and $(x_t - \rho x_{t-1})$ respectively, we may rewrite equation (3.78) as

$$y_t^* = \beta x_t^* + \varepsilon_t^*. \tag{3.79}$$

In this equation the error terms are serially independent and are drawn from statistical distributions with the same variance. However, the equation is based on only $T-1$ observations, whereas there are T observations in all. The observation corresponding to y_1^* and x_1^* is not defined because it involves observation corresponding to time period 0. This problem can be overcome by noting that the expected value of ε_1 is zero with variance $\sigma_v^2/(1-\rho^2)$. By a suitable transformation on ε_1 we can obtain ε_1^*, which will have the same statistical properties as that of the other ε^*'s. Since $(1 - \rho^2)$ is a constant, the following transformation on ε_1 will provide the required ε_1^*:

$$\varepsilon_1^* = \sqrt{(1 - \rho^2)}\,\varepsilon_1. \tag{3.80}$$

To obtain ε_1^* in the regression equation we have to transform the dependent and the independent variables as well. The y_1^* and x_1^* are therefore $\sqrt{(1 - \rho^2)}\,y_1$ and $\sqrt{(1 - \rho^2)}\,x_1$ respectively.

By including the first observation also in equation (3.79) we have T observations. The ordinary least squares estimation based on the T transformed variables yields the unbiased minimum variance estimate of β.

The estimation of parameter β from these transformed variables is called *generalized least squares*,[8] to distinguish it from the estimation using untransformed variables in equation (3.66). This estimation procedure is very general and can be applied to a regression with several independent variables. Consider the general case in which

$$Y_t = \beta_0 + \beta_1 X_{1t} + \beta_2 X_{2t} + \cdots + \beta_k X_{kt} + \varepsilon_t, \tag{3.81}$$

where the error term ε is generated by a first order Markov scheme with parameter ρ. The generalized least squares estimates of the β's, which are the minimum-variance unbiased estimates, are obtained by applying ordinary least squares estimation to the following regression equation in which all the variables, dependent and independent, are transformed:

$$Y_t^* = \beta_0^* + \beta_1 X_{1t}^* + \beta_2 X_{2t}^* + \cdots + \beta_k X_{kt}^* + \varepsilon_t^*. \tag{3.82}$$

In (3.82) the transformed variables are obtained as

$$Y_t^* = Y_t - \rho Y_{t-1}, \tag{3.83}$$

$$X_{it}^* = X_{it} - \rho X_{it-1}, \tag{3.84}$$

$$Y_1^* = \sqrt{(1 - \rho^2)}\,Y_1, \tag{3.85}$$

$$X_{i1}^* = \sqrt{(1 - \rho^2)}\,X_{i1}. \tag{3.86}$$

[8] This method is also called Aitken's estimation (see Specific References, p. 221).

Note:

Although the generalized least squares estimates are minimum-variance unbiased estimates, they cannot be attained, because they involve the parameter value ρ which is rarely known to the researcher.

Case where OLS is not best

When the researcher suspects that the error terms are serially correlated and believes that the value is some specified value, say ρ^*, he can obtain the estimates from the transformed variables by treating the specified ρ^* as though it were the true parameter. When the true parameter value ρ is different from ρ^*, the estimates of the β's from the transformed variables are no longer the minimum-variance unbiased estimates.

Sometimes, even when the error terms were generated by a first order Markov scheme, the use of a value ρ^* different from ρ can yield estimates that are even less efficient than those yielded by ordinary least squares estimation from the untransformed variables.

To study the consequences of using the wrong value ρ^* for ρ in such a case, let us consider a situation having one independent variable (3.66), in which the errors were generated by the first order Markov scheme with parameter ρ, and the independent variable is also generated by a first order Markov scheme with parameter λ as in (3.72). To simplify the algebra, let us consider the case with only $T - 1$ observations, in which the transformations on dependent and independent variables using a value ρ^* for ρ are

$$y_t^* = y_t - \rho^* y_{t-1} \tag{3.87}$$

$$x_t^* = x_t - \rho^* x_{t-1}. \tag{3.88}$$

After transforming the variables as in (3.87) and (3.88), the researcher estimates the regression equation:

$$y_t^* = \hat{\beta}^* x_t^* + e_t, \tag{3.89}$$

where

$$\hat{\beta}^* = \sum y_t^* x_t^* / \sum x_t^{*2}. \tag{3.90}$$

By expressing the transformed variables in the form of the original variables the researcher obtains

$$\hat{\beta}^* = \beta + \frac{\sum (x_t - \rho^* x_{t-1})(\varepsilon_t - \rho^* \varepsilon_{t-1})}{\sum (x_t - \rho^* x_{t-1})^2}. \tag{3.91}$$

Since the expected value of ε is zero, $\hat{\beta}^*$ is an unbiased estimate of β irrespective of the value of ρ^*. The estimate $\hat{\beta}^*$ has a theoretical distribution with mean β and variance given by

$$V(\hat{\beta}^*) = E\left[\frac{\sum (x_t - \rho^* x_{t-1})(\varepsilon_t - \rho^* \varepsilon_{t-1})}{\sum (x_t - \rho^* x_{t-1})^2}\right]^2 \qquad (3.92)$$

$$\begin{aligned}
= \frac{1}{[\sum (x_t - \rho^* x_{t-1})^2]^2} &\cdot \{\sum (x_t - \rho^* x_{t-1})^2 E(\varepsilon_t - \rho^* \varepsilon_{t-1})^2 \\
&+ 2 \sum\sum (x_t - \rho^* x_{t-1})(x_{t+s} - \rho^* x_{t+s-1}) \\
&\qquad \cdot E[(\varepsilon_t - \rho^* \varepsilon_{t-1})(\varepsilon_{t+s} - \rho^* \varepsilon_{t+s-1})]\}. \quad (3.93)
\end{aligned}$$

To simplify the algebra involved, we may use the following approximations:[9]

$$\sum (x_t - \rho^* x_{t-1})^2 \simeq \sum x_t^2 (1 + \rho^{*2} - 2\rho^* \lambda) \qquad (3.94)$$

$$\sum (x_t - \rho^* x_{t-1})(x_{t+s} - \rho^* x_{t+s-1}) \simeq \lambda^{s-1}(\lambda - \rho^*)(1 - \lambda\rho^*) \sum x_t^2 \qquad (3.95)$$

$$E(\varepsilon_t - \rho^* \varepsilon_{t-1})^2 = \sigma_\varepsilon^2 (1 + \rho^{*2} - 2\rho^* \rho) \qquad (3.96)$$

$$E[(\varepsilon_t - \rho^* \varepsilon_{t-1})(\varepsilon_{t+s} - \rho^* \varepsilon_{t+s-1})] = \rho^{s-1}(\rho - \rho^*)(1 - \rho\rho^*)\sigma_\varepsilon^2. \qquad (3.97)$$

By use of the expressions in (3.94) through (3.97), the variance of $\hat{\beta}^*$ may be simplified to

$$V(\hat{\beta}^*) \simeq \frac{\sigma_\varepsilon^2}{\sum x_t^2} \cdot \frac{(1 + \rho^{*2} - 2\rho^* \lambda)(1 + \rho^{*2} - 2\rho^* \rho) + 2(\lambda - \rho^*)(\rho - \rho^*)(1 - \lambda\rho^*)(1 - \rho\rho^*) \sum \rho^{s-1}\lambda^{s-1}}{(1 + \rho^{*2} - 2\rho^* \lambda)^2}. \qquad (3.98)$$

Since $\sum \rho^{s-1}\lambda^{s-1} = (1 - \rho\lambda)^{-1}$ we can write (3.98) as

$$V(\hat{\beta}^*) \simeq \frac{\sigma_\varepsilon^2}{\sum x_t^2} \left\{\frac{1 + \rho^{*2} - 2\rho^* \rho}{1 + \rho^{*2} - 2\rho^* \lambda} + \frac{2(\lambda - \rho^*)(\rho - \rho^*)(1 - \lambda\rho^*)(1 - \rho\rho^*)}{(1 - \rho\lambda)(1 + \rho^{*2} - 2\rho^* \lambda)^2}\right\}.$$

$$(3.99)$$

---

[9] Since ρ and λ are fractions, their higher powers converge to zero.

Though this expression for the variance of $\hat{\beta}*$ is messy and probably incomprehensible to most readers, it can answer a few specific questions.

When $\rho* = 0$ the estimate $\hat{\beta}*$ is nothing but the ordinary least squares estimate based on $T - 1$ observations. The variance (3.99) for $\rho* = 0$ is the same as the expression (3.74) obtained previously for ordinary least squares.

The least minimum variance obtainable corresponds to the generalized least squares estimate when $\rho* = \rho$. The expression for minimum variance is obtained by replacing $\rho*$ by ρ in (3.99) to obtain

$$V(\hat{\beta}*)_\rho = \frac{\sigma_\varepsilon^2}{\sum x_t^2} \left\{ \frac{1 - \rho^2}{1 + \rho^2 - 2\rho\lambda} \right\}. \tag{3.100}$$

Similarly, the variance corresponding to first-difference estimates can be obtained by replacing $\rho*$ with 1.

The information contained in the expression for variance (3.99) can also be summarized by defining the relative efficiency of an estimate obtained through use of a value of $\rho*$ different from ρ as

$$EFF = V(\hat{\beta}*)_\rho / V(\hat{\beta}*)_{\rho*}. \tag{3.101}$$

Since the relative efficiency of the estimate depends on $\rho*$, ρ, and λ, let us plot the relative efficiency with respect to $\rho*$ and λ for two arbitrarily selected values of ρ, namely $\rho = 0.2$ and 0.6. These plots are given in Figures 3.1 and 3.2.

When the $\rho*$ is different from the true value of the parameter ρ, the loss in precision of the estimation from the transformed variables can be extremely large. To take a few examples, let us consider the situation in which the true $\rho = 0.2$. The researcher suspects serial correlation in the errors but does not know the true value of ρ. Suppose he suspects the parameter to be "high" and selects $\rho* = 0.8$. In this situation he has the following alternatives: (1) to stop with the ordinary least squares, (2) to estimate the parameters from the transformed variables using $\rho* = 0.8$, or (3) to use first-difference estimates. As can be seen from Figure 3.1, the relative efficiencies of these alternatives are different for different values of λ, the serial correlation in the independent variable. When the independent variable is "trending," the parameter λ is large. Consider an economic series with $\lambda = 0.8$ as an independent variable. Of all the three estimates, ordinary least squares has maximum precision.

When researchers suspect high serial correlation in the errors they usually go ahead and estimate the parameters from the first-difference estimates.

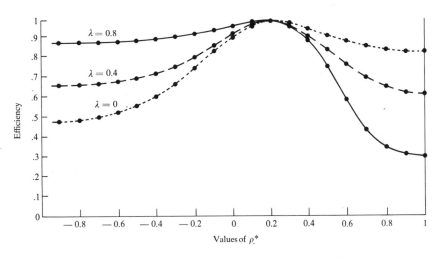

Figure 3.1. Efficiency of GLS for Various Values of ρ^* When True $\rho = 0.2$

Figures 3.1 and 3.2 show that a considerable amount of precision can be gained by *resisting* this temptation. The gain is substantial when the independent variable has "high" serial correlation, which is generally the case with economic time series data. Suppose the researcher suspects high serial correlation in the errors—in the neighborhood of, say, 0.6—and instead of going to the first-difference estimates he uses an arbitrary value of ρ^* from the interval (0.4–0.99); he will then obtain estimates with higher precision than the first-difference estimates.

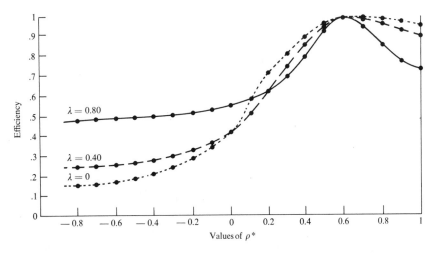

Figure 3.2. Efficiency of GLS for Various Values of ρ^* When True $\rho = 0.6$

In a practical situation, however, he rarely knows the parameter values. Unless the theory explicitly states it, there may be no strong reason to suspect any serial correlation in the error terms. Some researchers tend to blame serial correlation whenever their results are difficult to interpret, but such an attitude sometimes leads to serious consequences. To illustrate the point, let us consider the case in which there is no serial correlation in the errors and the independent variables; that is, $\rho = \lambda = 0$.

In this case $\hat{\beta}^*$ is an unbiased estimate of β and the variance obtained from (3.99) is

$$V(\hat{\beta}^*) = \frac{\sigma_\varepsilon^2}{\sum x_t^2} \left\{ 1 + \frac{\rho^{*2}}{(1 + \rho^{*2})^2} \right\}. \qquad (3.102)$$

The least variance is obtained when the arbitrary value ρ^* is equal to the true value of the parameter 0. (Remember, the true model has no serial correlation.) Whenever the value of ρ^* differs from zero, the variance is larger than the estimate using the true value of zero. When the true errors are, in fact, serially independent and the researcher suspecting serial correlation employs an arbitrary value to gain precision, he will actually be *losing* precision by so doing. Conversely, when the errors are serially correlated he may be able to increase the precision of the estimate (compared to the ordinary least squares approach) provided that he can obtain a "good" value of ρ^*. If the ρ^* value increases the variance of the estimate relative to ordinary least squares, then he may prefer to settle for the latter estimation procedure even though it does not provide the "best" estimate, for the alternative is even worse.

Typically the researcher obtains a ρ^* from the residuals of ordinary least squares estimation of (3.81) as

$$\rho^* = \sum e_t e_{t-1} / \sum e_{t-1}^2. \qquad (3.103)$$

Estimate ρ^* is not the true value ρ and has a statistical distribution. It is consistent but generally biased in small samples, the bias being negative and of the order of (ρ/T) in magnitude. When the independent variables in the estimated regression are also serially correlated, then the bias depends also on the parameters that generated their serial correlation. In the present case, in which ρ and λ are the parameters of serial correlation in the errors and in the independent variable respectively, the bias in ρ^* is of the order of magnitude of $[(\rho + \lambda)/T]$.[10]

Estimate ρ^* as obtained in (3.103) has a variance. The variance of ρ^* is of the order of $(1/T)$. For example, with a sample size of 49, the variance of ρ^* is approximately $(1/49)$ and the standard deviation is approximately $(1/7)$. In the case of serially independent errors the two-sigma limits for ρ^* cover the range $(-0.3$ to $+0.3)$. When the sample size is small, even though the true errors are serially independent, the chance is very high that ρ^* (obtained from the residuals in (3.103)) will show a sizable value. The researcher trying to improve the precision of his estimates should therefore be judicious in his selection of the arbitrary value for ρ^*.

3.4 Heteroscedasticity in Errors

Another situation in which the ordinary least squares method does not produce the best linear unbiased estimates occurs when the variance of the error term differs among various observations—that is, is non-constant. In such cases even though the errors in different observations are drawn at random, they are drawn from different distributions with zero means but different variances.

Consider the specification

$$y_t = \beta_1 x_{1t} + \beta_2 x_{2t} + \cdots + \beta_k x_{kt} + \varepsilon_t, \tag{3.104}$$

$$E(\varepsilon_t) = 0, \tag{3.105}$$

$$E(\varepsilon_t^2) = \sigma_{\varepsilon_t}^2. \tag{3.106}$$

In this specification all the errors are drawn from statistical distributions with zero mean but having different variances as indicated by the subscript of σ_ε^2 in (3.106).

Estimation of equation (3.104) by ordinary least squares, therefore, does not yield the best linear unbiased estimates because of the lack of constant variance in the error term. However, if the researcher knows the individual variances, $\sigma_{\varepsilon_t}^2$'s, then he can use the following transformation on the variables:

$$y_t' = y_t/\sigma_{\varepsilon_t}, \tag{3.107}$$

$$x_{it}' = x_{it}/\sigma_{\varepsilon_t}. \tag{3.108}$$

---

[10] See P. Rao and Z. Griliches, "Small Sample Properties of Several Two-Stage Regression Methods in the Context of Auto-Correlated Errors," *Journal of the American Statistical Association*, 64, March 1969, 253–72.

Instead of estimating equation (3.104), he may then estimate the following:

$$y_t' = \beta_1 x_{1t}' + \beta_2 x_{2t}' + \cdots + \beta_k x_{kt}' + \varepsilon_t'. \tag{3.109}$$

Transformation [This is a reduced form of equation (3.104), obtained by dividing each of the observations by the corresponding standard deviation of its error term. Hence, the error term in (3.109) is

$$\varepsilon_t' = \varepsilon_t / \sigma_{\varepsilon_t} \tag{3.110}$$

By assumption (3.106), the variance of the error term ε_t is $\sigma_{\varepsilon_t}^2$; hence,

$$V(\varepsilon_t') = \sigma_{\varepsilon_t}^2 / \sigma_{\varepsilon_t}^2 = 1. \tag{3.111}$$

That is, the transforming of (3.104) as indicated yields a regression equation with constant variance.

In the transformation version the error terms are serially independent and have the same variance, satisfying the assumptions under which the ordinary least squares estimation is best. Estimation of equation (3.109) yields the best linear unbiased estimates for the β's.

This technique has little relevance to empirical work because the researcher rarely knows the variances of the error terms, except that in some situations he may know the variance up to a constant of proportionality. That is, he may believe that the error term has a variance proportional to a quantifiable variable. Consider, for example, the following linear curve of crude oil requirements for refineries:

$$Y_t = \beta_0 + \beta_1 X_{1t} + \beta_2 X_{2t} + \beta_3 X_{3t} + \varepsilon_t, \tag{3.112}$$

where Y is the crude oil and X_1, X_2, and X_3 are gasoline, kerosene, and fuel oil respectively.

The refineries are of different sizes, and small refineries may perhaps be expected to exhibit small variance in the error term and large refineries to exhibit larger variance, even though the requirement function is assumed to be the same for all refineries. The nature of the variance of the error term may be specified as

$$V(\varepsilon_t) = X_{4t}^2 \cdot k, \tag{3.113}$$

where k is a constant of proportionality and X_{4t} is the capacity of the tth refinery.

In this case the transformation of the variables is of the form

$$Y_t' = Y_t/X_{4t}, \tag{3.114}$$

$$X_{it}' = X_{it}/X_{4t} \qquad i = 1,2,3 \tag{3.115}$$

This transformation adjusts the equation in such a way that its reduced form satisfies all conditions for the least squares estimation to yield best linear unbiased estimates. The data on the capacity of the refineries are available, hence equation (3.109) can be estimated.

The estimated equation is

$$(Y_t/X_{4t}) = \hat{\beta} + \hat{\beta}_0(1/X_{4t}) + \hat{\beta}_1(X_{1t}/X_{4t}) + \hat{\beta}_2(X_{2t}/X_{4t})$$
$$+ \hat{\beta}_3(X_{3t}/X_{4t}) + e_t, \tag{3.116}$$

where the constant term (β) is introduced even though it is not present in equation (3.112) to make the summary statistics meaningful.[11]

Another frequent example occurs when the data come from a published source in which the agency compiling information reports aggregate results rather than individual observations. For example, the Bureau of the Census reports only the aggregate income of all families in given geographic localities. If the researcher believes that the variance of the error term is the same to each individual, then the variance of error in the aggregate corresponding

---

[11] A common practice in examples of this type is to include X_4 also as a part of the specification (3.104) so that the constant term β can be legitimately interpreted as the coefficient of X_4. Even if X_4 does not belong in the true specification, we can introduce the constant term β as an irrelevant variable with mean value of zero. When the constant term is not estimated, the summary statistics (the R^2 and the standard errors) even though they can be computed, cannot be interpreted in the usual way.

to each locality cannot be the same unless the number of individuals in each is the same. When data on the number of individuals in each aggregate are also given, which is generally true in such reports, the researcher can use that information in transforming the variables to improve the precision of his estimates. (See p. 121 for an example.)

The problem of heteroscedasticity in the context of analysis of residuals is presented in Chapter 5.

4

Some ad Hoc
Procedures in Regression Analysis

Applied econometrics is not always as simple as a mere study of the distributional properties of regression estimates. These properties are derived under the suppositions that the researcher has his variables well defined and that the functional form has been clearly described. As every researcher in the empirical world sooner or later realizes, the reported regression equation represents only a small part of the work he has done. To report all the permutations and combinations he has tried in reaching his final results would be tedious and boring to his reader. But they can be intimated by saying that any reported result is the finished product, and not the sketchbook, of an artist. In this chapter we furnish the researcher with some of the tools he may frequently find useful in playing Sherlock Holmes with his data.

When a researcher is on a "fishing expedition" he should not forget that the usual statistical properties of his estimates need not be valid at all stages of the operation. Lack of validity in such a case is not a serious limitation, because the researcher is now interested simply in "feeling out the data" and not necessarily in obtaining an estimate of a parameter. This approach is something of an economic necessity; from insights thus obtained a researcher can minimize the cost of investigation by eliminating some alternative theoretical possibilities from his list of models. However, such a cavalier procedure is an art, and the successful use of these tools requires experience.

At the outset we want to warn the reader that the guidelines presented in this chapter may not seem to be "scientific" techniques of investigation, but they are being used quite extensively in empirical research albeit without specific reference to them.

4.1 Proxy Variables

In empirical research one often faces the problem of lack of data. Even though the theory clearly specifies the variables to be included in a regression equation, the researcher is at a loss when one of the variables cannot be measured or the data are missing. The ordinary least squares estimates of the parameters are unbiased only when all theoretically specified variables are included in the regression.

To avoid the bias which inevitably occurs when a variable is left out (see p. 31), the researcher can sometimes find a variable considered to be a "close substitute" for the missing one. For example, in production function estimation the theory may specify "weather" as an independent variable, but since this cannot be measured with any one quantity, "rainfall" may be considered a close substitute. Since data on rainfall are available, this may perhaps be an acceptable replacement.

The variable used as a substitute for the theoretically specified variable is called a *proxy variable*. Its use is quite extensive in empirical research, mainly because of the unavailability of data on some of the theoretically specified variables. To make good use of proxy variables the researcher should be well aware of the consequences of the substitution.

Let us consider a simple regression equation in which all the variables are measured as deviations from their respective means:

$$y_t = \beta_1 x_t + \varepsilon_t. \tag{4.1}$$

Since data are not available on the variable x, another variable, z, is used as its proxy. The estimated equation becomes

$$y_t = \hat{\beta}_1 z_t + e_t. \tag{4.2}$$

The ordinary least squares estimate $\hat{\beta}_1$ is obtained as

$$\hat{\beta}_1 = \sum z_t y_t / \sum z_t^2. \tag{4.3}$$

Since the true relation is given by (4.1), by substituting for y in (4.3) we obtain

$$\hat{\beta}_1 = \beta_1 \sum z_t x_t / \sum z_t^2 + \sum z_t \varepsilon_t / \sum z_t^2 \tag{4.4}$$

and

$$E(\hat{\beta}_1) = \beta_1 \cdot b_{xz}.$$
(4.5)

Thus $\hat{\beta}_1$ is not an unbiased estimate of β_1 unless b_{xz} (see p. 30 for the notation) is 1. The term b_{xz} is computationally equivalent to b in the regression

$$x_t = bz_t + \xi_t.$$
(4.6)

When x and z are measured in different units, the coefficient b measures the units of conversion. Note that when z is measured in different units than x the regression estimate $\hat{\beta}_1$ is also in different units compared to β_1, and b is the conversion factor. Even when both x and z are measured in the same units, the value of b may be different from unity, depending on the degree of similarity in the comovements of these two variables.

In empirical research a common situation is of the following type. Let the true relation be

$$y_t = \beta_1 x_{1t} + \beta_2 x_{2t} + \beta_3 x_{3t} + \varepsilon_t.$$
(4.7)

Suppose the researcher, unaware that x_2 and x_3 belong to the true specification, mistakenly specifies the following regression:

$$y_t = \beta_1 x_{1t} + \varepsilon_t.$$
(4.8)

When data on x_1 are not available he uses z as a proxy variable and obtains the equation

$$y_t = \hat{\beta}_1 z_t + e_t,$$
(4.9)

where

$$\hat{\beta}_1 = \sum z_t y_t / \sum z_t^2$$
(4.10)

$$= \beta_1 \sum z_t x_{1t} / \sum z_t^2 + \beta_2 \sum z_t x_{2t} / \sum z_t^2 + \beta_3 \sum z_t x_{3t} / \sum z_t^2 + \sum z_t \varepsilon_t / \sum z_t^2$$
(4.11)

and

$$E(\hat{\beta}_1) = \beta_1 b_{x_1 z} + \beta_2 b_{x_2 z} + \beta_3 b_{x_3 z}. \qquad (4.12)$$

The researcher may be under the impression that he is using z as a proxy for x_1 and, therefore, that it is measuring the influence of x_1 alone. He is correct only when equation (4.8) is the truth. If equation (4.7) is the truth, the proxy variable is measuring the influence of all variables not included in the equation, whether the researcher is aware of their relevance or not. This is true because even if the researcher used the variable x_1 in estimating $\hat{\beta}_1$ the estimate is biased by left-out variables (see p. 62). When z is used to replace x_1 it inherits the bias of x_1's regression coefficient as well. The bias in the estimate would differ depending on which of the two variables (x or z) is used in the regression. In general, the bias of the estimate with a proxy variable will be larger than with the true variable. But even so, when data on x are not available the researcher must of necessity depend on the proxy variable.

In interpreting the coefficient associated with a proxy variable the researcher should be extremely cautious. The extent of the influence of other omitted variables that is captured by the proxy variable depends on the closeness of the relationship between the proxy and those omitted. When the omitted variables and the proxy move very closely, which sometimes happens in the case of a trend or some such phenomenon, the proxy variable captures almost the total influence of all the left-out variables.

So far we have considered the situation with only one independent variable in the estimated regression. This exercise exposes the relevant concepts in analyzing the proxy variables. A more common practical problem, however, is the case with several independent variables. Consider the true relationship

$$y_t = \beta_1 x_{1t} + \beta_2 x_{2t} + \varepsilon_t. \qquad (4.13)$$

The researcher uses z as a proxy for the variable x_1 and obtains the estimated equation

$$y_t = \hat{\beta}_1 z_t + \hat{\beta}_2 x_{2t} + e_t. \qquad (4.14)$$

To study the consequences on $\hat{\beta}_1$ and $\hat{\beta}_2$ of the use of the proxy variable, let us rewrite equation (4.13) as

$$y_t = \beta_1 x_{1t} + \beta_2 x_{2t} + 0 \cdot z_t + \varepsilon_t. \tag{4.15}$$

Since the coefficient of z is zero in equation (4.15), its presence creates no conceptual problems and we introduce it for analytical convenience only.

Instead of estimating the true relation (4.15), the researcher now has estimated equation (4.14). Comparison of these two equations reveals that in (4.14) the variable x_1 is left out. When a theoretically specified variable is left out, then the ordinary least squares estimates of parameters are biased, and the expression for bias is

$$E(\hat{\beta}_1) = 0 + \beta_1 b_{x_1 z, x_2} \tag{4.16}$$

and

$$E(\hat{\beta}_2) = \beta_2 + \beta_1 b_{x_1 x_2, z}, \tag{4.17}$$

where

$$x_{1t} = b_{x_1 z, x_2} z_t + b_{x_1 x_2, z} x_{2t} + v_t. \tag{4.18}$$

When z is a good approximation to x_1, and both are measured in similar units, then $b_{x_1 z, x_2}$ and $b_{x_1 x_2, z}$ are approximately unity and zero respectively.[1] That is, the bias in the estimates of the parameters will decrease with the goodness of the proxy variable in approximating the left-out variable.

Using a proxy for the theoretically specified variable introduces bias into estimates of all the parameters. When the proxy is a good approximation, the extent of bias may be negligible for practical purposes. However, if the movements in the proxy variable do not correspond to those of the omitted variable, then the bias can be substantial. When the researcher has to choose

---

[1] This may perhaps seem clearer if we further consider equation (4.18). If z is a perfect approximation of x_1 and is measured in the same units, $b_{x_1 z, x_2}$ will equal unity and $b_{x_1 x_2, z}$ will be zero. The equation's multiple correlation coefficient will be unity and no part of x_1's movements will be left to be explained by x_2. If z is in different units of measurement than x_1 the results are the same, except that $b_{x_1 z, x_2}$ will not be unity. Its magnitude reflects the conversion factor. If x_1 were sales in dollars and z were sales in pennies, $b_{x_1 z, x_2}$ would be 0.01 and $b_{x_1 x_2, z}$ would be zero.

between using a proxy or leaving out the variable altogether, the choice must depend on the extent of bias in each case. When the variable x_1 is left out and not replaced by a proxy variable, the following equation results:

$$y_t = \tilde{\beta}_2 x_{2t} + e_t \tag{4.19}$$

and

$$E(\tilde{\beta}_2) = \beta_2 + \beta_1 b_{x_1 x_2}. \tag{4.20}$$

Comparison of (4.17) and (4.20) provides a basis for the choice. When $b_{x_1 x_2, z}$ is smaller than $b_{x_1 x_2}$, the extent of bias in the coefficient of x_2 can be reduced by including a proxy variable instead of leaving out the variable altogether. In many empirical cases it is possible to find proxy variables that are capable of reducing the bias in the regression coefficients.

The analysis of several omitted variables can be extended to the K variable case. In the Yule notation the only change in the formulae for a general case would be in the secondary subscripts.

Let the truth be

$$y_t = \beta_1 x_{1t} + \beta_2 x_{2t} + \beta_3 x_{3t} + \beta_4 x_{4t} + \varepsilon_t, \tag{4.21}$$

while the researcher mistakenly believes the true equation to be

$$y_t = \beta_1 x_{1t} + \beta_2 x_{2t} + \varepsilon_t. \tag{4.22}$$

When z is used as a proxy variable for x_1 he obtains

$$y_t = \hat{\beta}_1 z_t + \hat{\beta}_2 x_{2t} + e_t. \tag{4.23}$$

To analyze the consequences of using (4.23) on the bias of the estimates we shall rewrite (4.21) as

$$y_t = \beta_1 x_{1t} + \beta_2 x_{2t} + \beta_3 x_{3t} + \beta_4 x_{4t} + 0 \cdot z_t + \varepsilon_t. \tag{4.24}$$

Equation (4.23) may be viewed as (4.24) when x_1, x_3, and x_4 are left out in estimation. Using the previously derived expressions (see p. 62), we can express the bias in the estimates $\hat{\beta}_1$ and $\hat{\beta}_2$ as

$$E(\hat{\beta}_1) = 0 + \beta_1 b_{x_1 z, x_2} + \beta_3 b_{x_3 z, x_2} + \beta_4 b_{x_4 z, x_2}, \qquad (4.25)$$

$$E(\hat{\beta}_2) = \beta_2 + \beta_1 b_{x_1 x_2, z} + \beta_3 b_{x_3 x_2, z} + \beta_4 b_{x_4 x_2, z}. \qquad (4.26)$$

The extent of bias in each case depends on the various b's. The proxy variable is capturing the influence of all the variables that belong to the true equation but which were left out of the estimated equation. If the proxy variable moves closely with all the omitted variables, then the coefficient of the proxy variable contains influences additional to that of the variable it is replacing. The researcher should pay attention to such considerations in intepreting his results.

In the example of rice production for Guntur (p. 33) we obtained the following regression equation:

$$\text{RICE}_t = -739.9 + 0.578 I_t + 0.218 D_t + 46.6 R_t - 40.4 t \qquad R^2 = 0.61.$$
$$\quad (1755.4) \quad (0.442) \quad (0.959) \quad (10.9) \quad (26.9)$$

$$(4.27)$$

Suppose the researcher had started with the following model:

$$\text{RICE} = \beta_0 + \beta_1 I + \beta_2 D + \beta_3 R + \beta_4 E + \varepsilon_t, \qquad (4.28)$$

where E is the level of education of the people. Since no data are available on the level of education, the researcher may conjecture that the level of education has been steadily increasing with time, hence time is a reasonable proxy variable for education. When he uses this proxy he obtains (4.27), indicating that education makes a negative contribution to the yield of rice. This disturbing result is, however, a misinterpretation of the coefficient of the proxy variable.

The true specification may be as follows:

$$\text{RICE} = \beta_0 + \beta_1 I + \beta_2 D + \beta_3 R + \beta_4 E + \beta_5 F + \beta_6 M + \beta_7 L + \cdots + \varepsilon_t, $$
$$(4.29)$$

where F, M, and L are fertilizers, machinery, and labor respectively. All these variables have been left out in the estimated equation (4.27), and all are changing steadily with time.

Since

$$E(b) = \beta_4 \, b_{Et, IDR} + \beta_5 \, b_{Ft, IDR} + \beta_6 \, b_{Mt, IDR} + \beta_7 \, b_{Lt, IDR} + \cdots, \quad (4.30)$$

where b of $E(b)$ is the regression coefficient of the variable t in equation (4.27), the coefficient of time represents not only the influence of education, but the composite effect of all the omitted variables that move with time. Some of these effects can be positive and others negative, and their combined effect cannot be attributed to any *single* missing variable.

In this example, even though the coefficient of t cannot be used to isolate the effects of any of the omitted variables, its inclusion as a proxy for all of them considerably reduces the bias in the other regression coefficients; this reduction of bias is our primary objective in this particular problem. The coefficients are biased whether or not the proxy variable, t, is included, but t is useful as a variable because its inclusion produces a smaller bias.

4.2 Dummy Variables

In all the models discussed so far we have implicitly assumed that the specified equation is the same for all observations. In some situations in which this assumption may seem to be restrictive, it can be relaxed somewhat through the use of the dummy variable technique. This allows the researcher to separate information on certain variables into discrete categories by assuming "dummy" values (0 or 1) for each of the categories.

Though the dummy variables are usually associated with qualitative variables, recently they have been used in a variety of other situations, such as in preliminary investigations which are done to get a feel for the data. We shall now discuss some of these uses of dummy variables in empirical research.

Suppose the researcher has external information that allows him to separate the data into several categories. He has reason to believe that observations within each category have the same parameter values, but observations in different categories may have different sets of parameters. By distinguishing one category from the other, he can allow for such difference between them. The use of dummy variables is a convenient way of identifying the categories.

To understand the underlying concepts, consider the regression equation that tries to explain expenditure on entertainment (Y) by the number of movie houses (X_1) and the amount of liquor legally sold (X_2):

$$Y_t = \beta_0 + \beta_1 X_{1t} + \beta_2 X_{2t} + \varepsilon_t. \qquad (4.31)$$

The variable X_2 is zero for the prohibition period and nonzero for the post-prohibition period. Even if β_2 is nonzero, equation (4.31) can be used to explain behavior during the prohibition period, because the variable X_2 takes a zero value and essentially the equation becomes

$$Y_t = \beta_0 + \beta_1 X_{1t} + \varepsilon_t. \qquad (4.32)$$

The same reasoning can be employed in a situation in which the variable X_2 is relevant to one group of the data and not to the other. When X_2 is an irrelevant variable, this information may be incorporated in the specification either by assigning a zero coefficient to it as in equation (4.32) or by assigning a zero value to it whenever it is irrelevant. By taking X_2 as zero in the group to which it is irrelevant and retaining its observed values for the relevant group, the same regression equation may be used for both the groups.

When the researcher knows whether X_2 is relevant or not to a given observation, he can either copy the numbers accordingly—zero or observed value—or he may define a dummy variable, D, as zero when X_2 is irrelevant and as unity when it is relevant without altering the observed values of X_2. Instead of changing the data on X_2 to distinguish between the categories, he assigns the task to a properly defined dummy variable, D.

The main advantage of the dummy variable technique is that it allows a considerable amount of flexibility. Consider the case in which the data correspond to categories for which both the variables (X_1 and X_2) are relevant but in which the coefficient of X_2 is different in the two categories, whereas all other parameters are the same. In this situation the researcher can estimate the following regression, which makes use of the information on the two categories in the form of a dummy variable:

$$Y_t = \beta_0 + \beta_1 X_{1t} + \beta_2 X_{2t} + \beta_3(D \cdot X_{2t}) + \varepsilon_t, \qquad (4.33)$$

where D is the dummy variable that takes the value of zero when the observation belongs to one category and the value of unity for the other.

When the value of the dummy variable is zero, the data correspond to Category I, and the corresponding regression equation is

$$Y_t = \beta_0 + \beta_1 X_{1t} + \beta_2 X_{2t} + \varepsilon_t. \qquad (4.34)$$

When the value of the dummy variable is unity, the data correspond to Category II, and the regression is

$$Y_1 = \beta_0 + \beta_1 X_{1t} + (\beta_2 + \beta_3) X_{2t} + \varepsilon_t. \qquad (4.35)$$

Regression equation (4.33), corresponding to the two regression equations (4.34) and (4.35), has the same parameter values for all variables except X_2. By using information on the dummy variable, the researcher can allow for the coefficient of X_2 to differ in the two categories. This procedure can be extended to any number of variables. The coefficient of variable X_i can be allowed to differ in two categories by including the variables X_i and $(D \cdot X_i)$ in the same regression equation. It is readily seen that the introduction of D alone as an independent variable in the regression allows variation in the constant term in the two categories. This latter procedure is probably one of the most widely used aspects of the dummy variable technique.

Consider the following consumption function (see p. 9 for notation):

$$C_t = \beta_0 + \beta_1 Y_t + \beta_2 C_{t-1} + \varepsilon_t. \qquad (4.36)$$

Let the time series data be separated into two categories, namely a prewar period and a postwar period. Let the information on categorization be incorporated in the form of a dummy variable, D, which takes a value of zero for the prewar period and of unity for the postwar period.

When the researcher believes that the regression equations for the two time periods are different, he can allow for a difference in the parameters in the two categories. When all parameters are permitted to differ in the two categories, he has the equation

$$C_t = \beta_0 + \alpha_0 D + \beta_1 Y_t + \alpha_1 (D \cdot Y_t) + \beta_2 C_{t-1} + \alpha_2 (D \cdot C_{t-1}) + \varepsilon_t.$$

$$(4.37)$$

The researcher has another option: to separate the data for the two categories and to estimate equation (4.36) separately for each category. Either choice yields the same results for the regression coefficients; this is a mathematical certainty. The conditions imposed on the residuals are identical either in estimating (4.37) or in separately estimating the equation (4.36); the number of parameters estimated in either case is the same, and the researcher gains no additional information by estimating (4.37) instead of estimating the equations separately.

However, although the regression equations are the same for the alternative ways of obtaining the estimates, the standard errors of the estimates will not be the same. This is so because the standard errors in equation (4.37) are estimated under the assumption that the variance of the error terms is the same for all observations. When the equations are estimated for the two sets of data separately the underlying assumption is that the variance of the error terms is the same for all observations within each set, but that they may vary between sets. Which set of standard errors is appropriate depends on the assumptions regarding the variance of the error terms corresponding to the two categories. *The researcher should keep in mind that the computed standard errors do not necessarily reflect the true efficiency, or the appropriateness, of assumptions regarding the variance of the error terms.* When he chooses one procedure over the other, he has to state categorically what he believes to be the truth. He should also keep in mind that he cannot use the same data for testing a null hypothesis on equivalence of the variances in the two categories while also estimating the regressions under the assumption that the null hypothesis is true.

When the researcher has prior information that the coefficients of some of the independent variables are the same for the categories within the two regression sets, then he can incorporate this information into his estimation procedure by deleting the appropriate terms in (4.37). For example, deleting the term $(D \cdot Y_t)$ allows for the coefficient of Y_t to be the same for the prewar and the postwar data. The dummy variable approach may also be viewed as a way of incorporating prior information in the estimation procedure.

In the above example we used the same dummy variable for all independent variables because the data were clearly separated into two categories. Sometimes it may be desirable to classify them according to one criterion with respect to one independent variable and a different criterion for another. For example, the influence of education may vary among minority groups, and the influence of pay scale may vary among economic classes. Information on these categories may be incorporated by using one set of dummy variables for the education variable and another set for the pay scale variable.

The dummy variable procedure can also be used in situations in which the data are separated into more than two categories. To take an example, let us consider a situation in which equation (4.31) is used to explain the behavior of men, women, and children. The reseacher has reason to believe that only the parameter β_1 differs among the different categories. Since there are three categories, one dummy variable is not adequate; two are needed in order to distinguish three categories. In general, m categories can be distinguished by $m - 1$ dummy variables.

Let D_1 be a dummy variable that takes a value of unity when the observation corresponds to men, and of zero otherwise; then let D_2 take a value of unity when the observation corresponds to women, and zero otherwise. When there are only three categories, as in this case, and when the categories are mutually exclusive and exhaustive, then these two dummy variables can distinguish between the three. For example, when both D_1 and D_2 are zero, the observation does not correspond to men or women, therefore it must correspond to children. Similarly, when either of the two is unity the observation cannot correspond to children. Since information on the children is obtained from information on dummy variables D_1 and D_2, this is called the *excluded category*.

The choice of which category should be treated as the excluded category is completely arbitrary. The researcher will obtain the same implicit estimates and interpretation of the results regardless of the choice he makes.

A regression equation that provides for different regression coefficients for three categories is

$$Y_t = \beta_0 + \beta_1 X_{1t} + \alpha_1(D_1 \cdot X_{1t}) + \alpha_2(D_2 \cdot X_{1t}) + \beta_2 X_{2t} + \varepsilon_t. \qquad (4.38)$$

The excluded category corresponds to $D_1 = D_2 = 0$. The regression equation corresponding to the excluded category is

$$Y_t = \beta_0 + \beta_1 X_{1t} + \beta_2 X_{2t} + \varepsilon_t. \qquad (4.39)$$

When the dummy variable $D_1 = 1$, the regression equation corresponds to men and the coefficient of X_1 is $(\beta_1 + \alpha_1)$. Hence α_1 is the increase (or decrease) in the coefficient corresponding to men relative to the excluded category, namely children. Similarly α_2 is the increase (or decrease) of the regression coefficient of X_1 for women relative to children. The coefficients α_1 and α_2 thus measure the difference between the regression coefficient of X_1 for men and for women with respect to the excluded category.

This analysis can be extended to let all parameters be different for all categories, in which case the corresponding coefficients would be identical to those obtained by estimating regression equations separately for each of the categories. However, as noted before, the standard errors would be different because of implicit assumptions on the variance of the error terms in each of the cases.

4.3 Qualitative Variables

In the regression equations that we have been considering so far, all the variables are quantitative. However, information on some of the variables may be qualitative, and even if the variable is quantitative it may sometimes be less "sinful" to treat the available information as qualitative rather than quantitative.

Consider, for example, the regression equation that tries to explain the earnings of economists:

$$Y_t = \beta_0 + \beta_1 E_t + \beta_2 X_{2t} + \beta_3 X_{3t} + \varepsilon_t, \tag{4.40}$$

where Y is earnings, E is education, and X_2 and X_3 are other variables. Suppose the education is measured as B.A., M.A., and Ph.D. This information could be incorporated into the regression in several ways. One could rate the degrees according to some arbitrary scale. For example, B.A. $= 1$, M.A. $= 2$, Ph.D. $= 5$. Such arbitrary classifications require prior knowledge on the part of the researcher.

One way of solving this problem is to consider the "mean effects" of each of the university degrees. Assume, for example, fixed values for the other variables, X_2 and X_3. Given the values of these other variables, separate the observations into three categories according to the educational degree received. The difference in mean income is assumed to be attributable to differentials in education.

Since it is not possible to observe the data in which X_2 and X_3 are the same for all the observations in a group, we have to rely upon the regression technique. Let D_1 be a dummy variable defined as taking the value of unity when the observations corresponds to a B.A. and the value of zero otherwise; let D_2 be a dummy variable with value unity when the observation corresponds to an M.A. and zero otherwise; let the excluded category be Ph.D. We can rewrite regression equation (4.40) in the form

$$Y_t = \beta_0 + \alpha_1 D_1 + \alpha_2 D_2 + \beta_2 X_{2t} + \beta_3 X_{3t} + \varepsilon_t. \tag{4.41}$$

The education variable, E, has been replaced by dummy variables whose use allows for the mean effect of each of the three educational categories to differ for a given level of the other variables. The mean effects of B.A., M.A., and Ph.D. are given by $(\beta_0 + \alpha_1)$, $(\beta_0 + \alpha_2)$, and β_0 respectively.

This technique can be used even when data on a variable are quantitative in nature but cannot be expressed in a linear form in the regression equation. Consider, for example, the regression equation that tries to explain the re-offering yield of a bond by the number of bids received and some other variables:

$$RY_t = \beta_0 + \beta_1 NB_t + \beta_2 X_{2t} + \cdots + \beta_k X_{kt} + \varepsilon_t, \qquad (4.42)$$

where RY and NB are the reoffering yield and the number of bids respectively. In this example, the subscript "t" serves only to distinguish one bond from the other.

The variable representing the number of bids essentially measures the competitive nature of the bond. A bond with a large number of bids is assumed to be competitive, whereas a bond receiving very few bids is assumed to be less competitive and may be in a noncompetitive situation. When the number of bids is very small, the influence of an extra bid may have a substantial effect on the reoffering yield at the margin; but if the bond is already in a competitive market, the contribution of an additional bid in the market does not affect the reoffering yield by much. If the number of bids is introduced as a linear variable as in equation (4.42), it implies that the marginal effect of a bid is the same regardless of whether the market is competitive or noncompetitive. This may be too restrictive an assumption for the researcher.

Even though the information is quantitative in nature, it cannot be used linearly in the regression equation in obtaining any meaningful interpretation of the resultant coefficients. Therefore, instead of treating the number of bids as a quantitative variable the researcher may decide to treat it as qualitative information, just as in the above example concerning education. For given values of all the other variables, the data may be separated according to the number of bids received, with the mean effect in each category can then being used as a representation of the effect of that number of bids. In the regression form, the same effect can be obtained by using dummy variables. Let D_i be a dummy variable which takes the value unity when a bond receives i number of bids, and the value zero otherwise.

In this example, when a bond has twelve or more bids it may be considered to be in a competitive market and the marginal effect of an additional bid is negligible. Hence, bonds with twelve or more bids may be considered as the excluded category. In all, there are eleven dummy variables and an excluded category. The regression equation for 6503 bonds studied by Kessel[2] is

$$RY_t = \hat{\beta}_0 + 37D_1 + 24D_2 + 20D_3 + 15D_4 + 10D_5 + 6D_6 + 4D_7$$
$$\quad\quad (1.8) \quad (1.2) \quad (1.0) \quad (1.0) \quad (0.9) \quad (0.9) \quad (1.0)$$
$$+4D_8 + 3D_9 + 2D_{10} + 2D_{11} + \hat{\beta}_2 X_{2t} + \cdots + \hat{\beta}_k X_{kt}.$$
$$\quad (1.1) \quad (1.2) \quad (1.2) \quad (1.4)$$

$$(4.43)$$

Since the coefficients of the dummy variables indicate the partial influence relative to the excluded category for given values of all the other variables, we may present the information graphically as in Figure 4.1.

As would be theoretically expected, the marginal effect of the number of bids differs at different levels of bids offered on a bond. The mean effects on the bonds corresponding to a given level of number of bids was isolated by

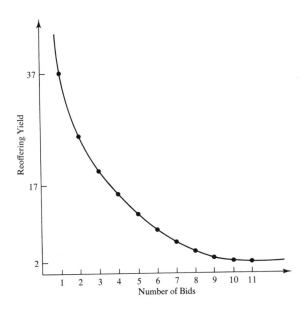

Figure 4.1. Effect of Bids on Reoffering Yield

---

[2] Reuben Kessel, "The Economic Effects of the Exclusion of Commercial Banks from the Underwriting of Revenue Bonds" (unpublished manuscript, University of Chicago, Dec. 1968).

treating the information as qualitative rather than quantitative, thus preventing problems of misspecification.

Now consider situations in which the information may be qualitative and not subject to measurement: for example, a regression equation that tries to explain the amount of output sold by firms to the government. The researcher knows that it is a function of certain well-defined variables, X_1, X_2, etc., but he is equally aware that the amount and effectiveness of lobbying in the Capitol is also a relevant variable. The information on lobbying cannot be measured, but it is sometimes reasonable to assume that the variable has the same value for several time periods for a given firm. When the data correspond to several firms with different lobbying forces in the Capitol and for different time periods, the missing information may be treated as a qualitative variable which has a different mean effect for each firm.

Instead of estimating

$$Y_t = \beta_0 + \beta_1 X_{1t} + \beta_2 X_{2t} + \cdots + \beta_k X_{kt} + \varepsilon_t, \qquad (4.44)$$

the researcher estimates

$$Y_t = \beta_0 + \beta_1 X_{1t} + \beta_2 X_{2t} + \cdots + \beta_k X_{kt} + \delta_1 D_1$$
$$+ \delta_2 D_2 + \cdots + \delta_N D_N + \varepsilon_t. \qquad (4.45)$$

The missing information has been incorporated in the form of dummy variables, $D_1, \ldots, D_N$ for the $N + 1$ firms.

The researcher should note that if other variables besides lobbying are missing in specification (4.44), then the dummy variables may capture their influence, provided that they are firm specific. See the discussion of proxy variables with several left-out variables (p. 86).

4.4 Scanning

In many empirical works data come from different countries, states, or industries. Many features may be common, while certain peculiarities may be specific to the different groups. In such cases we would be interested in capturing these divergences in order to improve upon the parameter estimates, but often it is not clear what causes the peculiarities. When several possible explanations appear, then the researcher is interested in laying his hands on one of them with a minimum of effort. Once the appropriate variable has been isolated, information on this variable may be incorporated into the regression equation. The technique of dummy variables may be used to *scan* the data when the observations are sufficient in number to allow it.

To illustrate this technique, let us consider a Cobb-Douglas production function:

$$Q = AL^{\alpha}K^{\beta}e^{\varepsilon}. \tag{4.46}$$

Assume that labor, L, should be measured in *efficiency* units of the work force rather than by the number of workers. Assume that we are at a loss to specify what causes the difference in efficiency in different states. This information cannot be ignored, because to do so would misspecify our regression equation.

For this problem, let us consider a variable specific to each state: that is, its value changes from state to state but remains the same for the same state over different observations through time. In our example, this specific variable may happen to be the quality-of-labor index. When a sufficient number of observations allows us to represent this specific factor by dummy variables, we shall write regression equation (4.46) in natural logarithms as

$$\log Q = \beta_0 + \alpha \log L + \beta \log K + \delta_1 D_1 + \delta_2 D_2 + \cdots + \delta_{49} D_{49} + \varepsilon, \tag{4.47}$$

where the 50th state is considered as the excluded category.

The estimates of the δ's provide information on the variable specific to the separate states. A researcher may *ex post* arrange the states according to high and low estimated values of the δ's and look for the appropriate attribute that would yield such a pattern. If average state educational levels of workers match the arrangement, then he may compute the quality index on the basis of the education level of the work force and use L as efficiency units of labor in order to improve the regression coefficients.

One should not forget that in this process dummy variables are being used to "feel the data out" and *not* as an alternative specification of the model. Dummy variables help reduce the cost of search for the variable that is causing a systematic variation in the production function. This approach is an alternative to searching through the residuals with the hope of shedding some light on the nature of the left-out variables.

4.5   *Dummy Variables as a Jackknife*

Consider the case in which theory strongly recommends that a specific independent variable should not enter into the regression equation linearly. It may well be that within the range of the data the simple linear approximation is adequate, but the researcher wants to "feel out" the data to make sure. He then may use dummy variables to "jackknife" the variable in question so that he can study its relation to the dependent variable at several values of the variable in question while at the same time holding constant all the other variables in the regression equation.

Let X_3 be the variable which the researcher believes should not enter the regression equation linearly:

$$Y_t = \beta_0 + \beta_1 X_{1t} + \beta_2 X_{2t} + \beta_3 X_{3t} + \varepsilon_t. \tag{4.48}$$

The researcher proceeds as follows: first the data are reorganized in terms of ascending order of magnitude of the variable in question, which is X_3 in this example. The data are then separated into, say, three equivalently sized groups. Each group is represented by a dummy variable, except that for ease of interpretation the lowest group is treated as the "excluded" category. The "jackknifed" variable is X_3. After the dummy variables have been inserted into the constant and into X_3, (4.48) becomes

$$\begin{aligned} Y_t = \beta_0 &+ \delta_1 D_2 + \delta_2 D_3 + \beta_1 X_{1t} + \beta_2 X_{2t} + \beta_3 X_{3t} \\ &+ \gamma_1 (D_2 \cdot X_{3t}) + \gamma_2 (D_3 \cdot X_{3t}) + \varepsilon_t. \end{aligned} \tag{4.49}$$

From this equation we can derive the partial effect of X_3 on Y for any given values of X_1 and X_2.

$$\text{For group 1:} \quad Y = \beta_0 + \beta_3 X_3 + Z. \tag{4.50}$$

$$\text{For group 2:} \quad Y = (\beta_0 + \delta_1) + (\beta_3 + \gamma_1) X_3 + Z. \tag{4.51}$$

$$\text{For group 3:} \quad Y = (\beta_0 + \delta_2) + (\beta_3 + \gamma_2) X_3 + Z. \tag{4.52}$$

In each case Z is the influence of all the other variables that are held constant. If the coefficients $\hat{\delta}$ and $\hat{\gamma}$ are not significantly different from zero, this implies that the partial regressions for the three groups are not different from each other; that is, a linear specification for X_3 is adequate within the sample data range. When $\hat{\delta}$ and $\hat{\gamma}$ are different from zero, we may draw the three partial equations as in Figure 4.2.

The gap between the extensions of these lines measures the seriousness of using an incorrect linear approximation. From studying these lines the researcher may conclude whether the evidence is strong enough to reject the linear approximation.

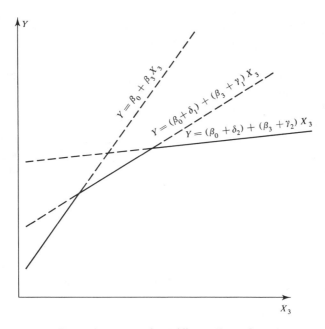

Figure 4.2. Partial Effects of X_3 on Y for Different Data Groups

4.6 Time as a Trend Variable

Sometimes the ordinary least squares estimation of a linear regression model leads to a spurious relation between the variables when their relation is not properly specified. Even though no causal relation exists between two variables, if they happen to be moving in the same direction because, for example, of the general economic activity or because of population growth, the researcher may find a significant association between the variables. Such a result is spurious and does not reflect the influence of one variable on the movements of the other. The problem of a spurious relation may be analyzed as a special case of left-out variables.

An enthusiastic researcher might find a significant association between capital investment expenditure and profits. It would be unwise to use this regression model as a basis for formulating policy recommendations. Both variables might happen to be moving in the same direction because of constantly increasing sales revenues. There may or may not be a causal relationship between the investment and profits, but the fact that the two series happen to move in the same direction results in a significant estimated relation within a linear regression model. The researcher is usually interested in isolating the causal effect of one variable on another and not in merely relating the comovements of one series with another.

When an increase in sales is causing both the investment and profits to go up steadily, the relation between the two variables cannot be extracted by the use of these variables alone. Suppose the researcher can find data corresponding to a time period when sales did not change. Then for these data the sales variable does not influence the comovements of the two series, and the regression equation corresponding to these data will yield the true relation between the two variables.

When the researcher cannot find a set of data for a period when a major influencing variable, such as sales, remains fairly constant, he can obtain the same effect by including the variable as an additional independent variable in the multiple-regression equation. Consider the equation

$$Y_t = \beta_0 + \beta_1 X_{1t} + \beta_2 X_{2t} + \varepsilon_t, \tag{4.53}$$

where Y, X_1, and X_2 are investment, profits, and sales respectively.

The parameter β_1 in equation (4.53) is the partial of Y with respect to X_1 when the value of X_2 is held constant. Hence the parameter β_1 measures the true relation between Y and X_1.

Suppose that instead of estimating equation (4.53), the researcher estimates that

$$Y_t = \alpha_0 + \alpha_1 X_{1t} + \varepsilon_{2t}. \tag{4.54}$$

Equation (4.54) ignores the information that the two variables, Y and X_1, are influenced by the third variable, X_2. The parameter α_1 is a measure of the *observed* relation between the variables, whereas β_1 in equation (4.53) is a measure of the *true* relation. Suppose no true relation exists between Y and X_1; that is, $\beta_1 = 0$. When equation (4.54) is estimated by least squares the result (see p. 31) is

$$E(\hat{\alpha}_1) = 0 + \beta_2 \cdot b_{21}. \tag{4.55}$$

When the sales variable, X_2, influences the variables Y and X_1, then both the terms β_2 and b_{21} are substantially different from zero. Even though $\beta_1 = 0$, the estimate $\hat{a}_1$ can be significantly different from zero. The significant observed relation between the variables Y and X_1 is a spurious result caused by the variable X_2. When either the relation between Y and X_2 (β_2) or the relation between X_1 and X_2 (b_{21}) is zero, the observed relation corresponds to the true relation.

As an illustration, consider using the data presented in Table 4.1 for the Indian engineering industry. If the researcher regresses investment on profits he obtains

$$I = 138.014 + 1.759P \qquad R^2 = 0.96,$$
$$(123.318) \quad (0.098) \tag{4.56}$$

where I is investment and P profits. The researcher interpreting (4.56) may consider that profits determine investment. But this is a spurious relation. Both profits and investment are affected by sales. When sales (S) enter into the equation, we obtain

$$I = -82.518 + 0.048P + 0.084S \qquad R^2 = 0.98.$$
$$(98.112) \quad (0.418) \quad (0.020) \tag{4.57}$$

Now the estimated coefficient of profits is very small. The researcher no longer will consider that profits determine investment; the spurious relation has been eliminated by the addition of sales to the regression equation.

When the researcher suspects that he may have obtained a false relation between the dependent variable and some or all of the independent variables, he can correct for it by including the suspected variable as an independent variable in the regression equation.

The problem of spurious association is frequent in the econometric analysis of time series data. When all or some of the variables move in the same direction because of general economic activity, the resulting relation may well be spurious. When such economic activity is assumed to be a smooth function of time, the series are said to contain a "trend" component because, though there is variation, the series is generally moving in one direction steadily over the time period.

When the researcher suspects that "trend" in the time series data underlies a spurious relation in the regression equation, he may abstract from this

Table 4.1. Data on Investment in Fixed Assets, Sales, and Profits in the Indian Engineering Industry

Year	Investment 10^5 Rs.	Profits after Tax 10^5 Rs.	Sales 10^5 Rs.	No. of Firms in the Industry Reported
1950	4280	154	369	54
51	5254	185	345	54
52	5756	189	371	54
53	5849	166	386	54
54	8249	250	660	54
55	14338	647	1204	88
56	19139	724	1498	88
57	22055	771	1668	88
58	22339	843	1608	88
59	25250	1182	2184	88
60	31283	1652	2676	131
61	34882	1703	2769	131
62	40220	1575	3703	131
63	47132	2208	4306	131
64	58265	2679	4585	131

Source: *Reserve Bank of Indian Bulletin*, Sept. 1957, July 1962, Dec. 1967.

influence by introducing time as an explicit variable in the regression equation We shall study the problems associated with the interpretation of the coefficient estimates in such cases.

The researcher should avoid the conclusion that all time series analyses yield spurious relations. When the specification of a regression is dynamic in nature, the trend components in the dependent variable are being explained by the equation. If the researcher mistakenly tries in such a case to eliminate the trend components from his series, he will be committing a conceptual error in specification. Time should not be used as an explicit variable to correct for trend when the objective is to explain the trend in one variable by the trend in others.

Consider the regression equation

$$Y_t = \alpha_0 + \alpha_1 X_{1t} + \alpha_2 X_{2t} + \varepsilon_t. \tag{4.58}$$

The researcher suspects that his data are subject to trend components, and to avoid a spurious relation he estimates the equation

$$Y_t = \beta_0 + \beta_1 X_{1t} + \beta_2 X_{2t} + \beta_3 t + \varepsilon_t. \tag{4.59}$$

The parameters β_0, β_1, and β_2 in equation (4.59) represent the true relation between the variables because they are the partial derivatives holding the time period constant.

When the data on all the variables are purged of the trend components, then of course there is no need for introducing the time variable in regression equation (4.59). In economic series some of the variables are available with a trend component and some without. In some cases an agency releasing information on a variable will correct for the trend component, and the researcher has no access to the raw (uncorrected) series. His only option then is to use whatever information he has. Fortunately, as we shall attempt to show, the problem turns out to be relatively minor.

Suppose that the variable X_1 has already been corrected for trend; that is, it contains no trend element. To distinguish this from the observed variables having trend components let us rename this variable as X_1'. The researcher has no information on X_1, but using X_1' he estimates the equation

$$Y_t = \beta_0 + \beta_1 X_{1t}' + \beta_2 X_{2t} + \beta_3 t + \varepsilon_t. \tag{4.60}$$

The parameter β_1 in equation (4.60) has the same interpretation as that in equation (4.59) because, once the variable t is maintained at a given level, increases in X_{1t} and X_{1t}' are the same. Therefore whether the researcher uses data on X_1 or on X_1' makes no difference in the interpretation of its regression coefficient so long as t remains in the equation.

When the variable X_1' was computed by the agency as

$$X_{1t}' = X_{1t} - k_1 \cdot t, \tag{4.61}$$

where k_1 is a constant and $(k_1 \cdot t)$ is the trend component removed from the observed series X_{1t}, then the researcher will obtain the same estimate for the parameter β_1 whether he estimates equation (4.60) or equation (4.59). This is true because a linear combination of any of the independent variables may be subtracted from another independent variable without altering the corresponding regression coefficients.

When the dependent variable is adjusted for the trend beforehand, then again the implicit regression results are unaltered by using the trend-free dependent variable instead of the raw series, as long as the trend component was computed as a linear function of the time variable. If the researcher estimates

$$Y_t' = \beta_0 + \beta_1 X_{1t} + \beta_2 X_{2t} + \beta_3 t + \varepsilon_t, \tag{4.62}$$

the regression estimates of the parameters in equations (4.62) and (4.50) will be implicitly the same when the trend-free Y' is computed as

$$Y'_t = Y_t - k_2 \cdot t, \tag{4.63}$$

where k_2 is a constant. The only difference will be in the computed R^2 for the two regression equations (see p. 15). In this case R^2 should not be used for any comparison among equations, because the dependent variables are different.

Thus, the correction for trend of some or all the variables in a regression will not affect the regression estimates or their interpretation as long as the trend is linear and the time variable appears in a linear form in the regression equation. This result is very general. When the trend component in some or all of the variables is computed as a quadratic function of time, the regression estimates and their interpretation will not be altered, provided that the time variable enters the regression equation in a quadratic form.

The researcher may note that whether he estimates equation (4.59) or some other equation with trend-corrected variables and the time variable as an explicit independent variable, he will obtain the same regression estimates for the X's, only the regression coefficient of the time variable will differ in these different cases. The regression coefficient of the time variable is capturing the trend component from all variables except the ones which are already corrected. The researcher is rarely interested in interpreting the regression coefficient of the time variable unless the study explicitly calls for it. When the objective of an investigation is to purge the trend components from the regression estimates, the researcher is interested in the regression coefficients of all the other independent variables, and not in that of the time variable. It is inappropriate to try to interpret the regression coefficient corresponding to the time variable when it is used to correct for trend components of the variables in the regression.

4.7   Dummy Variables as Seasons

Analogous to the problem of trend is seasonality in the variables. In the case of trend, the variables under investigation are steadily increasing or decreasing with time, but in other situations they may exhibit seasonal patterns. For example, the demand for currency has a seasonal peak during the Christmas holidays. If the researcher ignores seasonal patterns he may, as with trend, estimate spurious observed relations.

As in the case of a time trend, seasonal components may be eliminated from the observed data by including seasonality as an explicit independent variable in the regression analysis. Since the information on seasonality is qualitative in nature, it may be incorporated in the form of a set of dummy variables. Let D_i be a dummy variable that takes the value 1 when the data correspond to the ith season and 0 otherwise.

The regression equation corresponding to $m + 1$ seasons is

$$Y_t = \beta_0 + \beta_1 X_{1t} + \beta_2 X_{2t} + \delta_1 D_1 + \delta_2 D_2 + \cdots + \delta_m D_m + \varepsilon_t, \quad (4.64)$$

where the $(m + 1)$th season is the excluded category.

By introducing seasonality as an explicit variable we are abstracting the influence of seasonality from all other variables. The estimates of the regression coefficient of X_1 and X_2 in equation (4.64) reflect the true relation between the dependent variable and these independent variables, and not comovements in the series due to the presence of the same seasonal component in all the variables.

As long as the seasonality variable is present in regression equation (4.64), even if some of the variables (dependent or independent) are already corrected for seasonality, the researcher will obtain the same regression estimates of the parameters. When all variables are corrected for seasonality then, of course, there is no need for including the seasonality variable.

Estimated equations may contain both seasonal dummies and time as explicit variables. When this is done, the regression coefficients are purged of seasonal and trend influences.

4.8 Functional Forms

The basis for all empirical research is an hypothesized relation between a dependent and independent variables. In general

$$Y_t = f[X_1, X_2, \ldots, X_k] + \varepsilon_t, \quad (4.65)$$

where $f[\ ]$ refers to some as yet unspecified function. In any given situation the researcher cannot know with complete certainty the nature of $f[\ ]$. That is, he is ignorant of the true functional form of the hypothesized relation. Up to this point we have been approximating $f[\ ]$ by a linear function.

Implicit in the linear form is the assumption that all partial derivatives of the dependent variable with respect to the independent variables are constant and do not depend on the values of any of the independent variables.

Because this assumption may be unduly limiting in some cases, the researcher may wish to utilize less restrictive functional forms.

If the theory indicates unambiguously that the linear form is an adequate representation of the true relation, then the researcher need go no further. On the other hand, a theory may not sufficiently indicate which functional form should be used, and he must then consider other than linear equations.

For our purposes we will first examine the following set of alternatives, which represents the most commonly used forms:

$$Y_t = \beta_0 + \beta_1 X_{1t} + \beta_2 X_{2t} + \varepsilon_{1t}, \tag{4.66}$$

$$Y_t = \alpha_0 + \alpha_1 X_{1t}^2 + \alpha_2 X_{2t} + \varepsilon_{2t}, \tag{4.67}$$

$$Y_t = \gamma_0 + \gamma_1 \log X_{1t} + \gamma_2 X_{2t} + \varepsilon_{3t}. \tag{4.68}$$

Equation (4.66) is the standard linear model, whereas equation (4.67) utilizes X_1^2, and equation (4.68) utilizes $\log X_1$. In each case X_2 is unchanged, and it is to be understood that the following analysis holds for any number of independent variables. The implicit assumptions underlying these equations are

$$\text{for equation (4.66),} \quad \frac{\partial Y}{\partial X_1} = \beta_1, \qquad \frac{\partial Y}{\partial X_2} = \beta_2,$$

$$\text{for equation (4.67),} \quad \frac{\partial Y}{\partial X_1} = 2\alpha_1 X_1, \qquad \frac{\partial Y}{\partial X_2} = \alpha_2,$$

$$\text{for equation (4.68),} \quad \frac{\partial Y}{\partial X_1} = \frac{\gamma_1}{X_1}, \qquad \frac{\partial Y}{\partial X_2} = \gamma_2.$$

Equation (4.66) results in the marginal influence of X_1 on Y being a constant. Equation (4.67) carries the assumption that the marginal influence of X_1 on Y is a direct proportion of the level of X_1 but is unaffected by the level of X_2. Equation (4.68) indicates that the marginal influence of X_1 on Y is inversely proportional only to the level of X_1.

Given these possibilities the researcher must somehow choose the most appropriate functional form of the regression equation. Ideally, his theory tells him unambiguously which to choose; if he fails to utilize the appropriate one in this situation, his estimates will be biased and/or inefficient. Only if complete searching of the theory does not give the researcher any direction should he proceed to use the following *ad hoc* procedure, which can never completely substitute for a good theory.

4.9   Transformation of the Variables

Some functional forms are expressible as a linear function after a suitable transformation of the variables. For example, equation (4.67) is not a linear function in X_1, but by defining X_1', a new variable, as equal to X_1^2, we may express the equation in linear form as

$$Y_t = \alpha_0 + \alpha_1 X_{1t}' + \alpha_2 X_{2t} + \varepsilon_{2t}. \tag{4.69}$$

Since equation (4.69) is a linear function of its independent variables, X_1' and X_2, the researcher may estimate it by the standard least squares procedure.

In this case the problem is not with the technique of estimation. Since the researcher is generally interested in knowing which of the alternative non-linear forms of the variable X_1 is empirically appropriate, he may treat the alternative forms of the variable as alternative definitions of a specified variable. For example, in considering the alternative forms of X_1 given earlier, he may consider X_1, X_1^2, and log X_1 as the alternative definitions of X_1' in regression equation (4.69).

When a variable has alternative definitions, its empirically appropriate definition may be obtained by studying the residual sum of squares of the regressions under the various definitions. (See p. 18). As long as the dependent variable and the number of parameters are estimated the same, the residual sums of squares are comparable in different equations with different definitions of an independent variable.

This case is simple because we are dealing with the functional form of an independent variable. A problem frequently encountered in empirical research is the choice between a linear regression and a log-linear regression equation. To answer this question let us consider first the case in which the alternative functional forms are

$$Y_t = \beta_0 + \beta_1 X_{1t} + \beta_2 X_{2t} + \varepsilon_{1t}, \tag{4.70}$$

$$\log Y_t = \alpha_0 + \alpha_1 X_{1t} + \alpha_2 X_{2t} + \varepsilon_{2t}. \tag{4.71}$$

In this case the researcher cannot play the game of minimum residual sum of squares, because the dependent variables are different in the two equations.

We can trace the source of our trouble to a scaling factor. The variance of Y changes with the units of measurement of Y, but the variance of log Y does not, because $\log cY = \log c + \log Y$ and the addition of a constant ($\log c$) does not alter the variance. A direct comparison of residual sum of squares is therefore meaningless because by a proper choice of units of measurement one residual sum of squares may be made smaller than the other.

By standardizing the variable Y in such a way that its variance does not change with units of measurement we may bring these two equations onto a common footing. If we do the transformation so that the "Jacobian" of transformation is the same for Y^* and log Y^*, where Y^* is the transformed Y, we can directly compare the residual sums of squares.[3]

A transformation of Y that allows such a comparison of the residual sum of squares may be defined as

$$Y_t^* = c \cdot Y_t, \tag{4.72}$$

where

$$c = \exp\left(-\frac{\sum \log Y_t}{T}\right)$$

is the inverse of the geometric mean of Y.

By standardizing Y by its geometric mean and defining the standardized value as Y^* we may express the two equations (4.70) and (4.71) in terms of Y^* rather than Y as

$$Y_t^* = \beta_0^* + \beta_1^* X_{1t} + \beta_2^* X_{2t} + \varepsilon_{1t}^*, \tag{4.73}$$

$$\log Y_t^* = \alpha_0^* + \alpha_1^* X_{1t} + \alpha_2^* X_{2t} + \varepsilon_{2t}^*. \tag{4.74}$$

Since the residual sums of squares in these two equations, (4.73) and (4.74), are directly comparable, we choose the functional form yielding the minimum residual sum of squares as the empirically appropriate functional form.

---

[3] For a full discussion of this topic see G. E. P. Box and D. R. Cox, "An Analysis of Transformations," *Journal of the Royal Statistical Society, Series B*, 1964, 211–43.

The researcher may use a nonparametric test to see whether the difference between the residual sums of squares in these two functional forms is significant. The test is based on a statistic defined as

$$d = \frac{T}{2} \left| \log \frac{\sum e_{1t}^{*2}}{\sum e_{2t}^{*2}} \right|,$$ (4.75)

where $\sum e_{1t}^{*2}$ and $\sum e_{2t}^{*2}$ are the residual sums of squares in estimating equations (4.73) and (4.74) respectively. The d statistic follows a chi-squared distribution with one degree of freedom.[4] When the d statistic exceeds the chosen critical value, the researcher may reject the null hypothesis that these two functions are empirically equivalent.

This may seem to be an *ad hoc* procedure, but actually it is similar to so-called "maximum likelihood estimation," except that in this case we are not interested in the functional form that maximizes the likelihood value over the entire space. We are choosing one of the two well specified functional forms with the larger likelihood value.[5] The likelihood function may have a higher value outside the ranges of our inquiry, but we are not concerned with them because it may be difficult to interpret their relevance in a practical situation.

Once we understand the procedure of comparison between two regression equations with different dependent variables, we may extend our results to the choice of the linear versus the log-linear functional form. The choice is between the equations

$$Y_{1t}^* = \beta_0^* + \beta_1^* X_{1t} + \beta_2^* X_{2t} + \varepsilon_{1t}^*,$$ (4.76)

$$\log Y_{1t}^* = \gamma_0^* + \gamma_1^* \log X_{1t} + \gamma_2^* \log X_{2t} + \varepsilon_{3t}^*.$$ (4.77)

If the researcher has standardized his dependent variable by dividing it by its geometric mean, then the two equations are comparable. Using the residual sum of squares as the criterion, we choose the one with the minimum residual sum of squares. In this choice we are combining the rules for the transformation of a dependent variable and of independent variables.

To illustrate this procedure let us consider a numerical example. In Chapter 2 a production function was estimated for Indian woolen textiles as a log-linear function. We could just as well have expressed the production process as

---

[4] See Box and Cox, *op. cit.*

[5] We employ the same rationale in selecting empirically appropriate definitions of variables.

a linear function of the inputs. When the same notation is used as when the example was first presented (p. 41) but when the numbers are in millions of rupees in order to bring them to a manageable size, the linear and log linear functions for the data given in Table 2.2 are

$$q = 4.9669 + 2.3965k + 2.7031l \qquad \sum e_1^2 = 1471.0702, \qquad (4.78)$$

$$\log q = 1.6524 + 0.4133 \log k + 0.7082 \log l \qquad \sum e_2^2 = 1.7367 \qquad (4.79)$$

where $\sum e_1^2$ and $\sum e_2^2$ are the residual sums of squares in these two equations respectively.

Since the dependent variables in equations (4.78) and (4.79) are not the same we cannot directly compare the sums of squares of the residuals. To make them comparable we have to transform the dependent variable q as

$$q^* = c \cdot q, \qquad (4.80)$$

where c is the inverse of the geometric mean of q. The geometric mean of q is 19.2459, hence c is 0.05196.

To be able to compare the residual sums of squares we have to estimate the following regression equations:

$$q^* = \beta_0^* + \beta_1^* k + \beta_2^* l + \varepsilon_{1t}^*, \qquad (4.81)$$

$$\log q^* = \gamma_0^* + \gamma_1^* \log k + \gamma_2^* \log l + \varepsilon_{3t}^*. \qquad (4.82)$$

For our exercise we do not need the estimates but only the residual sums of squares. We know that the variance of $\log q^*$ and of $\log q$ is the same, because these q's are constant multiples of each other. The residual sum of squares in equation (4.79) is the same as in (4.82). We also know that multiplication of the entire equation (4.78) by a constant c is the same as changing the units of measurement of all the variables by the same scale. Hence, the residual sum of squares in (4.81) is the same as in (4.78) if they are expressed in the same units.

Thus the sums of squares of the residuals in equations (4.81) and (4.82)—respectively $\sum e_{1t}^{*2}$ and $\sum e_{2t}^{*2}$—are

$$\sum e_{1t}^{*2} = c^2 \sum e_{1t}^2 = 3.9715, \qquad (4.83)$$

$$\sum e_{2t}^{*2} = \sum e_{2t}^2 = 1.7367. \qquad (4.84)$$

The sum of squares of the residuals in equation (4.82) is smaller than that of (4.81). Hence, the log-linear function appears empirically more appropriate than the linear function for Indian woolen textiles.

To test whether these two functions are empirically equivalent, let us compute the d statistic:

$$d = \frac{15}{2} \left| \log \frac{3.9715}{1.7367} \right| = 6.2, \tag{4.85}$$

where the sample size is 15.

The d statistic follows the chi-squared distribution with one degree of freedom. The critical value for the 90 percent level of confidence is 2.706. The computed statistic, 6.2, exceeds the critical value. Hence we reject the null hypothesis that these two functions are empirically equivalent with 90 percent confidence.

5

Analysis of the Residuals

An applied econometrician often searches the residuals in hope of finding some clues for possible improvement of his estimates. Since residuals are similar to the error terms, they may be expected to throw some light on the nature of the true errors. But many researchers use the summary statistics derived from the residuals without recognizing all the resultant implications. In a given set of observed data the true error terms do not depend on the values of the independent variables, but the residuals do. The residuals are obtained in such a way as to satisfy a set of conditions imposed on the basis of the sample data relevant to the independent variables. The residuals therefore reflect the properties of the *independent variables* as well as those of the *errors*. Treating the residuals as though they are telling the story of the errors alone can often prove highly misleading.

In this chapter we study some common mistakes of researchers and suggest some ways of avoiding misuse of summary statistics derived from the residuals.

As a starting point, assume that the researcher estimates the parameters by the ordinary least squares procedure, even if he has reasons to believe that the errors may not be random. For reasonably large sample sizes when the estimated regression is the truth, the residuals provide, at least in principle, the needed information on the errors. In a real-world situation, however, the researcher cannot always meet this condition. The residuals in a regression equation are contaminated, *inter alia*, by left-out variables whenever there is a misspecification. If the researcher ignores this aspect in asking the residuals to answer questions regarding the error terms, he may obtain wrong answers.

In terms of precision of the estimates, the cost of incorporating wrong information is usually very high, and the researcher should be extremely cautious in attributing a relation among the residuals to the true relation among the error terms. Before reaching a conclusion about the nature of error terms on the basis of evidence furnished by the residuals, he should check for all sources of contamination and try to eliminate, or at least minimize, their influence.

We shall discuss some common sources of contamination and how they can be recognized from the analysis of the residuals.

5.1 Transcription Errors

In empirical work transcription errors do occur no matter how careful the researcher is. Usually the data are copied from several sources and change hands several times between the source and the computer input cards. A frequent mistake is a wrongly placed decimal point in some of the observations (or in the format instruction card).

The sequential plot of the residuals often reveals transcription errors. Consider the plot of residuals in Figure 5.1. The residuals identified by A and B are distinctly out of place with respect to the rest of the residuals and are called *outliers*.

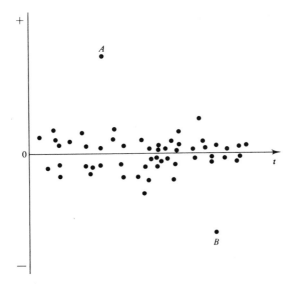

Figure 5.1. Outliers

Outliers may also be caused by abnormalities in the data. For example, during war years a government may impose controls or people may voluntarily refrain from certain consumption. In such cases the residuals corresponding to those years usually show up as outliers. A typical regression equation represents the behavior of individuals under the assumption of *ceteris paribus*. When unusual political or social conditions negate this assumption, the regression equation cannot be used for this particular time period. If the researcher incorporates the additional information in the form of an independent or a dummy variable, he may still be able to use the same regression equation to explain both war years and nonwar years. Otherwise, he may find it more appropriate to delete the abnormal years from the regression equations.

Sometimes the researcher may have theoretical reasons to believe that certain observations exhibit abnormal behavior. If the residuals corresponding to these observations do not show any conspicuous variation in behavior with respect to the rest of the residuals, he may decide to retain these observations in the sample. Even though theoretically the observations should exhibit abnormalities, the observed data may not.

5.2   Clustered Residuals

In many empirical works the residuals cluster to form definite patterns. When the researcher arranges the residuals in a systematic way with respect to an attribute or a variable not already in the regression equation, they may form into clusters. For example, when the dependent variable exhibits strong seasonality which is not captured by the independent variables of the regression equation, the residuals form into clusters according to season. When the residuals are arranged in such a way that all the residuals corresponding to a given season are plotted in a sequence, the residuals corresponding to various seasons may form into clusters if any seasonal effect has been left out.

The cluster effect in the residuals may be eliminated by incorporating the relevant independent variable, or it may at least be minimized by using dummy variables corresponding to each cluster, provided that the researcher can explain the cause for such behavior.

The cluster effect is often visible in cross-sectional studies when the nature of the regression equation includes significant variations on such aspects as geographic locality, climatic conditions, or educational background. Thus, for example, when the researcher suspects that the residuals may form into clusters according to the general level of education of each state in a cross-sectional study of all the states, he may arrange the residuals into groups of states ranked as having low, medium, and high levels of education. If these groups exhibit clusters of residuals, then he may minimize the contamination of the residuals by incorporating the education variable in the regression equation.

A typical graph of clusters of residuals is presented in Figure 5.2.

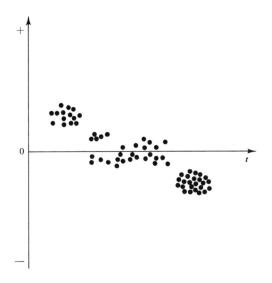

Figure 5.2. Clustering of Residuals

5.3 Left-Out Variables

When the researcher suspects that he may have left out a variable in the estimation equation, he might expect to be warned by the residuals. Unfortunately, residuals rarely provide any information on this subject unless the left-out variable is orthogonal (uncorrelated) to all the independent variables in the estimated regression. When a variable is left out, a part of its influence is captured by the included variables (see p. 29). The portion retained in the residuals depends on the values of the included variables. Should the researcher decide to correlate, or plot against, the suspected left-out variable with the residuals, he may not notice any significant relation even though, in fact, the variable was left out by misspecification.

It is more appropriate and economical to insert the suspected left-out variable in the regression equation and to estimate the new equation, rather than to try to match the residuals with the variable. When the questionable variable is included in the regression it captures its own share of influence on the movements of the dependent variable.

When the left-out variable is qualitative in nature, it is usually orthogonal to the independent variables and is often detected by the clustering of the residuals.

5.4   *Heteroscedastic Residuals*

Textbooks in econometrics often recommend plotting the residuals against the independent variables to check for heteroscedasticity. In some cases this may lead to wrong conclusions.

Heteroscedasticity relates to the *variance* of the error terms and not to patterns in the *values* of the error terms. The researcher expects to find the nature of the error of the variance of the error terms from the variance of the residuals. Since the number of residuals (observations) in a typical econometric research project is not large enough to accommodate any powerful techniques of test procedures based on inferences about the true variance, the researcher has to resort to other measures of dispersion.

A common measure in such situations is the range—the difference between minimum and maximum in a given subgroup. When the residuals are arranged according to a sequence believed to have caused heteroscedasticity, the researcher expects the range of the residuals to change when heteroscedasticity actually is present. There are several ways of approaching this problem; a commonly used procedure is to draw the envelope of all the residuals, as shown in Figure 5.3.

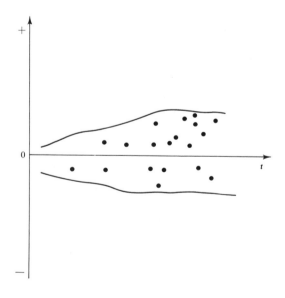

Figure 5.3. Envelope of Residuals

If the envelope expands or contracts systematically with respect to the arrangement of the residuals, then heteroscedasticity may be suspected. But this conclusion is valid only when the observations are reasonably large. In small samples, even though there is no heteroscedasticity in the true error terms, it may often be observed in the residuals arranged with respect to any of the independent variables in the regression that generated them. As we will now show, this is a consequence of the least squares estimation procedure; the researcher should guard against the possible misinterpretation of this phenomenon.

Consider the true relation

$$y_t = \beta x_t + \varepsilon_t, \tag{5.1}$$

where all the error terms (ε's) are randomly generated by the same statistical distribution with mean zero and variance σ_ε^2, and the variables are deviation from the means.

The residuals in the ordinary least squares estimation of (5.1) are

$$e_t = y_t - \hat{\beta} x_t. \tag{5.2}$$

Using (5.1) and the expression for the least squares estimation of $\hat{\beta}$ we obtain

$$e_t = \beta x_t + \varepsilon_t - \left(\sum x_t y_t / \sum x_t^2 \right) x_t \tag{5.3}$$

$$= \varepsilon_t - \left(x_t \cdot \sum x_t \varepsilon_t \right) / \sum x_t^2. \tag{5.4}$$

Since the residual e_t has a statistical distribution with mean zero, the variance of the distribution is

$$V(e_t) = E(e_t^2), \tag{5.5}$$

which, by using (5.4), equals

$$E\left[\varepsilon_t^2 + \frac{x_t^2 \left(\sum x_t \varepsilon_t \right)^2}{\left(\sum x_t^2 \right)^2} - 2 \cdot \frac{x_t \varepsilon_t \left(\sum x_t \varepsilon_t \right)}{\sum x_t^2} \right]. \tag{5.6}$$

Under the assumptions that the errors are serially independent and that the x's are nonstochastic (fixed in repeated samples) we obtain

$$V(e_t) = \sigma_\varepsilon^2 + \frac{x_t^2 \cdot \sigma_\varepsilon^2 \cdot \sum x_t^2}{(\sum x_t^2)^2} - \frac{2x_t^2 \sigma_\varepsilon^2}{\sum x_t^2} \tag{5.7}$$

$$= \sigma_\varepsilon^2 \cdot \left\{1 - \frac{x_t^2}{\sum x_t^2}\right\}. \tag{5.8}$$

Realizing that $V(\varepsilon) = \sigma_\varepsilon^2$, we note that the variance of the residuals is not the same as that of error terms; $V(e)$ depends on the values of x:

$$V(e_t) = V(\varepsilon_t) \cdot \left\{1 - \frac{x_t^2}{\sum x_t^2}\right\}. \tag{5.9}$$

If the error terms are homoscedastic and random, the residual correspond-ing to a given value of x has a statistical distribution with mean zero and variance (5.9). The variance of the residual depends on the value of x, even though the variance of the error term does not. The three-sigma limits for the error term and residuals differ for various values of x, as shown in Figure 5.4. If the researcher interprets the observed behavior of residuals as the behavior of errors, he may reach the wrong conclusion. It is advisable first to draw the expected three-sigma limits for the residuals on the basis of the maximum and the minimum values of the independent variable and on $\sum x_t^2$, before plotting the residuals against an independent variable as a search procedure for locating heteroscedasticity of the error terms.

When $\sum x_t^2$ is very large *compared* to the largest magnitude of observed x, the three-sigma limits for the residuals approach the three-sigma limits for the error terms.

In some empirical work the theory clearly indicates the nature of the vari-ance of the error term. When the theory specifies heteroscedasticity in the error terms then, of course, there is no need to search the residuals. Consider, for example, the case of an investment decision function in the Indian engineering industry (see p. 101 for the notation). For each firm, let the investment decision function be

$$I_j = \beta_0 + \beta_1 S_j + \beta_2 P_j + \varepsilon_j, \tag{5.10}$$

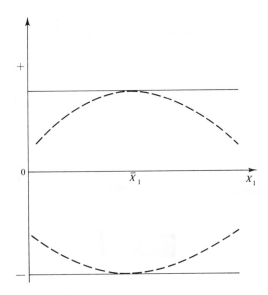

Figure 5.4. Three-Sigma Limits for Error Term and Residuals

where j denotes the jth firm. Let us assume that the variance of the error term for each firm is the same, σ^2.

When data are available for each firm then, of course, there is no problem of heteroscedasticity. But the data in each year relate to aggregates of several numbers of firms, and the number is not the same for all the time periods under investigation. For example there were 54 firms in 1950 and 131 in 1965. Since the data correspond to aggregates, we may express equation (5.10) in terms of the aggregates as

$$\sum_j I_j = \sum_j \beta_0 + \beta_1 \sum_j S_j + \beta_2 \sum_j P_j + \sum_j \varepsilon_j. \qquad (5.11)$$

Let N_t be the number of firms for the year t. When the aggregates corresponding to year t are denoted by a subscript t, the investment decision function in terms of the aggregates may be written as

$$I_t = \beta_0 N_t + \beta_1 S_t + \beta_2 P_t + \varepsilon_t. \qquad (5.12)$$

Even though equation (5.10) is homoscedastic, equation (5.12) is not. According to the Gauss-Markov theorem, estimation of (5.12) by ordinary least squares does not yield the minimum-variance unbiased estimates of the parameters (β's). However, by a suitable transformation of the variables we may reduce equation (5.12) to a Gauss-Markov case. Consider the variance of the error term ε_t:

$$V(\varepsilon_t) = V(\textstyle\sum \varepsilon_j) = N_t \cdot \sigma^2, \qquad (5.13)$$

since the error terms for each firm are independent of the errors in the other firms.

Suppose we define a new error term ε_t^* as

$$\varepsilon_t^* = \varepsilon_t / \sqrt{N_t}. \qquad (5.14)$$

Its variance is

$$V(\varepsilon_t^*) = \sigma^2. \qquad (5.15)$$

The transformed error term ε^* has the same variance for all t. Therefore, if we can express equation (5.12) in terms of ε^* the Gauss-Markov theorem holds and we obtain the minimum-variance unbiased estimates of β's by using ordinary least squares. Suppose we divide equation (5.12) by $\sqrt{N_t}$:

$$\frac{I_t}{\sqrt{N_t}} = \beta_0 \frac{N_t}{\sqrt{N_t}} + \beta_1 \frac{S_t}{\sqrt{N_t}} + \beta_2 \frac{P_t}{\sqrt{N_t}} + \frac{\varepsilon_t}{\sqrt{N_t}}. \qquad (5.16)$$

By rewriting, (5.16) becomes

$$\frac{I_t}{\sqrt{N_t}} = \beta_0 \sqrt{N_t} + \beta_1 \frac{S_t}{\sqrt{N_t}} + \beta_2 \frac{P_t}{\sqrt{N_t}} + \varepsilon_t^*. \qquad (5.17)$$

Equation (5.17) satisfies the Gauss-Markov conditions, hence ordinary least squares estimation of (5.17) provides best linear unbiased estimates.

Since the parameters of (5.12) are the same as those of (5.17), the $\hat{\beta}_0$ from (5.17) is the estimate of the constant term in equation (5.12).

The researcher may note that the general practice for this aggregation problem is to formulate equation (5.10) as though it corresponds to aggregates and then to divide by $\sqrt{N_t}$ to correct for heteroscedasticity. This is a bad practice; even worse, it gives wrong answers.

The investment decision function for the Indian engineering industry, adjusted for heteroscedasticity, is estimated as

$$\frac{I_t}{\sqrt{N_t}} = -61.36 + 7.43\sqrt{N_t} + 0.076\left(\frac{S_t}{\sqrt{N_t}}\right) + 0.036\left(\frac{P_t}{\sqrt{N_t}}\right) \qquad R^2 = 0.98.$$

$$\text{(53.37)} \quad \text{(7.36)} \qquad \text{(0.019)} \qquad\qquad \text{(0.437)} \qquad\qquad\qquad\qquad \text{(5.18)}$$

Given the level of sales, the movements in profits do not seem to influence the movements in investment. Whether we assume heteroscedasticity or not, we are reaching the same conclusions, for the coefficient of P_t in (4.57) was insignificant also.

In estimating (5.18) we introduced a constant term even though the theoretical specification (5.17) does not provide for it. The constant term in this context has no operational significance. It is there only to allow flexibility in the estimated equation and to simplify the interpretation of the summary statistics (R^2 and standard errors). See the discussion on interpretation of the constant term on page 5.

5.5 Serial Correlation in Residuals

In Chapter 3 it was shown that when the error terms are serially dependent the estimates by ordinary least squares are not the minimum-variance unbiased estimates of the parameters. We also studied an alternative estimation procedure (generalized least squares) using an estimate of the parameter (ρ) of serial correlation. Since a theory seldom provides unambiguous information on the serial correlation of the error terms, the researcher wants to infer the nature of serial correlation in the errors from analysis of the residuals with the hope of improving the precision of his estimates.

A point often overlooked by researchers is that correcting for serial correlation does not always give "better" results unless the parameter of serial correlation is known, which is rarely the case. Whenever an estimate of the serial correlation parameter used in reestimating the parameters is different from the parameter itself, the estimates of the β's no longer have minimum-variance.

In some cases, the use of an estimate of the serial correlation parameter from the least squares residuals may give even less efficient estimates than the original ordinary least squares estimates. Therefore, the researcher should be cautious in drawing inferences about the nature of serial correlation in the errors.

A widely used test for serial correlation in the error terms is the Durbin-Watson test[1] based on the least squares residuals. Consider the regression equation

$$y_t = \hat{\beta}_1 x_{1t} + \cdots + \hat{\beta}_k x_{kt} + e_t, \tag{5.19}$$

where $\hat{\beta}$'s are the least squares estimates of parameter β's and the e's are the residuals.

On the basis of residuals, the Durbin-Watson d statistic is defined as:

$$d = \sum_{t=2}^{T} (e_t - e_{t-1})^2 \Big/ \sum_{t=1}^{T} e_t^2 \tag{5.20}$$

where T is the sample size. When the error terms are serially independent, the d statistic has a theoretical distribution with mean 2; but sampling fluctuations may lead to a different computation of the d statistic even when the true errors are serially independent. Durbin and Watson computed a table of critical values for 95 percent confidence levels to test the null hypothesis that the error terms are serially independent against the alternative that the null hypothesis is false. These critical values are presented in Table 4 on page 228. Corresponding to a given sample size and the number of parameters estimated, there are two critical values: namely, the lower critical value d_l and the upper critical value d_u.

When the computed d statistic is smaller than the lower critical value d_l or above the critical value $(4 - d_l)$ then the null hypothesis is rejected. When the statistic is larger than d_u but smaller than $(4 - d_u)$ then the null hypothesis is accepted. When neither of these two cases is true then the test is inconclusive.

Let us consider the example of the multiplier equation for the Indian

---

[1] J. Durbin and G. S. Watson, "Testing for Serial Correlation in Least Squares Regression," parts I and II, *Biometrika*, 1950 and 1951.

economy (see p. 44 for notation). The regression equation of national income on investment is

$$Y_t = 77.267 + 2.997\, I_t \qquad R^2 = 0.852.$$
$$(4.404)\ (0.377)$$

$$(5.21)$$

The Durbin-Watson statistic computed from the residuals is $d = 1.0848$. Our sample size is 13, and the number of parameters estimated (other than the constant term) are $k' = 1$. The critical values corresponding to $n = 13$ and $k' = 1$ are not available in the table, but we may extrapolate to obtain $d_l = 0.81$ and $d_u = 1.21$. The computed statistic is not less than the lower critical value and not larger than the upper critical value, so the test is inconclusive.

This test procedure should not be misused. It is inapplicable when the constant term is not estimated in a regression equation; and if outliers or extreme observations are present in the residuals, then it may yield misleading conclusions. The researcher is advised to study the residuals for such exceptions before rejecting the null hypothesis of no first order serial correlation.

The Durbin-Watson test for serial correlation is valid for the regression equations in which the independent variables do not include any lagged dependent variables. When these are present, a different test is suggested by Durbin.[2] Consider the regression equation

$$y_t = \hat{\beta}_1 y_{t-1} + \hat{\beta}_2 y_{t-2} + \cdots + \hat{\alpha}_1 x_{1t} + \hat{\alpha}_2 x_{2t} + \cdots + e_t, \qquad (5.22)$$

where the $\hat{\beta}$'s and $\hat{\alpha}$'s are the ordinary least squares estimates. The test statistic h is defined as

$$h = (1 - \tfrac{1}{2}d)\sqrt{\frac{T}{1 - T \cdot \hat{V}(\hat{\beta}_1)}}, \qquad (5.23)$$

where d is the statistic defined by equation (5.20), T is the sample size, and $\hat{V}(\hat{\beta}_1)$ is the estimate of variance of $\hat{\beta}_1$.

---

[2] J. Durbin, "Testing for Serial Correlation in Least-Squares Regression When Some of the Regressions Are Lagged Dependent Variables," *Econometrica*, 38, No. 3 (May, 1970), 410–21.

The h statistic is distributed as standard normal with mean zero and variance unity.[3] By using the standard normal distribution tables the researcher may test for the null hypothesis.

To illustrate the test procedure, let us consider the impact multiplier equation for the Indian economy (see p. 44). The regression equation with one lagged dependent variable is

$$Y_t = 11.31 + 0.887\ Y_{t-1} + 0.406\ I_t \qquad R^2 = 0.97 \qquad (5.24)$$
$$\quad (11.41)\ (0.147) \qquad\quad (0.455) \qquad d = 2.67.$$

In this example, T, the sample size, is 12; $\hat{\beta}_1$, the estimate of coefficient of the dependent variable lagged by one time period, is 0.887; the estimate of the variance of $\hat{\beta}_1$, $\hat{V}(\hat{\beta}_1)$, is 0.0261 $(=(0.147)\cdot(0.147))$, and d, the Durbin-Watson statistic, is 2.67. From these data the h-statistic may be computed as

$$h = \left(1 - \frac{2.67}{2}\right)\sqrt{\frac{12}{1 - 12(0.0261)}} = -1.34. \qquad (5.25)$$

The h-statistic follows the standard normal distribution with mean zero and variance unity. For the 95 percent level of confidence the critical value is ± 1.645. Since the computed h-statistic (-1.34) does not exceed the critical value, we do not reject the null hypothesis that the errors are serially independent.

These tests are valid for the first order Markov processes. When the serial dependence in the error terms is caused by some process other than the first order Markov, the researcher may still reject the null hypothesis of serial independence in the error terms. In such cases, it may be inappropriate to use the generalized least squares estimation procedure on the basis of the serial correlation estimate from the residuals.

There are no clear-cut tests to determine whether the serial correlation is of the first order as opposed to higher order processes, but correlogram analysis sometimes helps. If the errors are generated by a first order Markov scheme then:

$$E(\varepsilon_t \varepsilon_{t-\tau}) = \rho^\tau. \qquad (5.26)$$

---

[3] This test is based on asymptotic properties, and h may not be defined in some cases when T is very small. When $T \cdot \hat{V}(\hat{\beta}_1)$ is larger than unity, which may happen with too few degrees of freedom, the h is not defined. This case is not frequent in applied econometrics.

A plot of ρ^τ against the value of τ is called the *correlogram* of the error terms. When these are generated by the first order Markov scheme, then the correlogram is a geometrically declining function of τ. If the plot of the lag correlation between the residuals defined as

$$r_\tau = \sum e_t e_{t-\tau} / \sum e_{t-\tau}^2 \qquad (5.27)$$

exhibits the same pattern as the correlogram of the first order Markov scheme, then this may be considered as some evidence in favor of the scheme. If the correlogram of the residuals does not match the hypothesized (geometrically declining) correlogram pattern of the error terms, then the researcher may wish to reconsider the evidence before proceeding to recompute the estimates of the β's by the generalized least squares procedure. If the process generating the error terms is not of the first order, then the use of the generalized least squares procedure is inappropriate.

In the equation (5.21) if the researcher proceeds with the assumption that errors are serially correlated with the estimate of serial correlation parameter as

$$\rho^* = \sum e_t e_{t-1} / \sum e_{t-1}^2 = 0.42 \qquad (5.28)$$

and if he uses this estimate in generalized least squares (see p. 71) to obtain the estimates of the β's, he will obtain

$$Y_t^* = 55.505 + 1.787 \, I_t^* \qquad R^2 = 0.368, \qquad (5.29)$$
$$(5.208) \quad (0.706)$$

where Y^* and I^* are transformed Y and I respectively using ρ^* from (5.28). (See p. 72.)

The summary statistic R^2 is not comparable with that in equation (5.22) because the dependent variables are different. The multiplier of 1.8 [which implies a marginal propensity to consume of (0.44)] seems to be an unreasonable value, and the generalized least squares estimate apparently did not provide a "better" estimate of the multiplier.[4]

---

[4] The coefficient of I_t in equation (5.29) is not the long-run multiplier. See p. 45 for a discussion of this.

This result could be because the first order Markov process is inappropriate to these data.[5] To check whether the correlogram of the residuals would provide information on the inappropriateness of the generalized least squares, the lagged serial correlation coefficients of residuals are computed:

$$r_1 = 0.42 \qquad r_2 = -0.31 \qquad r_3 = -0.41 \qquad r_4 = -0.36. \qquad (5.30)$$

If the serial correlation is of the order of 0.4, we expect these numbers to be of the order of 0.4, 0.16, 0.06, 0.02. The correlogram of the residuals seems to suggest that the first order Markov process is inappropriate to these data, and the estimates appear to agree with this opinion.

Some researchers have the habit of looking at the first lag correlation of the residuals (r_1) to see whether it exceeds a specified value and then to reestimate, using generalized least squares, if it does. Such a programmed attitude may sometimes lead to inefficient estimates. In the above case, for example, with the sample of 13 the variance of the estimate (r_1) is of the order of (1/13). The two-sigma limits cover the range (-0.56 to 0.56). Even if the first order Markov process is appropriate, the observed value $r_1 = 0.41$ could have come from the errors with zero serial correlation. The Durbin-Watson statistic is inconclusive even when it produces what may seem to be a "large" value for the serial correlation.

When a "significant" serial correlation in the residuals from the generalized least squares is noticed, some researchers proceed to do another round of generalized least squares by transforming the already transformed data. By so doing, the researcher hopes to eliminate the serial correlation in the *residuals* (not the *errors*). This is a bad habit and should be discouraged. A several-round generalized least squares procedure seldom results in theoretically meaningful estimates. Should the researcher decide to use the generalized least squares as an iteration procedure in obtaining the "maximum likelihood" estimates, he should compute the residuals at each iteration from the original data and *not* from the transformed data.

---

[5] Estimating equation (5.29) is inappropriate because the true model is a distributed lag specification (see p. 161). By estimating equation (5.29) we are forcing the data to satisfy a serial correlation model, which it cannot do. Equation (5.21) is a misspecification of the true model (5.24) to start with. The correlogram (5.30) is trying to convey this message.

6

Hypothesis Testing

Empirical research is often called for in testing a verifiable statement. When faced by several theories, the researcher interested in empirically testing which of them is appropriate in a given situation will apply the tools of hypothesis testing.

To understand the relevant concepts and their proper use, let us consider a situation in which there are two theories. The researcher wants to choose the appropriate one for the policy purposes of his given situation. There may be several ways of deciding which of the theories is appropriate. One is by the criterion of empirical relevance. If the real world, as observed by measured facts, proves to be inconsistent with a theory, then the researcher may decide to discard the theory.

To make effective use of empirical investigation in this way, one must be able to distinguish one theory from the other empirically. If both predict the same observable phenomena, there is no way of distinguishing between them; observed relations may lead to the conclusion that both theories are appropriate or both inappropriate. Reaching such a conclusion is simply a redundant exercise.

Only when the two theories disagree on an observable relation can empirical research determine the appropriateness of a given theory. Typically, the researcher should construct a statement regarding some observable phenomenon in such a way that one theory implies that the statement is false and the other implies it is true. By empirical verification the researcher can then determine which of the two contesting theories is appropriate to his needs.

When the testing of two theories has been thus reduced, the statement is rewritten in the terminology of statistics as two hypotheses: one declaring that the statement is true, referred to as the *null hypothesis*, and the other declaring that the statement is false, referred to as the *alternative hypothesis*. In this terminology only one of the two hypotheses can be true in a given situation. Prior to any testing the researcher must have both the null hypothesis and the alternative: hence the starting point in any test is a clear statement of the contrasting hypotheses and their relation to the corresponding theories. The researcher has need to test these as his only way of knowing which is the truth.

Having clearly stated the objective of his empirical investigation in the form of the null and alternative hypotheses, the researcher now turns to a test criterion—that is, how he intends to verify which of the two statements is the truth. He may set up a rule in such a way that if its terms are met by the data then he will accept the null hypothesis as the truth, otherwise he will accept the alternative.

When a rule is based on a statistic it may possibly give a wrong answer. When the null hypothesis is in fact true, the rule may indicate that it is false, which is clearly a wrong answer. This is called the *Type I error*. Though the researcher would like to have a rule that does not give wrong answers, it is hard to find one which always performs correctly. However, one may select a rule that gives right answers more frequently than others. By choosing such a rule the researcher can be confident that if it is used repeatedly on different occasions he will at least in a majority of the cases be getting correct answers, even though he does not know when he is getting wrong answers.

Any rule may give a wrong answer of the opposite kind: when the null hypothesis is actually false the rule may indicate that it is true. This is called the *Type II error*. Notice that the Type I error and the Type II error are different concepts. Any rule may give both kinds of wrong answers. Ideally, the researcher would prefer a rule that has the minimum chance of committing both of these errors. But unfortunately rules with a smaller probability of Type I error usually have a larger probability of Type II error and vice versa.

The problem of choosing a rule on the basis of *both* Type I and Type II errors is infrequent in applied econometrics, because we seldom know the probabilities of both of these two errors corresponding to any rule. It is true that their probabilities may be computed on the basis of the theoretical distributions of the estimates on which the rule is based, provided the null and the alternative hypotheses clearly state specific values of the corresponding parameters. But usually in applied econometrics only the null hypothesis is specific, and the alternative is usually the negation of the null hypothesis with no specific values assigned to the respective parameters. In such cases it is possible to obtain the probability of the Type I error but not of the Type II error.

When the researcher rejects a null hypothesis having a probability of Type I error of, say, 5 percent he is aware that his rejection on the basis of that rule will be wrong 5 percent of the time. Conversely, he is confident that he will get the correct answer in 95 percent of the cases. In other words, the rule is said to have a "95 percent level of confidence."

Unless the researcher knows the probability of the corresponding Type II error of a rule, he does not know the probability of getting a right answer when the rule indicates that the null hypothesis should be accepted. It may be that the null hypothesis is in fact false. That is, without knowing the probability of the Type II error the researcher cannot assess the chances of his getting the correct answer when the rule indicates acceptance of a null hypothesis.

Since the alternative hypothesis is usually the negation of the null hypothesis rather than a statement regarding the specific values of parameters, the researcher knows the chances of obtaining a wrong answer when he rejects the null hypothesis but not when he accepts. To maintain this distinction in reporting results, the applied econometrician either "rejects" or "does not reject" the null hypothesis, rather than "rejecting" or "accepting" it. Thus "not rejecting" a null hypothesis does not necessarily imply its acceptance.

The rule for rejecting or not rejecting a null hypothesis on the basis of empirical research is usually based on some test statistic (call it t) computed from the data. Typically, a rule rejects the null hypothesis when a test statistic exceeds a specified value, t_c, called the *critical value*. When the statistical distribution of the test statistic is known, then the researcher can compute the probability of the statistic exceeding the critical value when the null hypothesis is true, which is the probability of committing the Type I error corresponding to the rule.

6.1 Test Based on One Regression Coefficient

When the researcher wants to verify whether a theory is relevant to a given situation, he will want to test a null hypothesis on the basis of data relating to the situation. Sometimes it is possible to formulate the null hypothesis in the form of a specific value of a parameter. For example, consider a theory which states that, given the level of profits (P), investment (I) in an industry does not change with the sales (S) of that industry. This null hypothesis may be readily translated into a specific value of a parameter by expressing the relation between investment and profits as a linear regression equation:

$$I_t = \beta_0 + \beta_1 S_t + \beta_2 P_t + \varepsilon_t. \tag{6.1}$$

The null hypothesis implies that the parameter value of β_1 is zero. The alternative hypothesis may be stated simply as: the null hypothesis is false. In the standard notation the null hypothesis is expressed as

$$H_N: \beta_1 = 0$$

$$H_A: H_N \text{ is false.}$$

(6.2)

Since specification of the objective of a test is complete only when the null and alternative hypotheses have been clearly stated, expression (6.2) is usually referred to as the *null hypothesis* instead of the more accurate term, *null and alternative hypotheses*.

In this particular example, the rule to test the null hypothesis against the alternative is based on a statistic called the *t*-ratio, defined as

$$t = \hat{\beta}_1/\text{st. error of } \hat{\beta}_1.$$

(6.3)

Since the estimate $\hat{\beta}_1$ and its standard error are obtained from the results of the least squares procedure, the *t*-ratio has a statistical distribution. When the null hypothesis is true ($\beta_1 = 0$) and the error terms (ε's) are generated by a normal distribution, the *t*-ratio follows the "Student's *t*" distribution, with $T - K$ degrees of freedom, where T is the number of observations and K is the number of parameters estimated (including the constant).

The theoretical distribution of the *t*-ratio provides the probability that this statistic will exceed a specified value, say, t_c. When the null hypothesis is true, the probability of the statistic *t*-ratio exceeding a set critical value t_c is tabulated in Table 2 (p. 223) for various numbers of degrees of freedom.

Since the distributional properties of the *t*-ratio are known, we may set up the rule for testing the null hypothesis on the basis of this statistic. The rule may be set so that whenever the *t*-ratio exceeds a set critical value, t_c, the null hypothesis is rejected and not otherwise. Under this rule, the probability of a Type I error is solely the probability of *t* exceeding the value t_c when the null hypothesis is actually true. The critical value t_c may be chosen so that the level of confidence associated with it is acceptable.

Note that the researcher cannot forever increase the value of t_c to reach higher levels of confidence, because by so doing he would be increasing the probability of committing the Type II error associated with the test.

The null hypothesis is false when ($\beta_1 > 0$) and also when ($\beta_1 < 0$). When the alternative hypothesis, ($\beta_1 > 0$), is in fact true, we expect the *t* statistic to be positive; hence, the rule would be: "Reject the null hypothesis when *t* exceeds the critical value t_c." where t_c is a positive quantity. Testing a null hypothesis against an alternative that assigns values to the parameter which are greater than the value implied by the null hypothesis—for example in (6.2), $(\beta_1 > 0)$—is called the *right-tail* test. Similarly, when the alternative hypothesis, $(\beta_1 < 0)$, is in fact true, the t statistic will be negative and it will be inappropriate to use the rule of t exceeding a positive quantity. When t is negative and large in magnitude, it offers evidence in favor of the alternative. Therefore, the test rule for the alternative hypothesis $(\beta_1 < 0)$ should be different from that of the alternative $(\beta_1 > 0)$. When the alternative assigns values to the parameter which are less than the parameter value implied by the null hypothesis, the test is called the *left-tail* test; the rule is, then, " Reject the null hypothesis when t is smaller than t_c." where t_c is a negative quantity. When the alternative hypothesis includes both the right tail and left tail tests, both these rules should be applied; hence, the test rule may be stated as, " Reject the null hypothesis when the absolute value of the t statistic exceeds the value t_c in magnitude." Such a test is called the *two-tail* test.

Note that the probability of committing a Type I error in the case of a two-tail test is twice as much as in either of the one-tail tests for a given critical value t_c.

In our example (6.1), (6.2) we shall choose a 95 percent confidence level as acceptable. The critical value corresponding to 12 degrees of freedom (15 observations and 3 parameter estimates) may be obtained from Table 2 as 2.179. The rule for testing is, then, that if the computed statistic exceeds the value 2.179 we reject the null hypothesis, but not otherwise.

The estimated regression equation (6.1) for the Indian engineering data used before (see p. 101) is

$$I_t = -82.518 + 0.084\ S_t + 0.048\ P_t \qquad R^2 = 0.98. \qquad (6.4)$$
$$(98.112)\ \ (0.020)\quad\ (0.418)$$

In this case, $\hat{\beta}_1$ is 0.084, and its standard error is 0.020; so the t-ratio is

$$t = \frac{0.084}{0.020} = 4.2. \qquad (6.5)$$

Since the computed t-ratio satisfies our test rule, we reject the null hypothesis. Hence, the Indian engineering data provide enough evidence for rejecting the null hypothesis that " sales do not cause movements in investment." We are 95 percent confident that this test procedure will yield the correct answer when used in repeated samples.

This test procedure is based on one parameter and may be used for any specific value of the parameter and not necessarily zero as in the above example. Consider the null hypothesis

$$H_N: \beta_1 = 0.02$$

$$H_A: H_N \text{ is false.}$$

(6.6)

In this case the test statistic is defined as

$$t = (\hat{\beta}_1 - 0.02)/\text{standard error of } \hat{\beta}_1.$$

(6.7)

When the null hypothesis is true and error terms are normally distributed, the statistic defined by (6.7) follows the "Student's t" distribution with $T - K$ degrees of freedom. Once the distribution of the test statistic is known, the probability of committing a Type I error is known; hence, so are the critical value and the test rule.

In general, this test procedure may be used for any of the parameters of a regression equation, provided that the test involves only one parameter. Let the regression equation in the general case be

$$Y_t = \beta_0 + \beta_1 X_{1t} + \beta_2 X_{2t} + \cdots + \beta_k X_{kt} + \varepsilon_t,$$

(6.8)

and let the null hypothesis be based on the ith parameter β_i as

$$H_N: \beta_i = \mu$$

$$H_A: H_N \text{ is false,}$$

(6.9)

where μ is the chosen constant [0 in (6.2); 0.2 in (6.6)].

The test statistic is defined as

$$t = (\hat{\beta}_i - \mu)/\text{st. error of } \hat{\beta}_i.$$

(6.10)

When the null hypothesis is true and the errors are generated by a normal distribution, the t statistic follows the "Student's t" distribution with the appropriate degrees of freedom.

6.2 Consequences of Biased Estimates

In the preceding section the conventional t-statistic has been used as the test criterion. This statistic follows Student's t distribution only when the estimated regression equation is the truth and when errors are normally distributed. In many econometric investigations these assumptions need not hold, and the researcher will be interested in knowing the consequences of their violation. Though he can reasonably assume that the errors are normal, he may suspect that the estimated regression equation is not the truth. When such is the case, the resulting estimates of the parameter and the estimates of the variances may be biased, in which case the distribution of the statistic would be altered. In a typical econometric problem the researcher may have a misspecification of some sort which introduces bias in the estimate $\hat{\beta}_i$ and also in the estimate of the variance of $\hat{\beta}_i$.

To understand the concepts let us consider an extremely simple situation. Suppose that the null hypothesis (6.9) is true. Let the estimate of the true regression equation be $\hat{\beta}_i$, which is assumed to be unbiased. The t-statistic is computed as

$$t = (\hat{\beta}_i - \mu)/\sqrt{\hat{V}(\hat{\beta}_i)}, \qquad (6.11)$$

where $\hat{V}$ is the estimate of the variance of $\hat{\beta}_i$ and μ is the chosen value of β_i under the null hypothesis. The t-statistic has zero mean and follows Student's t distribution. The probability of Type I error corresponding to a specified critical value t_c is given by the shaded area in Figure 6.1.

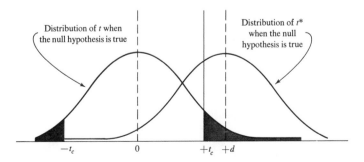

Figure 6.1. Distribution of t and t^* for the Case of Positive Bias

Suppose there is another estimate—say, $\hat{\beta}_i^*$—which is a biased estimate of β_1. When the null hypothesis (6.9) is true,

$$E(\hat{\beta}_i^*) = \beta_i + d = \mu + d, \qquad (6.12)$$

where d is the amount of bias, which may be positive or negative. If the researcher uses the biased estimate $\hat{\beta}_i^*$ instead of $\hat{\beta}_i$ in computing the t-statistic in (6.11), the distribution of t changes. Let the t-statistic based on $\hat{\beta}_i^*$ be called t^*. Then

$$t^* = (\hat{\beta}_i^* - \mu)/\sqrt{\hat{V}(\hat{\beta}_i)}. \qquad (6.13)$$

The t^*-statistic has a mean value of d whereas t has a mean value of zero. We shall suppose for purposes of exposition that only the mean of the distribution is affected by the substitution of $\hat{\beta}_i^*$ for $\hat{\beta}_i$ in equation (6.11). The distribution of t^* for a positive value of d is given in Figure 6.1. The distribution of t^* for a negative value of d can be drawn similarly to the left of the t distribution, as shown in Figure 6.2.

When the researcher uses the same critical value t_c for the test rule, the probability of Type I error will not be the same for the use of $\hat{\beta}_i^*$ as for the use of $\hat{\beta}_i$ in computing the test statistic. The probability of Type I error is the probability of the test statistic exceeding the critical value; as may be seen from Figures 6.1 and 6.2, this differs for the distribution of t and of t^*.

When the researcher is not aware that he is using $\hat{\beta}_i^*$, he may be under the impression that the probability of Type I error associated with his test criterion is the shaded area in Figure 6.1, whereas the implied Type I error is that corresponding to the t^* distribution. This changes the probability of Type I

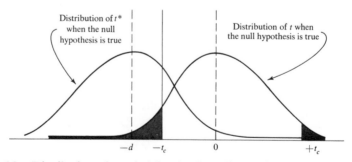

Figure 6.2.   Distribution of t and t^* for the Case of Negative Bias

error. In comparing the probability of actual Type I error (based on t^*) and the probability of theoretical Type I error (based on t), it can be seen that the difference between them increases with the value of d for the right-tail test and decreases for the left-tail test. This result is symmetric for negative values of d.

The consequences of bias in only the regression estimate is to underspecify the probability of Type I error implied by the test criterion for the case of positive bias and a right-tail test or of negative bias and a left-tail test. When the bias is small, the theoretical and the actual Type I error may be so close that the difference is of no real consequence. When the researcher suspects that his estimate is biased, he may opt for a conservative choice of the critical value to allow for such discrepancy. The situation becomes crucial only when bias in the estimates is of such size that the null hypothesis would be rejected under the theoretical t distribution but not under the t^* distribution. Should such a situation arise, the researcher is advised to seek more information or to try to reduce the bias of his estimate by inclusion of proxy variables (see Chapter 4) or by other means.

6.3 Consequence of Biased Estimates of Coefficient Variance

Now let us turn to the situation in which $\hat{V}(\hat{\beta}_i)$, the estimate of variance of $\hat{\beta}_i$, is biased. Once again, for the sake of exposition, let us suppose that instead of $\hat{V}(\hat{\beta}_i)$ the researcher uses a biased estimate in equation (6.11) to compute the t-statistic. Let the statistic with $\hat{V}'(\hat{\beta}_i)$ be

$$t' = (\hat{\beta}_i - \beta_i)/\sqrt{\hat{V}'(\hat{\beta}_i)}. \tag{6.14}$$

The t' is centered around zero because the estimate $\hat{\beta}_i$ is assumed to be unbiased. When $\hat{V}'(\hat{\beta}_i)$ is an overestimate of $\hat{V}(\hat{\beta}_i)$, the variance of t' will be smaller than that of t. Similarly, when $\hat{V}'(\hat{\beta}_i)$ is smaller than $\hat{V}(\hat{\beta}_i)$, the variance of t' will be larger than that of t.

The distributions of t and t' are presented in Figure 6.3. The critical value is t_c. The probability of a Type I error corresponding to t_c for a right-tail test is given by the areas under the respective distributions to the right of t_c. When $\hat{V}'$ is larger than $\hat{V}$, a frequent case in linear regressions, the probability of a Type I error associated with t' is smaller than that associated with t. When the researcher is not aware of the upward bias in the variance of his estimate, he may believe that he is testing with a lower level of confidence than is actually the case.

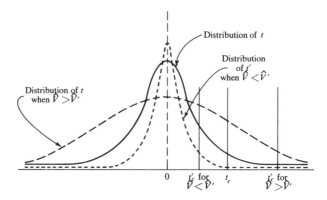

Figure 6.3.   Distribution of t' for Various Estimates of $\hat{V}(\hat{\beta}_i)$

In a practical situation, however, he may have bias both in his regression estimates and in his estimate of variance. In a right-tail test, downward bias in the parameter estimate and upward bias in the estimate of variance tend to indicate a probability of Type I error larger than the actual probability. When the researcher rejects a null hypothesis at the specified probability of Type I error, he will be rejecting it as well at other lower values, hence there is no problem. His test criterion is more "powerful" than he believes it to be.

When the bias in the estimate is positive and bias in the estimate of variance is also positive, the first tends to overstate and the other to understate the level of confidence. This also does not cause serious problems unless the test result is marginal: that is, for example, unless the researcher would reject the hypothesis at the 95 percent but not at the 99 percent level of confidence. In such a situation an applied econometrician cannot be sure whether the actual level of confidence is the same as the theoretical. If he rejects the null hypothesis at the 95 percent level on the basis of the theoretical level of confidence, he is completely ignoring the consequences of bias in his estimates.

Once having an idea of the extent of bias, at least whether the bias is considerable or not, a researcher may conjecture the maximum and minimum levels of confidence associated with a critical value t_c. If he then rejects the null hypothesis at the minimum actual probability of Type I error, he can be confident that, even though the estimates are biased, his test is conclusive.

So far we have presented the consequences of bias in the parameter estimates and in the estimate of variance. Now let us consider some typical problems in econometrics in order to study the *direction* of such bias.

Let the true relation between the economic variables be

$$y_t = \beta_1 x_{1t} + \beta_2 x_{2t} + \varepsilon_t, \qquad (6.15)$$

where the variables are deviations from their respective means. By misspecification the researcher estimates the following regression equation:

$$y_t = \hat{\beta}_1 x_{1t} + e_t.$$ (6.16)

We have already shown (p. 31) that the estimate $\hat{\beta}_1$ is biased and that the expression for bias is

$$E(\hat{\beta}_1) = \beta_1 + \beta_2 b_{21}.$$ (6.17)

To study the nature of bias in the estimate of variance of $\hat{\beta}_1$, let us consider the bias in the estimate of variance of the error term. This variance is usually estimated from the sum of squares of the residuals.

The residual corresponding to the tth observation is

$$e_t = y_t - \hat{\beta}_1 \cdot x_{1t}.$$ (6.18)

By substituting the true value of y_t given by equation (6.15) and the ordinary least squares estimate of β_1 in equation (6.16) we obtain

$$e_t = \beta_2 x_{2t} - \beta_2 x_{1t} b_{21} + \varepsilon_t - x_{1t} \frac{\sum x_{1t} \varepsilon_t}{\sum x_{1t}^2}.$$ (6.19)

When both sides of equation (6.19) are squared and the expected value of the summation over all the observations is taken,

$$E\left(\sum e_t^2\right) = \sigma^2(T-1) + \beta_2^2 \sum x_2^2 (1 - r_{x_1 x_2}^2).$$ (6.20)

The estimate of variance of the error term (e) based on the ordinary least squares residuals is biased whenever the equation is misspecified. This bias is nonnegative; that is, the variance of the error term is always overestimated (unless, of course, $\beta_2 = 0$ or $r_{x_1 x_2}^2 = 1$). The extent of this bias depends on the coefficient of and the sample variance of the left-out variable. It also depends on the correlation between the left-out and the included variable ($r_{x_1 x_2}$). Notice that as this correlation increases from zero to unity this bias goes from its maximum to its minimum value.

When the left-out variable is perfectly correlated with the included variable, $r_{x_1 x_2} = 1$, the included variable captures all the influence of the left-out variable in its coefficient, thus leaving no part of the left-out variable in the error terms. Since the residuals then represent only the error terms, and not any part of the left-out variable, the estimate of variance of errors computed from the residuals is unbiased. Note that these results are derived under the assumption that the x's are held constant in repeated trials.

6.4   Test on a Linear Function of Parameters

Often the researcher is interested in testing a null hypothesis on a linear function of the parameters rather than on the individual parameters. For example, he may want to test for returns to scale in the context of a Cobb-Douglas production function.

We shall study the general case of testing a linear combination of parameters in the linear regression

$$y_t = \beta_1 x_{1t} + \beta_2 x_{2t} + \cdots + \varepsilon_t. \tag{6.21}$$

Let the null hypothesis be

$$H_N: \delta = c_1 \beta_1 + c_2 \beta_2 + \cdots$$
$$H_A: H_N \text{ is false,} \tag{6.22}$$

where $\delta, c_1, c_2, \ldots$ are specified (chosen) constants.

When the researcher is testing for constant returns to scale with a Cobb-Douglas production function, $\delta = 1$ and all of the c's $= 1$, so that the null hypothesis (6.22) becomes

$$H_N: 1 = \beta_1 + \beta_2 + \cdots + \beta_k, \tag{6.23}$$

where there are k factors of production and the variables are in their logarithmic form.

The test statistic may be designed as

$$d = c_1\hat{\beta}_1 + c_2\hat{\beta}_2 + \cdots. \tag{6.24}$$

When the $\hat{\beta}$'s are unbiased estimates,

$$\begin{aligned} E(d) &= c_1\beta_1 + c_2\beta_2 + \cdots \\ &= \delta. \end{aligned} \tag{6.25}$$

The variance of the statistic d is

$$V(d) = c_1^2 V(\hat{\beta}_1) + c_2^2 V(\hat{\beta}_2) + \cdots + 2c_1 c_2 \text{COV}(\hat{\beta}_1, \hat{\beta}_2) + \cdots, \tag{6.26}$$

where COV stands for covariance between the estimates $\hat{\beta}_1$ and $\hat{\beta}_2$. In linear regression models the covariance term is usually nonzero and plays a prominent role in the testing of the hypothesis.

When the error terms are normally distributed the d-statistic follows a normal distribution with mean and variance given by (6.25) and (6.26). The d-statistic (6.24) may be standardized by the following transformation:

$$z = (d - \delta)/\sqrt{V(d)}. \tag{6.27}$$

The z-statistic follows the standard normal distribution with mean zero and variance 1. (See Table 1, p. 222.)

The researcher does not know $V(d)$ because it involves $V(\hat{\beta}_i)$, which is generally unknown. When an estimate of $V(\hat{\beta}_i)$ on the basis of the ordinary least squares estimation procedure is used instead of the true $V(\hat{\beta}_i)$ in computing $V(d)$, the resulting statistic follows Student's t distribution with $T - K$ degrees of freedom, where T is the number of observations and K is the number of parameters estimated by equation (6.21), including the constant term. When $V(d)$ is replaced by $\hat{V}(d)$, the z-statistic may be written as a t-statistic

$$t = (d - \delta)/\sqrt{\hat{V}(d)}. \tag{6.28}$$

Now let us turn to the production function in Indian woolen textiles to test whether there are constant returns to scale[1] (see p. 42). The regression equation is

$$\log q = \beta_0 + \beta_1 \log l + \beta_2 \log k + \varepsilon. \tag{6.29}$$

The null hypothesis may be stated as

$$H_N: 1 = \beta_1 + \beta_2$$
$$H_A: H_N \text{ is false.} \tag{6.30}$$

The regression equation estimated from the data is

$$\log q = 1.652 + 0.708 \log l + 0.413 \log k \qquad R^2 = 0.947. \tag{6.31}$$
$$ (0.154) \quad (0.138) \qquad\quad (0.161)$$

The value of $d\ (=\hat{\beta}_1 + \hat{\beta}_2)$ is 1.121, and the estimate of variance of d is

$$\hat{V}(d) = \hat{V}(\hat{\beta}_1) + \hat{V}(\hat{\beta}_2) + 2\hat{\text{COV}}(\hat{\beta}_1, \hat{\beta}_2)$$
$$= 0.0189 + 0.0260 + 2(-0.0013) \tag{6.32}$$
$$= 0.0423.$$

The t-statistic computed from d is

$$t = (d - 1)/\sqrt{\hat{V}(d)} = 0.121/0.2058 = 0.58. \tag{6.33}$$

---

[1] When the researcher has theoretical information which says that the null hypothesis is true, then there is of course no point in testing. The researcher may incorporate the truth into his estimation procedure by estimating the production function such that $1 = \hat{\beta}_1 + \hat{\beta}_2$. This can be acomplished by writing the regression equation under the truth as

$$\log q = \hat{\beta}_0 + \hat{\beta}_1 \log l + (1 - \hat{\beta}_1) \log k + e.$$

By rearrangement of terms

$$(\log q - \log k) = \hat{\beta}_0 + \hat{\beta}_1 (\log l - \log k) + e.$$

Estimating this equation with $y'(= \log q - \log k)$ as the dependent variable and $x'(= \log l - \log k)$ as the independent variable yields $\hat{\beta}_1$ under the restriction of constant returns to scale. The estimate $\hat{\beta}_2$ is obtained as $1 - \hat{\beta}_1$.

The t-statistic in equation (6.33) follows the Student's t distribution with 11 degrees of freedom (15 observations minus 3 parameter estimates minus 1). The critical value corresponding to the 95 percent confidence level is 2.201. The test rule is that we reject the null hypothesis whenever the computed t-statistic exceeds the critical value 2.201 in magnitude. The computed t-statistic does not satisfy the rule. Therefore we do not reject the null hypothesis that there are constant returns to scale in the woolen textile industry in India.

6.5 Simultaneous Test on Several Parameters

In some situations the theory may make a statement regarding several parameters at the same time. The theory is true only when the entire statement is true and not when just a part of it is true. In such a case the researcher has to treat the statement as a whole and should not try to test parts of it separately. For example, a theory may state that the parameters β_1 and β_2 in a regression equation take the specific values $\beta_1 = \mu_1$ and $\beta_2 = \mu_2$. If the researcher should test null hypotheses separately on β_1 and β_2, he would be misinterpreting the implications of the theory, that both of them must be simultaneously true.

Consider, for example, the case of tea imports into the United States. Let a theory state that the imports of Ceylonese tea do not depend on the price of Indian tea *and* that the price elasticity of Ceylonese imports is unity. This theory makes a statement regarding the price sensitivity of Ceylonese tea imports with respect to both Indian price and Ceylonese price. Hence, we cannot treat the statement as two different parts and test them separately.

Let the demand for Ceylonese imports be (see p. 38):

$$\log \text{TEA} = \beta_0 + \beta_1 \log P_{cy} + \beta_2 \log P_I + \beta_3 \log P_{bz} + \beta_4 \log Y + \varepsilon.$$

$$(6.34)$$

The null hypothesis may be posed in the general framework as

$$H_N: \beta_1 = \mu_1 \quad \text{and} \quad \beta_2 = \mu_2$$

$$H_A: H_N \text{ is false.}$$

$$(6.35)$$

In the context of our example, $\mu_1 = -1$ and $\mu_2 = 0$.

The required test statistic may be based on the two separate values for the sum of squares of the residuals under the null and under the alternative hypotheses. The alternative hypothesis implies no conditions on the parameters; hence, the residual sum of squares under the alternative hypothesis, $RSS(H_A)$, using ordinary least squares estimation, is the minimum value of sum of squares.

When the regression equation is estimated under the presumption that the null hypothesis is true, the residual sum of squares, $RSS(H_N)$, will be larger than the $RSS(H_A)$. Since the null hypothesis implies some specific values for the parameters, there is no need for estimating these parameters. In estimating the regression under the null hypothesis the researcher is forcing the estimation procedure, so that the estimates are, in fact, the true values of the parameters under the null hypothesis. This necessarily increases the residual sum of squares, because the least residual sum of squares is obtained under no restrictions.

The increase in the residual sum of squares due to imposing the condition that the null hypothesis is true provides a basis for the test. When the null hypothesis is actually true, then imposing the condition that the null hypothesis is true should not increase the residual sum of squares. Because of sampling fluctuations we cannot hope to obtain a zero increase; hence we should test to see whether the increase in the residual sum of squares is significantly different from zero.

The increase in the sum of squares depends on the number of observations, on the number of restrictions implied by the null hypothesis, and also on the units of measurement of the dependent variable. Since we want the test statistic to be independent of these factors we shall standardize the increase in the residual sum of squares as

$$F = \frac{[RSS(H_N) - RSS(H_A)]/n}{RSS(H_A)/(T - K)}. \tag{6.36}$$

The numerator shows the increase in the residual sum of squares due to the restrictions imposed on the parameters, adjusted for the number of restrictions n. As the number of restrictions increases, the difference between $RSS(H_N)$ and $RSS(H_A)$ also increases. By dividing by the number of restrictions we are, in a way, correcting for this.

The denominator is the residual sum of squares based on $T - K$ degrees of freedom; hence, it is divided by the number of degrees of freedom. Since the numerator and the denominator are in the same units, namely the square of the dependent variable, even if the unit of measurement of the dependent variable changes we still obtain the same value for the statistic.

The F-statistic depends crucially on two parameters (the number of restrictions (n), called the *number of degrees of freedom in the numerator*, and the degrees of freedom of the regression equation when no restrictions are imposed on the estimation, called the *number of degrees of freedom in the denominator*. As the number of degrees of freedom change in the numerator and the denominator, the distribution of the *F*-statistic changes when the null hypothesis is true. Under the assumption that the errors are normally distributed, the theoretical properties of the *F*-statistic follow Snedecor's *F*-distribution with the corresponding number of degrees of freedom of the numerator and the denominator.

The researcher may specify an arbitrary critical value for the *F*-statistic as F_c. When the statistic exceeds the critical value the researcher rejects the null hypothesis. The probability of Type I error associated with the critical value F_c can be obtained by the area under the *F*-distribution corresponding to the value of *F* that implies rejection of the null hypothesis when in fact it is true. The Type I errors corresponding to specified critical values are readily available in tabular form in any standard textbook in statistics. (See Table 3, pages 224–227.)

Now we turn to the problem of obtaining the sum of squares of residuals under the null and the alternative hypotheses. When the alternative hypothesis is true, there are no restrictions on the estimates, and the residual sum of squares is exactly that obtained under the ordinary least squares estimation of the specified regression equation (6.34). To obtain the residual sum of squares under the null hypothesis the researcher has to impose the condition that the resulting estimates are the same as the parameter values implied by the null hypothesis. In equation (6.34) with four independent variables the null hypothesis $\beta_1 = \mu_1$ and $\beta_2 = \mu_2$ may be imposed as

$$\log \text{TEA} = \hat{\beta}_0 + \mu_1 \log P_{cy} + \mu_2 \log P_I + \hat{\beta}_3 \log P_{bz} + \hat{\beta}_4 \log Y + e. \tag{6.37}$$

Since μ_1 and μ_2 are specified constants, the corresponding terms may be taken to the left side to obtain

$$\log \text{TEA} - \mu_1 \log P_{cy} - \mu_2 \log P_I = \hat{\beta}_0 + \hat{\beta}_3 \log P_{bz} + \hat{\beta}_4 \log Y + e, \tag{6.38}$$

which may be rewritten as:

$$Y' = \hat{\beta}_0 + \hat{\beta}_3 \log P_{bz} + \hat{\beta}_4 \log Y + e \tag{6.39}$$

where $Y' = \log \text{TEA} - \mu_1 \log P_{cy} - \mu_2 \log P_I$.

Obtaining equation (6.39) by ordinary least squares is identical to imposing the restrictions $\hat{\beta}_1 = \mu_1$ and $\hat{\beta}_2 = \mu_2$ in equation (6.37). By defining a new variable, Y', and running regression equation (6.39) the researcher has obtained the residual sum of squares under the null hypothesis. Once the residual sums of squares under the null and the alternative hypotheses are known, the F-statistic can be computed by using expression (6.36).

In the specific example of Ceylonese tea, the regression equations under the alternative and null hypotheses are

$$\log TEA = 2.837 - 1.481 \log P_{cy} + 1.181 \log P_I$$
$$(2.000)\ (0.987)\qquad\ (0.690)$$

$$+\ 0.186 \log P_{bz} + 0.257 \log Y \qquad RSS(H_A) = 0.4277,$$
$$(0.134)\qquad\quad (0.370)$$

$$(6.40)$$

$$(\log TEA + \log P_{cy} - 0 \cdot \log P_I) = -0.738 + 0.199 \log P_{bz}$$
$$(0.820)\ \ (0.155)$$

$$+0.261 \log Y \qquad RSS(H_N) = 0.6788.$$
$$(0.165)$$

$$(6.41)$$

The null hypothesis imposes two restrictions on the estimates. The F-statistic may be computed as

$$F = \frac{(0.6788 - 0.4277)/2}{(0.4277)/17} = 4.99. \qquad (6.42)$$

Since the numbers of degrees of freedom in the numerator total 2 and in the denominator 17, the F-statistic follows $F(2, 17)$. Corresponding to the 95 percent level of confidence we obtain the critical value F_c as 3.59 (see Table 3, pp. 224–227). The test rule is, "Whenever the computed F-statistic exceeds the critical value $(F_c = 3.59)$ we reject the null hypothesis." The computed statistic $(F = 4.99)$ exceeds the critical value; therefore at the 95 percent level of confidence we reject the null hypothesis.

Notice that if the researcher had treated the stated null hypothesis as two independent statements regarding the parameters β_1 and β_2 he would have reached a different answer. Since the theory makes a statement on the parameters jointly rather than independently, a test procedure should be based on the total statement. Testing only a part of a complete statement may lead to wrong conclusions.

A null hypothesis frequently found in empirical research is the case in which $\mu_1 = 0$ and $\mu_2 = 0$. The residual sum of squares under the null hypothesis is obtained by merely deleting the corresponding independent variables from the regression equation.

This test procedure can be extended to regression equations with several independent variables and several restrictions on the parameters. Formula (6.36) is given for a general case with n restrictions implied by the null hypothesis and K parameters, including the constant term implicit in our discussion. It may be noted that when $n = 1$, the test procedure is identical to that which we used for testing a single parameter. When the number of degrees of freedom in the numerator is 1, the F-statistic is nothing but the square of the t-statistic with the number of degrees of freedom of the denominator.

6.6 Test for Equivalence of Two Parameters

Another null hypothesis involving several parameters that is frequently encountered by empirical researchers is

$$H_N: \beta_1 = \beta_2$$
$$H_A: H_N \text{ is false.}$$
(6.43)

This null hypothesis (6.43) is similar to the one discussed earlier. The F-statistic can be used once the residual sum of squares has been obtained under the null and the alternative hypotheses.

The residual sum of squares under the alternative hypothesis is identical to that obtained under the ordinary least squares estimation. The sum of squares of the residuals under the null hypothesis can be obtained by imposing the condition that the resulting estimates for β_1 and β_2 are the same. This may be accomplished in the writing of the regression equation. For example, in the case of three independent variables;

$$y_t = \hat{\beta}_1 x_{1t} + \hat{\beta}_2 x_{2t} + \hat{\beta}_3 x_{3t} + e_{3t}.$$
(6.44)

Since the estimates of β_1 and β_2 are the same, under null hypothesis (6.43) equation (6.44) may be rewritten as

$$y_t = \hat{\beta}_1(x_{1t} + x_{2t}) + \hat{\beta}_3 x_{3t} + e_{3t},$$
(6.45)

which becomes

$$y_t = \hat{\beta}_1 x_t' + \hat{\beta}_3 x_{3t} + e_{3t}. \tag{6.46}$$

By defining the variable x' as $x_1 + x_2$ and using ordinary least squares estimation for regression equation (6.46), we are able to estimate equation (6.44) with the restrictions implied by the null hypothesis.[2] The residual sum of squares given by equation (6.46) is the RSS(H_N). The F-statistic given by (6.36) can be computed for testing the null hypothesis.

To illustrate the test procedure, let us consider the rice production function for Guntur district (see p. 33):

$$Q = \beta_0 + \beta_1 I + \beta_2 D + \beta_3 R + \beta_4 t + \varepsilon. \tag{6.47}$$

Assume that the null hypothesis states that the marginal yield of a dry acre is the same as that of an irrigated acre. The null hypothesis may be expressed as:

$$H_N: \beta_1 = \beta_2$$
$$H_A: H_N \text{ is false.} \tag{6.48}$$

To compute the test statistic, F, we need to estimate equation (6.47) under the null hypothesis and the alternative hypothesis. Under the alternative

---

[2] This null hypothesis may be generalized to a test involving several parameters. Consider for example

$$H_N: \beta_1 = \beta_2 = \beta_3$$
$$H_A: H_N \text{ is false.}$$

The null hypothesis involves two restrictions on parameters, namely $\beta_1 = \beta_2$ and $\beta_2 = \beta_3$. The residual sum of squares under the null hypothesis is obtained by defining x' as $x_1 + x_2 + x_3$.

hypothesis the parameter values can take any value; hence, we estimate the equation without imposing any restrictions:

$$Q = -739.950 + 0.578 I + 0.218 \, D + 46.588 \, R - 40.388 \, t$$
$$\text{RSS}(H_A) = 1,614,627.$$

$$(6.49)$$

When the null hypothesis is true we estimate the equation in such a way that we obtain the same regression coefficient for the two independent variables (I and D) as[3]

$$Q = -669.241 + 0.520 \, (I + D) + 47.603 \, R - 32.246 \, t$$
$$\text{RSS}(H_N) = 1,626,856. \qquad (6.50)$$

The residual sums of squares under the null and the alternative hypotheses are 1,626,856 and 1,614,627 respectively. The corresponding F-statistic is

$$F = \frac{(1,626,856 - 1,614,627)/1}{(1,614,627)/16} = 0.1211. \qquad (6.51)$$

Corresponding to one degree of freedom in the numerator and sixteen degrees of freedom in the denominator, the critical value for the F distribution for the 95 percent level of confidence is obtained from Table 3 as 4.49. The test rule is, "Whenever the computed F-statistic exceeds the value of 4.49 we reject the null hypothesis."

The computed statistic 0.121 does not satisfy the rule. Hence, the null hypothesis is not rejected at the 95 percent level of confidence. We do not reject the null hypothesis that the marginal yields of irrigated acre and of dry acre are the same.

This test procedure may also be used when the null hypothesis implies

---

[3] When the researcher has external theoretical information that states that the null hypothesis is true, he may incorporate the truth into his estimation by forcing the coefficients of the appropriate variables to be the same by using this procedure.

that one parameter is a constant proportion of another.[4] For example, let the null hypothesis be

$$H_N: k \cdot \beta_1 = \beta_2$$

$$H_A: H_N \text{ is false}$$

(6.52)

where k is a given constant.

Under null hypothesis (6.52) the estimated regression equation (6.45) now becomes

$$y_t = \hat{\beta}_1(x_{1t} + kx_{2t}) + \hat{\beta}_3 x_{3t} + e_{3t}.$$

(6.53)

Testing of the null hypothesis in many practical situations involves either the t- or the F-statistic, and the necessary ingredients for computing these statistics may be obtained by simple least squares regression. Once the researcher translates the restrictions implied by the null hypothesis into an estimable regression equation, the rest is a mechanical standard process of estimation.

6.7 Testing across Several Sets of Data

All the test procedures discussed so far relate to a linear regression for a given set of data. When the researcher estimates a regression equation separately for several sets of data, he may want to test whether some or all of the parameters are the same for all different sets of data. Instances are numerous in econometric research. The researcher may, for example, want to test whether the demand schedule for Indian imports in the U.S. is the same before and after India's independence. He will then estimate one regression for pre-independence and another for post-independence, and test the null hypothesis that they are the same for both periods. As another example, he may be interested in testing the null hypothesis that the marginal productivity of labor is the same in all southern as in all northern states of the United States.

Consider the following regression equations for two sets of data in which

---

[4] This problem is reduced essentially to the problem of units of measurement. By appropriate choice of units of measurement we can always express constant proportionality between parameters in the form of null hypothesis (6.48).

the same definitions of the variables and the same general regression model are used:

$$Y_t = \beta_0 + \beta_1 X_{1t} + \beta_2 X_{2t} + \beta_3 X_{3t} + \varepsilon_{1t} \tag{6.54}$$

$$Y_{t'} = \beta_0^* + \beta_1^* X_{1t'} + \beta_2^* X_{2t'} + \beta_3^* X_{3t'} + \varepsilon_{2t'}. \tag{6.55}$$

Equation (6.54) corresponds to the first set of data and (6.55) corresponds to the second set. In this case the t and t' subscripts (respectively distinguishing the two sets of data) are used only to identify separate observations and do not necessarily imply time-series data. The following results hold for cross-sectional as well as time-series data.

The researcher is interested in testing the null hypothesis

$$H_N: \beta_1 = \beta_1^*$$

$$\tag{6.56}$$

$$H_A: H_N \text{ is false.}$$

The test procedure may be based on the residual sum of squares under the null and the alternative hypotheses. To pose this as a special case of preceding problems, let us introduce a dummy variable, D (see p. 88), to distinguish between the two sets of data. Let D take on a value of zero when corresponding to the first set of data and of unity for the second set. Since the variables used in equations (6.54) and (6.55) have the same definitions, we may combine the two sets of data into a pooled set having the original variables and then utilize a dummy variable to distinguish the sets.

Taking advantage of the information contained in the dummy variable, we may rewrite equations (6.54) and (6.55) as one regression equation:

$$Y_t = \beta_0 + \alpha_0 D + \beta_1 X_{1t} + \alpha_1 (X_{1t} \cdot D) + \beta_2 X_{2t} + \alpha_2 (X_{2t} \cdot D) + \beta_3 X_{3t}$$
$$+ \alpha_3 (X_{3t} \cdot D) + \varepsilon_t. \tag{6.57}$$

When the dummy variable takes the value zero, the data correspond to the first set, and equation (6.57) is identical to equation (6.54). When the dummy variable is unity the data correspond to the second set, and equation (6.57) becomes

$$Y_t = (\beta_0 + \alpha_0) + (\beta_1 + \alpha_1)X_{1t} + (\beta_2 + \alpha_2)X_{2t} + (\beta_3 + \alpha_3)X_{3t} + \varepsilon_t,$$

$$(6.58)$$

which can be rewritten as

$$Y_t = \beta_0^* + \beta_1^* X_{1t} + \beta_2^* X_{2t} + \beta_3^* X_{3t} + \varepsilon_t. \qquad (6.59)$$

Equation (6.58) is nothing but equation (6.55) rewritten in terms of the parameters, β's and α's. By using equation (6.57) instead of the two equations (6.54) and (6.55) we neither gain nor lose any information in terms of interpretation of the parameters. As we have already shown (p. 91), estimation of equation (6.57) from the pooled data gives the same regression estimates as those obtained by estimating equations (6.54) and (6.55) separately to the respective sets of data. The sum of squares of the residuals in equation (6.57) is equal to the addition of the two sums of squares of residuals from the estimation of equations (6.54) and (6.55) separately. Also, the number of degrees of freedom corresponding to equation (6.57) is equal to the sum of the separate numbers of degrees of freedom corresponding to the two regression equations (6.54) and (6.55).

To repeat: whether the researcher estimates the two equations (6.54) and (6.55) separately to the two sets of data, or estimates equation (6.57) to the pooled data, he will obtain identical information regarding the estimates, the residual sum of squares, and the number of degrees of freedom. There is no loss or gain in estimation or interpretation.

In the form of equation (6.57), null hypothesis (6.56) is *analytically* equivalent to null hypothesis (6.43) discussed above. The test procedure developed for null hypothesis (6.43) is equally applicable for (6.56) when the latter is considered to be the regression equation for a single set of data.

To compute the test statistic we need the residual sum of squares under both the null and the alternative hypotheses. Under the alternative hypothesis no restrictions are imposed on the estimates. The ordinary least squares estimation of equation (6.57) for the pooled data gives the residual sum of squares under the alternative hypothesis. If the researcher has already computed the regression equations for the two sets of data, he may obtain the RSS(H_A) by simply summing the two residual sums of squares and the respective numbers of degrees of freedom to obtain the residual sum of squares and the number of degrees of freedom corresponding to equation (6.57).

The residual sum of squares under the null hypothesis may be obtained by estimating equation (6.57) with the restrictions implied by the null hypothesis. The null hypothesis implies that $\beta_1 = \beta_1^*$, which is the same as $\alpha_1 = 0$ in equation (6.57). This condition may be easily imposed by deleting the term $(X_{1t} \cdot D)$ in equation (6.57) (see p. 90). The residual sum of squares obtained in estimating the following equation for the pooled data is the RSS(H_N):

$$Y_t = \beta_0 + \alpha_0 D + \beta_1 X_{1t} + \beta_2 X_{2t} + \alpha_2(X_{2t} \cdot D)$$
$$+ \beta_3 X_{3t} + \alpha_3(X_{3t} \cdot D) + \varepsilon_t.$$
$$(6.60)$$

Equation (6.60) implies the same estimate corresponding to the coefficient of X_{1t} for the two regressions (6.54) and (6.55), whereas all estimates of other parameters are different for the two equations. It may be noticed that the number of restrictions imposed by the null hypothesis in estimation of equation (6.57) also equals the number of terms deleted in equation (6.57) to obtain equation (6.60). When a null hypothesis implies several restrictions, the corresponding residual sum of squares may be obtained by deleting the appropriate terms in equation (6.57).

Once the researcher obtains the RSS(H_N) and RSS(H_A), the corresponding F-statistic given by (6.36) may be computed. The appropriate critical value, F_c, corresponding to a given level of confidence may be used for the test criterion.

The F-test may be used for any number of restrictions, provided that the researcher can obtain the residual sum of squares under the null hypothesis. A frequent case in applied econometrics is the case in which, instead of testing for a subgroup of parameters, the researcher is interested in testing the null hypothesis that all parameters are the same for the two sets of data. For example, in the case under consideration examine the null hypothesis on equations (6.54) and (6.55):

$$H_N: \beta_i = \beta_i^* \text{ for all } i \ (i = 0, 1, 2, 3)$$
$$H_A: H_N \text{ is false.}$$
$$(6.61)$$

This null hypothesis implies four restrictions; we may use an F-test. The residual sum of squares under the alternative hypothesis is the same as in the above examples. The residual sum of squares under the null hypothesis is obtained by estimating (6.57) after deleting all the appropriate terms applied by the null hypothesis. As can be seen, the equation implied by the null hypothesis is

$$Y_t = \beta_0 + \beta_1 X_{1t} + \beta_2 X_{2t} + \beta_3 X_{3t} + \varepsilon_t, \tag{6.62}$$

which is in the same form as equations (6.54) and (6.55).

The $RSS(H_N)$ is obtained by simply estimating equation (6.62) for the pooled data with no dummy variables. The RSS (H_A) is obtained by estimating equation (6.62) separately for the two sets of data. When the null hypothesis implies that all parameters are the same for the two sets of data, there is no need to introduce a dummy variable, because the researcher can now obtain all ingredients necessary to compute the F-test by estimating the equations separately to the two sets of data and estimating the same equation to the pooled data.

The F-test may be used in the context of linear regression equations with several independent variables and for several sets of data. With M sets of data the researcher has to introduce $M - 1$ dummy variables to distinguish the sets. By rewriting the regression equations corresponding to various sets of data in the form of equation (6.57) he can clearly see the restrictions implied by the null hypothesis and may estimate the $RSS(H_N)$ by the standard regression techniques.

The reader may already have noticed that in hypothesis testing, whether the null hypothesis is based on one set of data or on several sets, on one parameter or on several parameters, the test procedure is to obtain the residual sum of squares by using the least squares estimation of a regression equation. Once the researcher obtains the basic form of the regression (for example, equation (6.57)) all regression equations that need to be computed are obtained by deleting the appropriate independent variables. With the availability of regression programs, the cost of obtaining an additional regression equation is negligible.

The test procedures discussed so far have been based on regression coefficients. In econometric research, however, one also encounters hypotheses not readily expressible in the form of linear regression models. Some such hypotheses and the relevant test procedures are now considered.

6.8   Test for Association

Often in empirical investigations the researcher proceeds on the basis of conjectures, regardless of theoretical reasoning. Such investigations are used to find out whether any systematic relation exists between two observed variables even if there is no reason for any causal relationship. These results are "empirical observations" and need not imply any theoretical relations. For example, a statistician may observe, on the basis of empirical investigation, that the proportion of lung cancer among smokers is higher than among non-smokers. This empirical observation does not imply that smoking is *the cause* of lung cancer; any such causal relation would need to be established by the medical profession on the basis of its theories. Lack of any underlying theory does not, however, invalidate empirical observations.

When based on strong evidence, such observations call for explanation, and the search for explanation has resulted in much of the feedback from empirical work to theory. In econometric research, the making of empirical observations on the basis of evidence, even if no theory already exists, is a task equal in importance to the testing of a specified theory for appropriateness.

Any systematic relation between two qualitative variables is called association. When there is no systematic relation between the variables, they are called independent; that is, the value of one variable is not associated with the observed value of the other. Association does not imply causal relationship.

Any variable qualitative in nature may be categorized into one of two groups: with, or without, a specified attribute. For example, information on a set of farmers may be classified as "with" or "without" education. When the variable is agricultural productivity, the yield may be classified as "high" and "low." Even though the information on the two variables is, in principle, quantitative, they may be treated as qualitative variables. When the above two variables, education and agricultural productivity, are precisely measured, the researcher may use a better test procedure (p. 156). When the variables are inadequately defined, or when it is less "sinful" to treat the information as qualitative rather than quantitative, or when the information is purely qualitative, then the researcher may decide to use the *test for association* between the two variables.

In our example, if the per-acre yield is independent of the education of the farmers, and if farmers are classified as producing high or low yield, we would expect to observe the same proportion of high-yield farmers among the educated as among the illiterate; and a similar situation for the low-yield farmers.

When the researcher actually observes the same percentage of educated and of illiterate farmers having high yield, then empirically the two variables are independent. Because of sampling fluctuations, however, the researcher may rarely find the percentages to be exactly equal. He is then interested in testing a null hypothesis that the difference is due to the sampling fluctuations. If the evidence rejects the null hypothesis, then the difference in percentages is greater than can be attributed to sampling fluctuations, and some systematic relationship is implied.

In our example, the null hypothesis may be stated as

$$H_N: \text{education and yield are independent}$$
$$H_A: H_N \text{ is false.} \tag{6.63}$$

To test the null hypothesis we need a test statistic. This may be obtained on the basis of what the researcher would expect to observe if the null hypothesis were true. Under the null hypothesis the proportion of high-yield farmers is the same for the non-educated as for the educated category, and this is the same proportion of high yield as for the total sample. Since the proportion of high-yield farmers in the total sample is known, the researcher can readily compute the number of farmers with high yield to be expected in each category if the null hypothesis were true.

The data corresponding to 256 districts in India are given in Table 6.1.

Table 6.1. Data on Education and Yield per Acre in India

Level of Education	Yield per Acre		
	Low	High	Total
Illiterate	16	40	56
Educated	49	151	200
Total	65	191	256
Proportion	0.254	0.746	1.000

Source: D. P. Chaudhri, "Education and Agricultural Productivity in India" (unpublished Ph.D. dissertation, University of Delhi, Delhi, India, April, 1968).

Each number in the table represents the attributes corresponding to its column and row. For example, 40 families are illiterate and have high yield. In all, 191 families out of 256 have high yield. The proportion of high yield in the total sample is $p = 191/256 = 0.746$. If the two variables are independent, then we expect 0.746 of the total educated farmers to have high yield and the same proportion of illiterate farmers to have high yield. The number of expected observations corresponding to each category may be presented as in Table 6.2.

Table 6.2. Expected Numbers in Each Category When Education and Yield Are Independent

Level of Education	Yield per Acre		
	Low	High	Total
Illiterate	14	42	56
Educated	51	149	200
Total	65	191	256

The observed numbers differ from those expected under the null hypothesis. The researcher wants to test whether the difference is due to sampling fluctuations or not.

In all, there are four separate categories, and their corresponding expected and observed values may be arranged as in Table 6.3. The test statistic is defined as

$$\text{Chi-square} = \sum_{i=1}^{4} (d_i^2/E_i). \tag{6.64}$$

The test statistic defined by (6.64) follows the chi-squared (χ^2) distribution with 1 degree of freedom. By setting up a critical value for the chi-square (χ_c^2) the researcher may use as a test rule: "Whenever the chi-squared value exceeds the critical value χ_c^2, the null hypothesis is rejected." The levels of confidence associated with given levels of critical value are presented in Table 5, p. 229. For the 95 percent level of confidence the critical value of

Table 6.3. The Difference between the Observed and Expected Numbers in the Four Categories

Number i	Expected E_i	Observed O_i	Difference d_i
1	14	16	2
2	42	40	2
3	51	49	2
4	149	151	2

chi-square with one degree of freedom is 3.84 (see p. 229). Hence, our test rule is, "Whenever the computed χ^2 exceeds 3.84 the null hypothesis is rejected." By definition in (6.64) the computed χ^2 statistic is

$$\chi^2 = 4/14 + 4/42 + 4/51 + 4/149 = 0.44. \tag{6.65}$$

The test statistic does not satisfy the test rule. We do not reject the null hypothesis on the basis of available evidence. That is, within the population covered by the data there is not enough evidence to reject the statement, "Education of farmers and their yield per acre have no systematic empirical relation."

This chi-squared test may be applied to numerous instances in economic and business studies.[5] When the researcher finds a systematic relation between the variables, he may be interested in knowing whether the association is positive or negative. When low literacy and low yield are more frequently observed than would be expected if the two variables were independent, then it may be called *positive association*; a reverse case is *negative association*.

Sometimes the systematic relation between two variables may be the result of a third variable influencing them both. In such cases the researcher can make a valid inference from the data only if the third variable is held constant. This may be accomplished by separating the data into several groups within which the third variable is kept constant; the association within each subgroup is then called the *partial association*. If the systematic relation between the variables is not due to the presence of the third variable, the same systematic relation should be observed within all the subgroups classified according to the third variable. If the relationship changes in a systematic way according to which values the third variable takes, then it becomes apparent that the observed systematic relation cannot be independent of the third variable. In this case the observed association is called a spurious association. The researcher should be alert for such misleading results.

6.9   Test for Correlation

Association between two quantitative variables is called a correlation. We used a 2×2 table in the context of qualitative variables, but when the data on variables are more precise than mere "high" and "low" we should be able to

---

[5] See L. A. Goodman and W. H., Kruskal, "Measures of Association for Cross-Classifications," *Journal of the American Statistical Association*, 49(1954) 723–64 and "Measures of Association for Cross-Classifications, II: Further Discussion and References," *Journal of the American Statistical Association*, 54 (1959) 123–63.

improve the test procedure by taking advantage of this information. The correlation between two quantitative variables provides such a test.

Let X and Y be two variables under investigation, and let the data correspond to T observations. The correlation between the variables is defined as

$$r = \frac{\sum (X_t - \overline{X})(Y_t - \overline{Y})}{\sqrt{\sum (X_t - \overline{X})^2 \cdot \sum (Y_t - \overline{Y})^2}}, \tag{6.66}$$

where $\overline{X}$ and $\overline{Y}$ are the means of X and Y respectively.

When the value of X does not depend upon the value of Y, then the correlation between the two is zero, and they are called independent. Suppose the values of X and Y are taken from a population with zero correlation. Since the correlation coefficient r is based on a sample of only T observations from this population it need not be zero, because of sampling fluctuations.

The researcher is interested in testing whether the correlation between the two variables in the population is zero. If the observed correlation in the sample is more than would be expected due to sampling fluctuations, then he may reject the null hypothesis that the two variables are independent in the population. The null hypothesis is

H_N: correlation between X and Y in the population is zero

H_A: H_N is false. $\tag{6.67}$

The test statistic is defined as[6]

$$t = \frac{r\sqrt{T - 2}}{\sqrt{1 - r^2}}. \tag{6.68}$$

If the null hypothesis were true and the variables are drawn from a normal distribution, the t-statistic defined in (6.68) follows Student's t distribution with $T - 2$ degrees of freedom. The test rule is to reject the null hypothesis whenever the computed t-statistic exceeds the critical value t_c. The alternative

---

[6] For a full discussion on this topic see M. G. Kendall and A. Stuart, *The Advanced Theory of Statistics*, Vol. 2., 2nd edition, Griffin & Co. Ltd. (London), 1967, p. 296.

hypothesis implies a two-tailed test. The critical value for a two-tailed test must have two values, $+t_c$ and $-t_c$, or the test criterion may be restated as $|t| > t_c$. The probability of Type I error for the two-tailed test associated with the given critical value may be obtained from Table 2, p. 223.

6.10   The d-Test

A common problem in empirical investigation is to study the effectiveness of a policy in the short run. The time period for such studies is often so limited that almost all the independent variables determining the value of the dependent variable—the variable under investigation—remain unchanged. A regression analysis for such situations seems inappropriate and uneconomical. A simple test based on the differences of the dependent variable before and after the policy implementation provides an answer.

When no other variable except the policy has changed between two time periods, and there is a difference in the observed values of the dependent variable, the difference is attributable to the policy. In real life we rarely observe a situation in which the difference is zero even if the policy did not change. The researcher is, therefore, interested in testing whether the difference is due to randomness of the data or whether there is any systematic difference.

For example, consider the case of free reserves of commercial banks. Suppose the researcher wants to study whether a recent increase in the Central Bank's rediscount value (bank rate) has altered the free reserves of the commercial banks. Suppose no change has occurred in other variables that would determine the bank's policy as to the free reserves. The researcher may collect information from the various banks on their free reserves before and after the change in the rediscount rate. Let the data correspond to T commercial banks, and let the difference in free reserves corresponding to the ith bank be

$$d_i = (\text{free reserves before the change}) - (\text{free} \qquad (6.69)$$
$$\text{reserves after the change}).$$

The null hypothesis, based on the mean difference for all banks in the total population rather than for the T selected banks, states that the mean difference for the population is zero:

$$H_N: \text{mean of } d \text{ in the population is zero}$$
$$\qquad (6.70)$$
$$H_A: H_N \text{ is false.}$$

The test statistic is based on the observed mean and variance of the d's, corresponding to the sample of T observations:

$$t = \frac{\bar{d}}{\sqrt{\dfrac{\sum (d - \bar{d})^2}{T - 1}}} \ . \tag{6.71}$$

Under the null hypothesis, if the d's were drawn randomly from a normal distribution, then the t-statistic follows Student's t distribution with $T - 1$ degrees of freedom. The test rule rejects the null hypothesis whenever the computed t-statistic exceeds the critical value.

7

Special Topics in Linear Regression

The standard linear regression model specifies a causal relation between the dependent and independent variables. This specification implies that a unit change in one of the independent variables causes a change in the dependent variable during the same time period and during that period alone. In some situations, however, this specification may seem restrictive. For example, an advertisement placed by a company may influence sales of the commodity advertised over various periods, exerting some influence today, some tomorrow, some the day after tomorrow, and so on. Such a causal relation—in which the influence of a change in an independent variable is spread over a long stretch of time periods—is called the *distributed lag* effect. The linear regression estimation procedure may be tailored to incorporate such effects.

Another frequent problem in applied econometrics is due to *errors in the variables*. It goes without saying that all economic data are subject to errors of measurement. In many situations an applied econometrician can do nothing about the data. However, he can protect himself from possible misinterpretation of his results if he becomes aware of the extent and consequences of these measurement errors. In many practical situations the errors of measurement pose no great threat to the validity of the standard interpretation of the estimates, though researchers frequently include the problem of errors in the variables as one excuse for not obtaining " good " results.

In this chapter we shall study the problems of estimation and interpretation in the context of distributed lags and errors in the variables.

7.1   Distributed Lags

A simple specification of a distributed lag model may be described by the statement

$$\frac{\Delta Y_{t+\tau}}{\Delta X_t} = \omega_\tau, \tag{7.1}$$

where ΔX_t is the change in a variable X during time period t, and $\Delta Y_{t+\tau}$ is the change in variable Y after τ time periods due to ΔX_t. The proportional change in Y after τ periods because of a change in X_t is expressed by the constant term ω_τ. When the causal relation between the variables does not depend on the time period in which the change in X took place, the proportional increase in Y after τ periods of time should not depend on t. It depends only on τ, the time difference between the change in X and the change in Y.

When the influence of a change in X_t is spread over several periods of time, then the constants, ω_τ's, would be nonzero for many values of τ. The distributed lag effect of a variable X on the variable Y may be described by the specification of these constants (ω's).

The distributed lag effect is fully described when the values of the ω's are known. Different sets of values for the ω's describe different distributed lag schemes. When the researcher is interested in studying the impact of an advertisement on the sales of a product, all needed information is supplied by the ω's. But the ω's are seldom known, and to estimate these parameters from the observed data the researcher has to formulate the problem as an estimable functional form.

When the change in the independent variable is expressed as a continuous change, at least for analytical purposes, we may rewrite specification (7.1) in the form of partial derivatives as

$$\frac{\partial Y_{t+\tau}}{\partial X_t} = \omega_\tau. \tag{7.2}$$

Since the distributed lag specification is independent of t we may then rewrite equation (7.2) as

$$\frac{\partial Y_t}{\partial X_{t-\tau}} = \omega_\tau. \tag{7.3}$$

Equation (7.3) states one differential equation for each value of τ. The functional form yielding these differential equations may be written as

$$Y_t = c + \omega_0 X_t + \omega_1 X_{t-1} + \omega_2 X_{t-2} + \cdots + \omega_\infty X_{t-\infty}, \qquad (7.4)$$

where c is a constant.

Equation (7.4) is in the familiar form of a linear regression, though it has "too many" parameters. Technically speaking, one should go back an infinite number of time periods to complete the specification of the distributed lag effect described by equation (7.4), but for all practical purposes it may be adequate to assume that the ω's are zero beyond a certain number of time periods, say Υ. By deleting terms beyond Υ time periods in the past and expressing the variables as deviations from their means we may write equation (7.4) as

$$y_t = \omega_0 x_t + \omega_1 x_{t-1} + \omega_2 x_{t-2} + \cdots + \omega_\Upsilon x_{t-\Upsilon} + \varepsilon_t, \qquad (7.5)$$

where ε is the error term to account for the remaining terms and for other sources of errors such as "pure noise."

The distributed lag effect described by the ω's may also be expressed graphically by the "time profile," which plots ω_τ against the value of τ as shown in Figure 7.1. Different distributed lag schemes have different ω's and, hence, different time profiles.

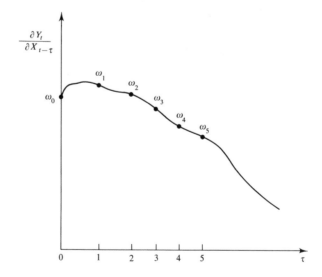

Figure 7.1. Typical Time Profile

The reader should note here that, even though the underlying scheme is the same, a change in the units of measurement of one of the variables will yield a different time profile and the profile curve will shift by a constant of proportion while keeping the same shape. When the researcher wants to compare two distributed lag schemes by the use of time profiles, he should adjust for the scale problem. One way of overcoming this difficulty is by normalizing the time profile; that is, by reducing all the time profiles to comparable units. One process of normalization is to adjust the scale of the time profiles in such a way that all those corresponding to a specified time lag, say τ^*, will have the same parameter value ω_{τ^*}. The choice of τ^* is, of course, arbitrary and may be set according to convenience. We may define the scale of the vertical axis of the time profile in such a way that ω_{τ^*} is unity for all the time profiles. Figure 7.2 describes some normalized time profiles for $(\tau^* = 0)$.

When the time profile implied by equation (7.5) has been normalized on $(\tau^* = 0)$ we may rewrite the equation as

$$y_t = \alpha(1x_t + \mu_1 x_{t-1} + \mu_2 x_{t-2} + \cdots + \mu_\Upsilon x_{t-\Upsilon}) + \varepsilon_{6t}, \qquad (7.6)$$

where α is the parameter of units of measurement and μ's are the normalized ω's. By expressing the independent variables as

$$x_t^* = 1x_t + \mu_1 x_{t-1} + \mu_2 x_{t-2} + \cdots + \mu_\Upsilon x_{t-\Upsilon}, \qquad (7.7)$$

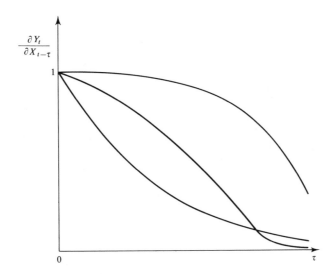

Figure 7.2. Normalized Time Profiles

regression equation (7.6) may be rewritten as

$$y_t = \alpha x_t^* + \varepsilon_{6t}. \tag{7.8}$$

Any particular set of μ's in (7.6) yields a different time profile of the distributed lag effect of x. The researcher must somehow choose the appropriate time profile. This problem may be viewed as a special cases of choosing the empirically appropriate definition of the independent variable x^* (see p. 18). Therefore the empirically appropriate time profile may be selected as that set of μ's in (7.6) that yields the highest R^2 for (7.8).

Since obviously the researcher could employ an infinite number of sets of μ's, the above rule is not operational. Construction of the infinite number of series on x^* would be an extremely difficult task. Simplification has become necessary in order to minimize the computational burden.

In many economic problems the researcher may know *a priori* something about the time profile. For example, consider a help-wanted advertisement. It may yield a large number of applicants the first week, with smaller and smaller numbers in successive weeks. This may be represented in a time profile of the form shown in Figure 7.3 and approximated by a simple geometrically declining function. Now x_t^* may be rewritten as

$$x_t^* = 1 \cdot x_t + \lambda x_{t-1} + \lambda^2 x_{t-2} + \cdots + \lambda^\Upsilon x_{t-\Upsilon}, \tag{7.9}$$

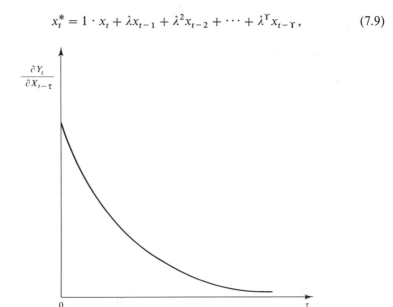

Figure 7.3. Time Profile for Help-Wanted Advertisements

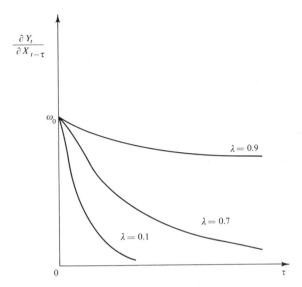

Figure 7.4. Time Profile for Different Values of λ

where λ is a constant less than unity. Different values of λ yield different time profiles as shown in Figure 7.4. Instead of having to choose between an infinite number of sets of μ's, the researcher may now have to choose between an infinite number of λ's. However, he usually will use a number of λ's only up to the accuracy of a first or second decimal place. That λ which when used in constructing x^* yields the highest R^2 for equation (7.8) is the empirically appropriate one.[1]

7.2 Other Forms of Distributed Lag Equations

Forms of the regression equation other than (7.4) may also be used to generate a distributed lag scheme described by equation (7.9). Consider, for example, the regression equation

$$y_t = \alpha x_t + \beta y_{t-1} + \varepsilon_{10t}. \tag{7.10}$$

This equation implies an exponential decay scheme similar to the one in Figure 7.3. To understand the underlying time profile implicit in equation (7.10) consider a one-unit, once-and-for-all, increase in x so that $\Delta x_t = 1$ in

---

[1] Usually the researcher computes x^* with λ at intervals of 0.1 apart, then within the relevant range chooses finer intervals.

equation (7.1). To help trace its influence on future values of y we construct Table 7.1. The zeros in the row corresponding to $t = 0$ indicate that we are arbitrarily starting from a zero equilibrium position so that future values of y are nothing but $\Delta y_{t+\tau}$. Then a unit change in x is shown by the unity in the row corresponding to $t = 1$. The effect of this change on y_t is given by equation (7.10) as α. Since y_{t-1} in period 1 is zero, it does not affect y_t in this period.

Table 7.1. Distributed Lag Effect on y_t of One-Unit, Once-and-for-All Increase in x_t for the Equation $y_t = \alpha x_t + \beta y_{t-1} + \varepsilon_t$

Time Period t	y_t	x_t	y_{t-1}	Lag τ
0	0	0	0	
1	α	1	0	0
2	$\alpha\beta$	0	α	1
3	$\alpha\beta^2$	0	$\alpha\beta$	2
4	$\alpha\beta^3$	0	$\alpha\beta^2$	3
5	$\alpha\beta^4$	0	$\alpha\beta^3$	4
.	.	.	.	.
.	.	.	.	.
.	.	.	.	.

Now we go to period 2; x is zero and remains so thereafter in this experiment because we are considering a once-and-for-all change in x in period 1. The value of y_{t-1} is merely the previous value of y_t, namely α. The current value of y_t—that is, the distributed lag effect of a one-unit increase of x one period before—is given by $\beta \cdot y_{t-1}$, that is, $\alpha\beta$. By continuing this process we may generate all the future values of y.

It may be seen that the distributed lag effect for equation (7.10) follows the exponential scheme given in the column under y_t in Table 7.1. This column is merely the ω's of the differential equation (7.5) because $\Delta x_t = 1$ and future values of y are $\Delta y_{t+\tau}$. Therefore, we may represent equation (7.10) as

$$y_t = \omega_0 x_t + \omega_1 x_{1t-1} + \cdots + \omega_\Upsilon x_{t-\Upsilon} + \varepsilon_t \qquad (7.11)$$

or

$$y_t = \alpha x_t^* + \varepsilon_t, \qquad (7.12)$$

which are the same as equations (7.5) and (7.8). To normalize the coefficients given in the column for y_t of Table 7.1 we choose τ^* as zero. The normalized column y_t (or ω_τ) is presented in Table 7.2 as μ_τ, which obviously represents the exponentially declining distributed lag scheme, as given in Figure 7.3. Notice that the normalized time profile does not depend on α.

To illustrate the use of this technique, let us consider the consequences of a once-and-for-all increase of Indian investment. The effect is felt not only during that period; rather, it is spread over all future values of the national income. The causal relation between national income (y) and investment (x) is a distributed lag scheme. We may assume that its effect is an exponentially decaying scheme[2] of the form shown in Figure 7.3. To estimate the underlying distributed lag scheme we have two techniques, one to estimate equation (7.8) for various values of λ in (7.9), and the other to estimate equation (7.10). The data we have, however, rule out the first choice and we are left with estimation by equation (7.10).

The regression equation (7.10) for the Indian data is estimated (see p. 44) as

$$y_t = 0.406\, x_t + 0.887\, y_{t-1} \qquad R^2 = 0.96.$$
$$ (0.455) \quad\ (0.147) \tag{7.13}$$

The estimates of α and β are 0.406 and 0.887 respectively. By substituting these values in Table 7.2 we may obtain the time profile and the normalized time profile of the estimate of the underlying distributed lag scheme.

Table 7.2. Distributed Lag Effect of x_t on y_t, Normalized on $\tau^* = 0$ for the Equation $y_t = \alpha x_t + \beta y_{t-1} + \varepsilon_t$

Lag τ	ω_τ	μ_τ
0	α	1
1	$\alpha\beta$	β
2	$\alpha\beta^2$	β^2
3	$\alpha\beta^3$	β^3
4	$\alpha\beta^4$	β^4
.	.	.
.	.	.
.	.	.

[2] The macroeconomic theory actually tells us that the distributed lag effect of investment on income is an exponentially decaying scheme.

From this exercise one may get the impression that the estimation of equation (7.10) is computationally more economical and requires fewer observations than estimation of equation (7.8). This may be the case, but it should be noted that the estimates obtained by these two procedures do not have the same statistical properties. If equation (7.6) were true and the error terms ε_6's were generated randomly, the error terms in equation (7.10), the ε_{10}'s, could not be random. To see this point let us write equation (7.6) (with $\Upsilon = \infty$) corresponding to the time periods t and $t - 1$ as:

$$y_t = \alpha(1 \cdot x_t + \lambda x_{t-1} + \lambda^2 x_{t-2} + \cdots \lambda^\infty x_{t-\infty}) + \varepsilon_{6t}, \qquad (7.14)$$

$$y_{t-1} = \alpha(1 \cdot x_{t-1} + \lambda x_{t-2} + \lambda^2 x_{t-3} + \cdots \lambda^\infty x_{t-\infty}) + \varepsilon_{6t-1}. \qquad (7.15)$$

By multiplying equation (7.15) by λ and subtracting the result from equation (7.14) we obtain

$$y_t - \lambda y_{t-1} = \alpha x_t + (\varepsilon_{6t} - \lambda \varepsilon_{6t-1}) \qquad (7.16)$$

or

$$y_t = \alpha x_t + \lambda y_{t-1} + (\varepsilon_{6t} - \lambda \varepsilon_{6t-1}). \qquad (7.17)$$

A comparison of equations (7.17) and (7.10) reveals that we cannot assume that both ε_6's and ε_{10}'s are random. If one is random, the other is not.

If the error terms ε_6's are serially independent then the ε_{10}'s are serially correlated, and vice versa. Which of the two errors is serially independent is a difficult question to answer. Several theoretical models have been developed to study which of these two assumptions is appropriate in a given situation.[3] In applied econometrics, however, life is not that refined. The researcher is interested in obtaining estimates of his parameters even though they may not be the "best."

As developed by Durbin, a test procedure for serial correlation in the presence of lagged dependent variables was discussed on page 123. In our example, Durbin's test did not reject the null hypothesis of serial independence

---

[3] For a survey of these theories see Z. Griliches, "Distributed Lags: A Survey," *Econometrica*, Vol. 35, No. 1, Jan. 1967, pp. 15–49.

in the error terms ε_{10}'s (see p. 124). Of course there is a chance that this conclusion is a "wrong answer," but we have to take that chance in statistical estimation.

Estimation of equation (7.10) implies that the distributed lag effect is exponentially decaying, starting from the time of change in the independent variable (x). In some practical problems this may be a restrictive specification. In some situations, there may not be any visible effect in y for some time, then a sudden effect is felt and a gradually decaying effect follows. For example, if we consider the influence of investment in "Building and Equipment," the distributed lag effect is negligible until the plant is completed; thereafter, its effect on production has "significant" ω's. In other kinds of situations, the effect of a change in an independent variable is felt "heavily" during the first few time periods and decays gradually thereafter. Problems of this kind of distributed lags may also be handled easily by redesigning equation (7.10).

Consider, for example, the following equation, which is merely (7.10) with x_{t-1} included as an independent variable:

$$y_t = \alpha x_t + \beta y_{t-1} + \delta x_{t-1} + \varepsilon_t. \tag{7.18}$$

This equation implies a distributed lag effect of x on y. To study the underlying lag structure, let us examine the effect of a one-unit, once-and-for-all, increase in x_t, starting with equilibrium values of all variables as zero. The future values of y may be derived in a manner similar to the exercise for equation (7.10). These values are presented in Table 7.3.

The ω's of the underlying distributed lag scheme are given by the future values of y as shown in the row corresponding to y in Table 7.3. In this case it

Table 7.3. Distributed Lag Effect on y_t of a One-Unit, Once-and-for-All Increase in x_t for the Equation $y_t = \alpha x_t + \beta y_{t-1} + \delta x_{t-1} + \varepsilon_t$

Time Period t	y_t	x_t	y_{t-1}	x_{t-1}	Lag τ
0	0	0	0	0	
1	α	1	0	0	0
2	$\alpha\beta + \delta$	0	α	1	1
3	$(\alpha\beta + \delta)\beta$	0	$\alpha\beta + \delta$	0	2
4	$(\alpha\beta + \delta)\beta^2$	0	$(\alpha\beta + \delta)\beta$	0	3
5	$(\alpha\beta + \delta)\beta^3$	0	$(\alpha\beta + \delta)\beta^2$	0	4
6	$(\alpha\beta + \delta)\beta^4$	0	$(\alpha\beta + \delta)\beta^3$	0	5
.	.	.	.	.	.
.	.	.	.	.	.
.	.	.	.	.	.

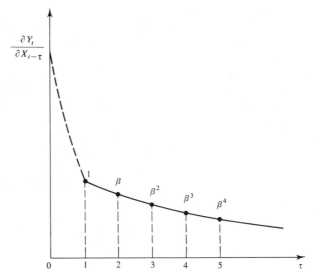

Figure 7.5. Normalized Time Profile

is convenient to normalize the ω's corresponding to $\tau^* = 1$, because starting from this point the μ's exhibit the familiar exponential decay. The normalized time profile is presented in Figure 7.5.

By including further lagged values of the independent variable (x) in equation (7.18) we may shift the starting point of the exponential decay to any value of τ. When the maximum lag on x is s periods of time, the exponential decay segment of the time profile starts from $\tau = s$.

Suppose now that instead of equation (7.18) the following equation is estimated:

$$y_t = \beta y_{t-1} + \delta x_{t-1} + \varepsilon_t. \tag{7.19}$$

The difference in equations (7.18) and (7.19) is that the current value of x, namely x_t, is dropped in estimation. The underlying time profile for equation (7.19) may be obtained as a special case of equation (7.18) when α is zero. In this case ω_0 is zero. The normalized time profile, starting from $\tau^* = 1$, follows the familiar geometrical decay form. By deleting x_t we set ω_0 to zero in the distributed lag scheme. This procedure may be generalized. When the lagged values of x start from x_{t-s}, the time profile has exponential decay from $\tau = s$; all earlier ω's are zeros.

The reader now will realize that when a lagged dependent variable is present in a regression equation the researcher may obtain the desired distributed lag scheme by appropriate choice of the lagged independent variables.

With only one lagged dependent variable, we obtained a variety of distributed lag schemes depending on the lags used on the independent variable. All these schemes have some common characteristics, the most obvious being that they all exhibit exponential decay over some range of τ. Even more important is that all these schemes start with an outburst and then decay afterward. In some situations it may be more appropriate to specify a causal relation where the effect of a change in the independent variable is realized gradually, reaches a peak after some time periods, and thereafter decays. Such schemes may be estimated by lagging the dependent variable more than once in equation (7.10).

Consider, for example, the following equation, which includes the lagged dependent variables as independent variables:

$$y_{\scriptscriptstyle{d}} = \alpha x_t + \beta y_{t-1} + \gamma y_{t-2} + \varepsilon_t. \tag{7.20}$$

To study the distributed lag scheme implied by this regression equation, consider a once-and-for-all unit increase in x. The future values of y may be obtained as in the previous cases. These values are presented in Table 7.4.

It is obvious that the ω's given in the y_t column of Table 7.4 are somewhat more complicated than in previous tables in which only y_{t-1} appeared. Nonetheless the ω's follow a very simple recursive scheme:

$$\omega_j = \omega_{j-1}\beta + \omega_{j-2}\gamma, \tag{7.21}$$

where ω_{j-1} refers to ω of the previous period, and ω_{j-2} refers to the ω obtained in the period before that. It is necessary to compute the first two ω's before this recursive solution may be used.

Table 7.4. Distributed Lag Effect on y_t of a One-Unit, Once-and-for-All Increase in x_t for $y_t = \alpha x_t + \beta y_{t-1} + \gamma y_{t-2} + \varepsilon_t$

Time Period t	y_t	x_t	y_{t-1}	y_{t-2}	Lag τ
0	0	0	0	0	
1	α	1	0	0	0
2	$\alpha\beta$	0	α	0	1
3	$\alpha\beta^2 + \alpha\gamma$	0	$\alpha\beta$	α	2
4	$(\alpha\beta^2 + \alpha\gamma)\beta + (\alpha\beta)\gamma$	0	$\alpha\beta^2 + \alpha\gamma$	$\alpha\beta$	3
.	.	.	.	.	.

The time profile of the distributed lag scheme implicit in equation (7.20) depends uniquely on two parameters, β and γ, if we normalize on the first time period and divide through by α. A change in the values of β and γ will vary the shape of the unimodal time profile curve. The distributed lag schemes corresponding to selected values of these parameters are presented in Figure 7.6.

The implied time profiles in equations (7.10) and (7.20) have distinct features. In one case, equation (7.20), the ω's gradually increase and then start decaying with τ, whereas in equation (7.10), they decay from the first non-zero ω. Which of these schemes is appropriate to a given empirical problem should be determined by the nature of the problem itself rather than on the basis of any summary statistics computed from the data.

At this point we must warn against injudicious use of more than two lagged values of the dependent variable. As more and more such variables are added to the regression equation, the implied time profile curve comes to depend on more and more distinct parameters and to take on increasingly complex shapes. The specific shape becomes very sensitive to the parameter values, and given that these are never known, the particular form of the estimated time profile becomes extremely sensitive to sampling fluctuations in the estimates.

Once the researcher has determined the appropriate distributed lag equation he must realize that the parameters cannot take on all conceivable real values.

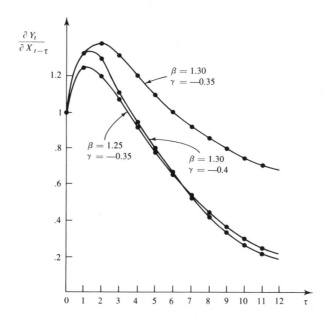

Figure 7.6. Normalized Time Profile of $y_t = \alpha x_t + \beta y_{t-1} + \gamma y_{t-2} + \varepsilon_t$ for Various Values of β and γ

In the first place the implicit μ's must of necessity be non-negative, otherwise he will be hard-pressed to rationalize the causal relation. Any distributed lag equation which yields negative implied μ's within the relevant range of operation may not be considered a reasonable *distributed lag scheme*. Negative μ's may, however, be consistent with other causal relations.

We therefore suggest that after estimating the regression equation, the researcher draw the underlying time profile. He should be satisfied that it is of acceptable shape—that is, that none of the μ's are negative in the relevant range and that the mode occurs at what he theoretically considers a reasonable time period. For example, if the mode in the distributed lag effect of a change in fiscal policy is shown to occur 18 years after the policy change, most researchers will not consider this theoretically reasonable.

7.3 Serial Correlation Model

In some situations the researcher, suspecting a causal relation of a distributed lag type between two variables, may estimate the equation as

$$y_t = \alpha x_t + \beta y_{t-1} + \varepsilon_{1t}. \tag{7.22}$$

It is possible that he may thereby obtain sensible estimates of α and β even though the true causal relation is not of the distributed lag type. For example, consider the model

$$y_t = \alpha x_t + \varepsilon_{2t} \tag{7.23}$$

with

$$\varepsilon_{2t} = \rho \varepsilon_{2t-1} + w_t. \tag{7.24}$$

The specification of this model does not imply any distributed lag effect of x on y. The error terms are, however, serially correlated with serial correlation parameter ρ. By multiplying equation (7.23) corresponding to time period $t - 1$ by ρ and subtracting the result from equation (7.23) we have

$$y_t = \alpha x_t + \rho y_{t-1} - \rho \alpha x_{t-1} + w_t. \tag{7.25}$$

Equation (7.22) may, therefore, also be viewed as a misspecified equation (7.25) in which the variable x_{t-1} is left out. If such is the case, the researcher may get sensible values for α and β of (7.22) in terms of signs and magnitudes, as though the estimates were consistent with a distributed lag scheme. When the true model is (7.25), we therefore need to guard against interpreting (7.22) as a distributed lag model merely because this estimated and misspecified equation "makes sense."

It is necessary to check to make sure that the data were not generated by a serial correlation model. Suppose the researcher estimates equation (7.25) directly; he may still be under the impression that what he has is a distributed lag model similar to equation (7.18). Even though equations (7.25) and (7.18) look similar in terms of the independent variables, the researcher may notice that the underlying time profiles differ. The time profile corresponding to equation (7.25) has all zero ω's except for ω_0, whereas equation (7.18) has a gradually decaying time profile. This distinction between the serial correlation model and the distributed lag model may be used to identify the specification.

In a practical situation, however, the researcher may not obtain zero ω's in the serial correlation model because of sampling fluctuations, but the time profile in serial correlation specification is usually made conspicuous by its "weak" ω's for all τ except ω_0. When the researcher makes a habit of drawing the implicit time profile before interpreting his estimates, he will usually notice the serial correlation specification if that is really what he is estimating. If he were to estimate only equation (7.22) he would not be able to distinguish the serial correlation specification from the distributed lag specification. If the true relation is that of a distributed lag, estimation of equations (7.22) and (7.25) will yield similar time profiles. In the case of serial correlation specifications, equation (7.22) yields a time profile because of the left-out variable, but equation (7.25) does not.

Similarly, when two lagged dependent variables enter an equation, the use of x_t, x_{t-1}, and x_{t-2} as independent variables will not yield a strong time profile if the true specification is a serial correlation model.

7.4 Average Lag

Among several distributed lag schemes, one method of comparison is to draw their time profiles. Unless all the time profiles are from a single parameter family, as in the case of exponential decay, such comparison may not be easy. To aid in comparing these schemes, a summary-statistic "average lag" is defined as

$$\theta = \sum \tau\omega_\tau / \sum \omega_\tau. \tag{7.26}$$

The average lag, θ, is the weighted average of the τ's, the weights being proportional to ω_τ. The statistic θ in a sense measures how the various values of the ω's are distributed on the time profile. When the ω's corresponding to earlier lags are relatively larger than for the latter ones, the average lag will be small. When the average lag is "large," much of the distributed lag effect is felt at larger values of τ.

The average lag may be computed directly from the estimates without going through the values of all the ω's. Consider, for example, the equation

$$y_t = \alpha x_t + \delta x_{t-1} + \beta y_{t-1} + \varepsilon_t. \tag{7.27}$$

The ω's are given by the future values of y in Table 7.3. The average lag, as defined by (7.26) is

$$
\begin{aligned}
\theta = \frac{\sum \tau \omega_\tau}{\sum \omega_\tau} &= \frac{(\alpha\beta + \delta)(1 + 2\beta + 3\beta^2 + 4\beta^3 + \cdots)}{\alpha + (\alpha\beta + \delta)(1 + \beta + \beta^2 + \beta^3 + \cdots)} \\
&= \frac{(\alpha\beta + \delta)/(1 - \beta)^2}{\alpha + (\alpha\beta + \delta)/(1 - \beta)} \\
&= \frac{\alpha\beta + \delta}{(1 - \beta)(\alpha + \delta)} \\
&= \frac{\delta}{\alpha + \delta} + \frac{\beta}{1 - \beta}.
\end{aligned}
\tag{7.28}
$$

The average lag of the time profile implied by equation (7.27) is $\delta/(\alpha + \delta) + \beta/(1 - \beta)$. If that equation were generated by a serial correlation model rather than by a distributed lag model, the average lag will be zero. The researcher may verify this by computing the average lag for the time profile implied by equation (7.25).

The average lag of the time profile implied by the equation

$$y_t = \alpha x_t + \beta y_{t-1} + \varepsilon_t, \tag{7.29}$$

may be obtained as a special case of equation (7.27) when δ is zero. The average lag is therefore $[\beta/(1 - \beta)]$.

A general expression may be derived for the average lag when several lags occur in the dependent and the independent variables. The algebra involved in this derivation does not provide any insights, hence we shall furnish the researcher only the final formula. Let the regression equation be

$$y_t = \alpha_0 x_t + \alpha_1 x_{t-1} + \cdots + \alpha_m x_{t-m} + \beta_1 y_{t-1} + \cdots + \beta_n y_{t-n} + \varepsilon_t.$$

$$(7.30)$$

The average lag, θ, is given by the formula[4]

$$\theta = \frac{\sum_{i=0}^{m} i\alpha_i}{\sum_{i=0}^{m} \alpha_i} + \frac{\sum_{i=1}^{n} i\beta_i}{1 - \sum_{i=1}^{n} \beta_i}.$$

$$(7.31)$$

7.5 A Note on Estimation

The ordinary least squares estimation procedure is not the "best" when lagged dependent variables enter the regression equation as independent variables. In small samples the least squares estimates are biased, although they are consistent when the errors are serially independent.[5] Because of the bias in the estimates the computed standard errors are also biased. These problems associated with least squares estimation do not mean, however, that it is an inappropriate procedure. No other estimation procedure has been shown to be "better" in small samples when lagged dependent variables are on the right-hand side of the equation.

7.6 Several Independent Variables

Up to this point, equations having only one independent variable have been considered. We were able to describe the implicit distributed lag effect for different numbers of lagged dependent variables and of independent

---

[4] This formula is derived by the use of the "lag operator." For a discussion on the use of this concept in deriving the average lag, see Z. Griliches, *op. cit.*

[5] When the lagged dependent variable appears as an independent variable the ordinary least squares estimates are inconsistent whenever the errors are serially dependent. The technique of estimation with serially dependent errors has not been perfected. For some suggested procedures involving nonlinear estimations see Z. Griliches, *op. cit.*

variables. If theory dictates that more than one independent variable belongs in a regression equation, we can still obtain the underlying time profiles. Consider a regression equation with two independent variables and a lagged dependent variable:

$$y_t = \beta y_{t-1} + \alpha_1 x_{1t} + \alpha_2 x_{2t} + \varepsilon_t. \tag{7.32}$$

As before, we consider the effect of a one-unit, once-and-for-all change in the independent variable. But now we must consider change in variables separately, holding the value of the other constant. This is done in Table 7.5.

Table 7.5.   Distributed Lag Effect of x_{1t} on y_t with x_{2t} Held Constant and Distributed Lag Effect of x_{2t} on y_t with x_{1t} Held Constant

Time Period	$y_t \mid x_{2t = \text{constant}}$	x_{1t}	y_{t-1}	$y_t \mid x_{1t = \text{constant}}$	x_{2t}	y_{t-1}
0	0	0	0	0	0	0
1	α_1	1	0	α_2	1	0
2	$\alpha_1\beta$	0	α_1	$\alpha_2\beta$	0	α_2
3	$\alpha_1\beta^2$	0	$\alpha_1\beta$	$\alpha_2\beta^2$	0	$\alpha_2\beta$
4	$\alpha_1\beta^3$	0	$\alpha_1\beta^2$	$\alpha_2\beta^3$	0	$\alpha_2\beta^2$
5	$\alpha_1\beta^4$	0	$\alpha_1\beta^3$	$\alpha_2\beta^4$	0	$\alpha_2\beta^3$
.	.	.	.	.	.	.

We normalize the lag structure (the ω's) by dividing by the lead coefficient, which is α_1 when x_2 is constant and α_2 when x_1 is held constant. After normalization, each of the independent variables exhibits exactly the same lag structure—exponentially decaying and having the same parameter (β).

Similar analysis may be applied to the use of any number of independent variables. For many empirical problems this is a very restrictive result. Unless the researcher is willing to assume that every x has the same distributed lag effect on y with exactly the same parameters, he cannot include a lagged dependent variable in the regression equation and then consider that he has a distributed lag model.

Suppose that, instead of estimating equation (7.32), the researcher estimates

$$y_t = \beta y_{t-1} + \alpha_1 x_{1t} + \alpha_2 x_{1t-1} + \gamma_1 x_{2t} + \gamma_2 x_{2t-1} + \varepsilon_t. \tag{7.33}$$

Now we compute the usual implied time profile values in Tables 7.6 and 7.7.

Table 7.6. Distributed Lag Effect of x_{2t} on y_t with x_{1t} Held Constant in the Equation: $y_t = \beta y_{t-1} + \alpha_1 x_{1t} + \alpha_2 x_{1t-1} + \gamma_1 x_{2t} + \gamma_2 x_{2t-1} + \varepsilon_t$

Time Period	$y_t \mid x_{1t-\text{constant}}$	x_{2t}	x_{2t-1}	y_{t-1}
0	0	0	0	0
1	γ_1	1	0	0
2	$(\beta\gamma_1 + \gamma_2)$	0	1	γ_1
3	$\beta(\beta\gamma_1 + \gamma_2)$	0	0	$(\beta\gamma_1 + \gamma_2)$
4	$\beta^2(\beta\gamma_1 + \gamma_2)$	0	0	$(\beta\gamma_1 + \gamma_2)$
.	.	.	.	.

Remember that we are considering the partial effects, holding one or the other independent variables constant. If the parameter estimates are such that $\hat{\beta}\hat{\gamma}_1 = -\hat{\gamma}_2$, then it is obvious that the column in Table 7.6 for y_t with x_1 held constant has only zeros after the first time period. That means that x_2 has no distributed lag effect on y. Notice that for this to be true the number of lags on x_2 must be the same as the number of lags on y.

If the estimates do not satisfy $\hat{\beta}\hat{\gamma}_1 = -\hat{\gamma}_2$, then we have a distributed lag effect of x_2 on y. Note, however, that if γ_2 is not estimated this condition is not met. If the researcher wants a distributed lag effect of x_2 on y then there is no restriction on the number of lags of x_2 which may be included in the regression equation.

Similarly, when $\hat{\beta}\hat{\alpha}_1 = -\hat{\alpha}_2$ the independent variable x_1 will not have any distributed lag effect on y. Lagging an independent variable by the same number of time periods as that of the dependent variable does not automatically eliminate the distributed lag effect, however. It only gives the variable a chance to express itself.

In a practical situation these constraints, $\hat{\beta}\hat{\gamma}_1 = -\hat{\gamma}_2$ or $\hat{\beta}\hat{\alpha}_1 = -\hat{\alpha}_2$, are

Table 7.7. Distributed Lag Effect of x_{1t} on y_t with x_{2t} Held Constant in the Equation: $y_t = \beta y_{t-1} + \alpha_1 x_{1t} + \alpha_2 x_{1t-1} + \gamma_1 x_{2t} + \gamma_2 x_{2t-1} + \varepsilon_t$

Time Period	$y_t \mid x_{2t-\text{constant}}$	x_{1t}	x_{1t-1}	y_{t-1}
0	0	0	0	0
1	α_1	1	0	0
2	$(\beta\alpha_1 + \alpha_2)$	0	1	α_1
3	$\beta(\beta\alpha_1 + \alpha_2)$	0	0	$(\beta\alpha_1 + \alpha_2)$
4	$\beta^2(\beta\alpha_1 + \alpha_2)$	0	0	$\beta(\beta\alpha_1 + \alpha_2)$
.	.	.	.	.

rarely met because of sampling fluctuations in the estimates. When an independent variable does not have a distributed lag effect on y, the researcher will observe a "weak" time profile from his estimates, except for $\tau = 0$, because of sampling fluctuations. In such a case, if he does not include the required number of lags on that particular independent variable, he is forcing it to exhibit a distributed lag effect.

Suppose the researcher has estimated equation (7.33) and now realizes that both the independent variables have "weak" time profiles. His model then corresponds to the serial correlation specification with two independent variables, x_1 and x_2, and not to a distributed lag specification.

This procedure may be extended to several independent variables. It is necessary, of course, to lag all the independent variables to match the number of lags on the dependent variable.

When the researcher has access to nonlinear estimation procedures, then by imposing the required constraints on the estimates he may even force some of the independent variables not to have distributed lag effects.

7.7 Errors in the Variables

In all regression equations considered so far we have treated the variables as though they had no errors, whether of measurement or of other kinds. It is true that most data have some errors, however small. We shall now analyze the consequences of these errors on the variables.

Let us first consider the case in which the independent variables have no errors, but the dependent variable does. Let y^* be the true value of the dependent variable and y the observed value, so that

$$y_t = y_t^* + d_t, \tag{7.34}$$

where d is the error in the observed value. Let the true relation between the dependent and the independent variable (x) be

$$y_t^* = \beta x_t + \varepsilon_t. \tag{7.35}$$

Instead of estimating equation (7.35), the researcher estimates

$$y_t = \beta x_t + v_t. \tag{7.36}$$

By substituting equation (7.34) in equation (7.36) we see that $v = \varepsilon + d$.

When the error term in the dependent variable d is uncorrelated with the independent variable, the estimates of β from equations (7.35) and (7.36) have the same mean value β. However, the variances of these distributions are different. The variances of the least squares estimate of β from equations (7.35) and (7.36) are, respectively, $\sigma_\varepsilon^2/\sum x^2$ and $\sigma_v^2/\sum x^2$. It is thus obvious that when the error terms ε and d are independent ($\sigma_v^2 = \sigma_\varepsilon^2 + \sigma_d^2$), the estimate of β from equation (7.36) has a larger variance than the estimate from equation (7.35).

When both the dependent variable and the independent variable have errors, the situation is different. Consider the case in which y^* and x^* are the true values, and their respective observed values are y and x:

$$y_t = y_t^* + d_t, \tag{7.37}$$

$$x_t = x_t^* + f_t, \tag{7.38}$$

where f is the error of measurement in x. Let the true relation between the true values of the variable be

$$y_t^* = \beta^* x_t^* + \varepsilon_t^*. \tag{7.39}$$

Instead of estimating equation (7.39), the researcher estimates the following regression:

$$y_t = \beta x_t + \varepsilon_t. \tag{7.40}$$

The least squares estimate of β is obtained as

$$\begin{aligned}\hat{\beta} &= \sum xy/\sum x^2 \\ &= [\sum (x^* + f)(y^* + d)]/\sum (x^* + f)^2.\end{aligned} \tag{7.41}$$

If we assume that the error terms are uncorrelated with the true values of the variables but that the same forces cause errors in both the variables, then for large values of the sample size we may treat $\sum fy^*$, $\sum x^*d$, $\sum x^*f$ as zero, but not $\sum fd$. Using this assumption, we may rewrite expression (7.41) as

$$\text{plim}(\hat{\beta}) = \frac{\beta^* + k\lambda}{1 + \lambda}, \tag{7.42}$$

where

$$k = \text{plim}(\sum df / \sum f^2) \tag{7.43}$$

and

$$\lambda = \text{plim}(\sum f^2 / \sum x^{*2}). \tag{7.44}$$

It is easily seen that k represents the regression coefficient of d on f. When the error terms in x and y are caused by different forces so that d and f are independent, then k is zero. The coefficient λ measures the proportion of the variance in f to the variance of x^*. When the errors in x are dominant, the value of λ tends to be large. Typically, λ is less than unity because the variance of the errors is usually smaller than the variance of the variable. In many practical situations, even though errors do occur in the variables their variance relative to that of the variable may be very small. In such cases λ is very close to zero. This is an important observation, because the researcher should keep in mind that the relevant point in estimation for the errors in the variables model is the value of λ and not the *mere presence* of errors in the variables.

From equation (7.42) we readily see that the least squares estimate $\hat{\beta}$ is asymptotically biased toward the value of k. The two common situations in applied econometrics correspond to $k = 0$ and $k = 1$. When the errors in the variables are independent—that is, when $k = 0$—the regression estimate $\hat{\beta}$ is downward biased in absolute value, that is, toward zero. When $k = 1$, $\hat{\beta}$ is biased toward unity in absolute value.

The case of $k = 1$ typically occurs in estimation of the elasticity of substitution between capital and labor in the CES production function estimated from wage data. Here the bias favors acceptance of the Cobb-Douglas production function, which has substitution elasticity of unity. In the framework of the CES production function, if we assume constant returns and competitive equilibrium the elasticity of substitution may be shown to equal b in the following equation:[6]

$$\log (Q/L) = a + b \log W, \qquad (7.45)$$

where Q/L is real output per man-hour, and W is the real wage rate per man-hour.

The researcher may not have exact information on the variables specified by the theory underlying equation (7.45). Specifically, labor should be measured in constant quality units, but the researcher typically must rely on total number of employees or total man-hours as reported, for example, in the Census of Manufacturing. Here no account is taken of differences in labor quality. Given that L is measured incorrectly, if the researcher estimates W by dividing the total wage bill by L then both the dependent and the independent variables in (7.45) are measured with error. In fact, since both variables are expressed in their logarithms, these errors will be identical.

Realizing that these errors are merely the d's and f's of equations (7.37) and (7.38), we know that k as defined by (7.43) must equal 1. Therefore the ordinary least squares estimate of b is biased toward 1—that is, toward the acceptance of unitary elasticity between capital and labor.

Errors in the variables do not affect only the coefficient of x; they also affect the constant term. This fact is often the source of misinterpretation of empirical results.

Consider the problem of testing for constant proportionality between two variables, both of which are measured with errors. Say, for example, that the researcher wishes to know whether the production of gasoline is a constant proportion of crude oil input in petroleum refineries. He considers the two possible truths, $T1$ and $T2$:

$$T1: G_t = \beta_1 C_t + \varepsilon_{1t} \qquad (7.46)$$

and

$$T2: G_t = \beta_0 + \beta_1 C_t + \varepsilon_{2t}, \qquad (7.47)$$

[6] K. J. Arrow, H. B. Chenery, B. S. Minhas, and R. M. Solow, "Capital-Labor Substitution and Economic Efficiency," *The Review of Economics and Statistics*, August 1961, pp. 225–50.

where G = gasoline and C = crude oil. Unlike $T1$, $T2$ includes a constant term, β_0. $T1$ implies constant proportionality between the dependent and the independent variables. When β_0 is positive, $T2$ implies that the proportion of gasoline produced decreases as a percentage of crude oil.

A common procedure is to estimate the regression equation (7.47) and to test the null hypothesis $\beta_0 = 0$. When the null hypothesis is rejected, this is considered as evidence against constant proportionality.

The question arises, though, whether this commonly used test procedure is still valid when G and C are measured with errors. Let us consider a case in which the measurement errors are uncorrelated—that is, a case in which k from equation (7.43) is zero. The underlying model with errors of measurement is

$$G = G^* + d, \tag{7.48}$$

$$C = C^* + f, \tag{7.49}$$

where the starred variables are true values and d and f are errors in the variables. Suppose that the true relation is that of constant proportionality; that is, $\beta_0 = 0$, so that

$$G^* = \beta^* C^* + \varepsilon^*. \tag{7.50}$$

Repeating equation (7.42), we see that the least squares estimate of β_1 in (7.47) will be biased downward (since β^* is positive):

$$\text{plim}(\hat{\beta}_1) = \beta^* \left(\frac{1}{1 + \lambda} \right). \tag{7.51}$$

Now let us consider the ordinary least squares estimate of the constant term β_0 in equation (7.47). It is merely

$$\hat{\beta}_0 = \bar{G} - \hat{\beta}_1 \bar{C}. \tag{7.52}$$

For large samples, we may replace the expression for $\hat{\beta}_1$ in terms of the true β^*.

$$\text{plim}(\hat{\beta}_0) = \bar{G} - \left(\frac{\beta^*}{1 + \lambda} \right) \bar{C}. \tag{7.53}$$

Since $\beta^* \bar{C} = \bar{G}$, (7.53) simplifies to

$$\text{plim}(\hat{\beta}_0) = \bar{G}\left[\frac{\lambda}{1 + \lambda}\right]. \qquad (7.54)$$

We easily observe that, whenever $\lambda = 0$ (that is, when there are no errors in crude oil), the ordinary least squares estimate of β_0 will indeed have an expected value of zero. However, when λ is greater than zero, the expected value of $\hat{\beta}_0$ will not be zero, and the researcher may even find his estimate significantly different from zero. Thus, the conclusion is that, although the true variables are in constant proportion, errors in the variables may cause the theory of constant proportionality to be rejected.

A classic example of this problem involves the estimation of the consumption function. Typically, estimated linear consumption functions contain a positively significant nonzero constant term. This has led many economists to hypothesize that the average propensity to consume decreases as the income level increases. That is, the rich supposedly would save a larger proportion of income than the poor. We merely note here that if income were measured with error, a "significant" ordinary least squares estimate of the constant term is not inconsistent with a consumption function with constant average and marginal propensity to consume.

 The above examples have dealt with only one independent variable. The same analysis applies to cases with several independent variables when only one of them has measurement errors. However, when more than one has measurement errors the expression for bias cannot be readily simplified.[7]

Every researcher is aware that all data contain errors of measurement, but he should not immediately jump to the conclusion that all his estimates are biased due to these errors. In many cases in which λ is very small whatever bias is present may for all practical purposes be negligible. Whether the bias is, or is not, "large" calls for external information on the magnitude of λ.

---

[7] See H. Theil, *Economic Forecasts and Policy*, 2nd Revised Edition, North Holland Publishing Company (Amsterdam), 1965, p. 329.

8

Simultaneous-Equations Model

The specification of some economic models involves more than one equation; these are called simultaneous-equations models because their variables simultaneously satisfy all these equations. In such models the single-equation estimation procedures discussed in the previous chapters may not be appropriate, and several alternative estimation procedures have been developed. Although the theoretical properties of these procedures have been extensively studied, their use in applied econometric work has been limited.

It is widely believed that whenever the model is simultaneous in nature, the use of single-equation estimation procedure necessarily yields "bad" estimates. This is not always the case. True, the single-equation procedure yields biased estimates of the parameters; but so do all the others in small samples. In some situations it may happen that single-equation estimation procedures are "better" than the simultaneous-equations estimation procedures, even though the true model involves simultaneous equations. When to use single-equation and when to use simultaneous-equations procedures is a topic often ignored by textbooks. This is not an easy question to answer, but we shall try to bring out some of the considerations that determine the choice. When the researcher has some external information on these characteristics, then he may take advantage of the following guidelines.

The theoretical properties of various alternative estimation procedures in the context of simultaneous-equations models have been extensively studied to derive the exact distributions and properties of the estimates. We see no merit in reproducing these results here, since the derivations are usually in terms of matrix jugglery and seldom provide insights into what is actually happening. For this reason we avoid the conventional approach to the problem and, instead, deal in terms of *approximate* expressions rather than *exact* expressions. By so doing, we hope to provide a feel for what is actually happening in the shadows of incomprehensible matrix manipulations.

8.1 Single-Equation Estimation

Estimating a single equation from a simultaneous-equations model introduces bias in the estimates even though the estimated equation is the truth, because the procedure ignores information on the other equations. The bias resulting from the presence of other equations in the model, rather than from left-out variables or misspecification of the functional form, is called *simultaneity bias*.

Estimating an equation as though it were from a single linear equation model by using the ordinary least squares estimation procedure is called the *direct least squares procedure*. To illustrate the source of bias in this procedure, let us consider the standard textbook example in which the price of a commodity, P, and the quantity sold, Y, are determined by the demand and supply schedules. Let these be

$$Y_t^d = \beta_0 + \beta_1 P_t, \tag{8.1}$$

$$Y_t^s = \alpha_0 + \alpha_1 P_t, \tag{8.2}$$

with the equilibrium condition

$$Y_t^d = Y_t^s. \tag{8.3}$$

The equilibrium price and the amount of commodity sold at that price are given by the intersection of the demand and supply schedules.

The researcher rarely knows the parameters of demand and supply curves and wants to estimate them from observed data. The data are the equilibrium prices and amounts sold in the market—that is, the market-clearing prices and quantities. Given only these equilibrium values of Y and P, the researcher wishes to estimate the demand and supply curves.

In this situation each observation gives only one price and one value for the amount sold. In the real world, and depending on the commodity in question, we observe variation through time in the price of a product and in the amount sold, but we assume that these variations are all market-clearing. Thus, they occur because there are error terms shifting the demand and supply curves. Consider, for example, the case in which the supply curve of the commodity has shifted due to some unusual climatological conditions. The consequences of the changes may be analyzed by incorporating this information as an error term in the supply curve, written as

$$Y_t^s = \alpha_0 + \alpha_1 P_t + v_t. \tag{8.4}$$

The new equilibrium value for the price and for the amount of the commodity sold is obtained by the intersection of the demand curve and the new supply curve (8.4) corresponding to the specified error term. As the error term changes in different time periods, the equilibrium values also change. Similarly, if the demand function for the commodity has some error component, the equilibrium values will change in accordance with those error values. When both supply and demand curves are subject to errors, the equilibrium values of P and Y may (and usually will) vary for different time periods; hence we have a theoretical justification for the variation exhibited in our sample data.

In this model the values of P and Y depend on error terms in the demand and in the supply curves. Let us rewrite such a model as

$$y_t^d = \beta p_t + u_t, \tag{8.5}$$

$$y_t^s = \alpha p_t + v_t, \tag{8.6}$$

where the variables are expressed as deviations from their respective means.

8.2   Bias in Direct Least Squares Estimates

When a researcher tries to estimate the demand curve (8.5) from observed data on y and p by the direct least squares estimation procedure, he obtains $\hat{\beta}$ as

$$\hat{\beta} = \sum py / \sum p^2. \tag{8.7}$$

Using the true relation for y as given by equation (8.5) we obtain

$$\hat{\beta} = \beta + \sum pu / \sum p^2.$$
(8.8)

Since the value of p systematically depends on the value of u because the values of y and p are simultaneously determined by equations (8.5) and (8.6), we cannot treat the values of p as fixed in repeated experiments (nonstochastic) as we did in the previous chapters. The value of p may be expressed completely in terms of u and v. First consider the equilibrium condition (8.3) expressed as

$$\beta p + u = \alpha p + v.$$
(8.9)

By rearrangement

$$p = (u - v)/(\alpha - \beta).$$
(8.10)

When multiplied through by u and summed, equation (8.10) becomes

$$\sum pu = \left(\sum u^2 - \sum uv \right)/(\alpha - \beta).$$
(8.11)

Also, when squared and then summed, equation (8.10) becomes

$$\sum p^2 = \left(\sum u^2 + \sum v^2 - 2 \sum uv \right)/(\alpha - \beta)^2.$$
(8.12)

By substituting equations (8.11) and (8.12) we obtain a new expression for the bias of the direct least squares estimate:

$$\hat{\beta} = \beta + (\alpha - \beta) \frac{\sum u^2 - \sum uv}{\sum u^2 + \sum v^2 - 2 \sum uv}.$$
(8.13)

The estimate $\hat{\beta}$ has a statistical distribution. It has been shown that the mean value of this distribution does not fluctuate with much increase in sample size.[1] Using this property we may treat the mean of $\hat{\beta}$ for any sample size as *approximately* equal to the mean of $\hat{\beta}$ as the sample size tends to infinity. The mean of the distribution of $\hat{\beta}$ is approximately

$$E(\hat{\beta}) \simeq \beta + (\alpha - \beta)\frac{T \cdot \sigma_u^2 - T \cdot \text{cov}(u, v)}{T \cdot \sigma_u^2 + T \cdot \sigma_v^2 - 2 \cdot T \cdot \text{cov}(u, v)} \qquad (8.14)$$

where T is the sample size, and σ_u^2 and σ_v^2 are the variances of u and v respectively. When u and v are generated independently of each other, $\text{cov}(u, v) = 0$, and (8.14) simplifies to

$$E(\hat{\beta}) \simeq \beta + (\alpha - \beta)\frac{\sigma_u^2}{\sigma_u^2 + \sigma_v^2}. \qquad (8.15)$$

The direct least squares estimate $\hat{\beta}$ is biased. This bias does not decrease with the sample size. Hence, the direct least squares estimation of β yields a biased and inconsistent estimate even though the estimated equation is the truth. This result occurs because the estimated equation is a part of the simultaneous-equations model.

The bias in direct least squares depends also on the other parameter of the model, namely α. The crucial factors, however, are the variances of the error terms in the model, namely σ_u^2 and σ_v^2.

The bias is least when the error term u has least variance, namely zero. That is, when no error terms are present in the demand curve the ordinary least squares estimation of the demand curve (8.5) gives an unbiased estimate of β. When the demand curve has no error terms the observed data correspond to movements along the demand curve. This is because the changing error values of the supply curve (v_t in equation (8.6)) are causing the supply curve to intersect at different points *along* the demand curve. The observed price-quantity pairs represent intersections of a shifting supply curve on a stable demand curve, as shown in Figure 8.1.

[1] T. Sawa, "The Exact Sampling Distribution of Ordinary Least Squares and Two Stage Least Squares Estimators," *Journal of the American Statistical Association*, September 1969, pp. 923–38.

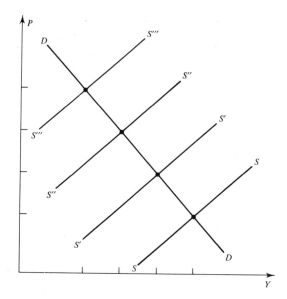

Figure 8.1. Stable Demand Curve with Shifting Supply Curve

The maximum bias is obtained when the errors in the supply curve, v_t, have zero variance, in which case (8.15) reduces to

$$E(\hat{\beta}) \simeq \beta + (\alpha - \beta) = \alpha. \tag{8.16}$$

In this situation, the researcher ends up estimating the coefficient of the supply curve even though he may be thinking that he is estimating the demand curve (8.5). When only the demand curve has nonzero errors, all observed price-quantity pairs represent movements *along* a stable supply curve, as represented in Figure 8.2.

Comparable results may be obtained for the case of estimating a supply curve, (8.6). The minimum bias occurs when errors in the supply curve have zero variance, the maximum bias occurs when those in the demand curve have zero variance.

In a practical situation, however, these extreme cases are rarely encountered. The direct least squares estimate always has a mean which is a function of both demand and supply parameters, namely, α and β. We see this by rewriting (8.15) as

$$E(\hat{\beta}) \simeq \beta + (\alpha - \beta)\lambda, \tag{8.17}$$

where

$$\lambda = \frac{\sigma_u^2}{\sigma_u^2 + \sigma_v^2}. \tag{8.18}$$

When the variance of errors in the demand curve is very small *relative* to the variance of errors in the supply curve, then λ will be close to zero and the estimated regression equation will be a very close representation of the demand curve.

The researcher should not confuse the bias in direct least squares with the problem of "identification." The concept of identification relates to what the researcher *thinks* he is estimating. In this example, when the researcher is estimating the demand curve (8.5) there is no reason why he should not have thought that he was estimating the supply curve (8.6), which is a look-alike of equation (8.5). For that matter the estimated equation could have been thought to be a linear combination of equations (8.5) and (8.6).

Thus, when the regression is estimated and the researcher is asked to interpret the results, he is hard pressed because he does not know on theoretical grounds whether he has produced a demand curve, a supply curve, or a linear combination of both—because they all look alike. No matter what he

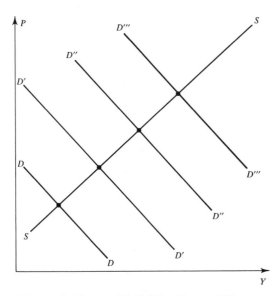

Figure 8.2. Stable Supply Curve with Shifting Demand Curve

has tried to estimate, the resultant parameter is still a linear combination of the parameters of the model. The relevant question in applied econometrics is, then: Is the estimated equation closer to the demand curve or to the supply curve? The answer depends on the magnitude of λ, the relative variance of the error terms, and not on whether an equation is identified or not. As shown later, the use of "exogenous" variables to identify an equation does not eliminate this problem.

8.3   Variance of Direct Least Squares Estimates

The variance of the direct least squares estimates can be obtained from the exact distribution; but we use, instead, an approximation (analogous to equation (3.15)) which is more revealing than the exact expression. For reasonably large samples the variance of the estimate $\hat{\beta}$ is approximately

$$V(\hat{\beta}) \simeq \frac{V(e)}{T \cdot \sigma_p^2},$$ (8.19)

where e is defined analogous to ε of equation (3.15) as

$$e_t = y_t - E(\hat{\beta})p_t.$$ (8.20)

By substituting in (8.20) the true value for y (equation (8.5)) and the least squares estimate $\hat{\beta}$ given by equation (8.7) we obtain

$$e_t = u_t - (\alpha - \beta)\lambda p_t.$$ (8.21)

The variance of e from equation (8.21) may be obtained as

$$V(e) = V(u) + (\alpha - \beta)^2\lambda^2\sigma_p^2 - 2(\alpha - \beta)\lambda COV(p, u)$$ (8.22)

or

$$V(e) = \sigma_u^2 + (\alpha - \beta)^2\frac{\lambda^2(\sigma_u^2 + \sigma_v^2)}{(\alpha - \beta)^2} - 2(\alpha - \beta)\frac{\lambda\sigma_u^2}{\alpha - \beta}.$$ (8.23)

By using the definition of λ, (8.18), and simplifying, we arrive at:

$$V(e) = \sigma_u^2(1 - \lambda).$$

(8.24)

Substitution of (8.24) into (8.19) yields

$$V(\hat{\beta}) \simeq \frac{(\alpha - \beta)^2}{T(\sigma_u^2 + \sigma_v^2)} \cdot \{\sigma_u^2(1 - \lambda)\}.$$

(8.25)

By use of the definition of λ, (8.18), this becomes

$$V(\hat{\beta}) \simeq \frac{(\alpha - \beta)^2}{T} \lambda\{1 - \lambda\}.$$

(8.26)

The variance of the direct least squares estimate $\hat{\beta}$ depends on both the parameters, α and β. Since λ is a positive fraction, the variance decreases with the value of λ. That is, as the relative variance of error in the estimated equation decreases with respect to the variance of error in the other equation of the model, the precision of the direct least squares estimate increases.

It is interesting to note that this increase also occurs as λ approaches unity; that is, as the relative variance of the error term v compared to u approaches zero. In this case, as we have noted earlier, direct least squares estimation gives the supply curve instead of the demand curve. Hence, using direct least squares in estimating the "wrong" parameter may yield a pretty good estimate of the "wrong" parameter.

These results, both of bias and of variance, are crucially dependent on the coefficient λ, which is generally unknown. When the researcher has external information on the relative variances of u and v, there is no problem. But in many instances in which the researcher is not that fortunate, he may expect that the use of summary statistics will shed some light on the value of λ. With this possibility in mind let us turn to the summary statistic R^2:

$$R^2 = 1 - \frac{\sum e^2}{\sum y^2}.$$

(8.27)

From the equilibrium condition (8.3) we may express y completely in terms of u and v as

$$y = \frac{\alpha u - \beta v}{\alpha - \beta},$$

(8.28)

$$V(y) = (\alpha^2 \sigma_u^2 + \beta^2 \sigma_v^2)/(\alpha - \beta)^2,$$

(8.29)

since u and v are assumed to be independent. For reasonably large sample sizes we may *approximate* the value of R^2 as:

$$R^2 \simeq 1 - \frac{V(e)}{V(y)}.$$

(8.30)

By use of equations (8.24) and (8.29):

$$R^2 \simeq 1 - \frac{\sigma_u^2(1 - \lambda)(\alpha - \beta)^2}{\alpha^2 \sigma_u^2 + \beta^2 \sigma_v^2}.$$

(8.31)

By the definition of λ, (8.18), this becomes

$$R^2 \simeq 1 - (\alpha - \beta)^2 \cdot \frac{\sigma_v^2}{\sigma_u^2 + \sigma_v^2} \cdot \frac{\sigma_u^2}{\alpha^2 \sigma_u^2 + \beta^2 \sigma_v^2}$$

(8.32)

which may be rewritten as:

$$R^2 \simeq 1 - (\alpha - \beta)^2 \frac{k}{(1 + k)(\alpha^2 + \beta^2 k)}$$

(8.33)

where

$$k = \sigma_v^2/\sigma_u^2.$$

(8.34)

It may be seen by computing the values of R^2 for various values of k (for given values of α and β) that the theoretical R^2 approaches unity as k approaches zero or infinity. Since there is a one-to-one correspondence between k and λ, the value of the theoretical R^2 is close to one whenever λ is close to zero or unity. When λ is zero the bias in $\hat{\beta}$ is zero, and we are estimating the demand curve; when λ is unity the bias is maximum, and we are estimating the supply curve.

When λ is close to zero, the value of theoretical R^2 is close to unity, the bias in $\hat{\beta}$ is close to zero, and the estimated equation is close to the demand curve. The variance of the estimate is also close to zero. As a practical policy, whenever the computed R^2 is close to unity, even though the estimated equation is a part of a simultaneous-equations model, direct least squares is doing a "good job." When λ is close to unity we have similar results, except that the estimated equation is the supply curve instead of the demand curve. The reader should note that these results do not depend on "identification" of the model. When a researcher obtains high R^2 his result is a good estimate either of the supply curve or of the demand curve. Which is which is to be identified from economic theory (expected values and signs of parameters) and not from "rules of identification."

8.4 Extension to More Than One Independent Variable

The above exercise illustrates some basic concepts. A simultaneous-equations model usually includes several other variables in its specification. A simple case with several independent variables is

$$y_t^d = \beta p_t + \gamma x_t + u_t, \tag{8.35}$$

$$y_t^s = \alpha p_t + \delta z_t + v_t, \tag{8.36}$$

$$y_t^d = y_t^s. \tag{8.37}$$

This model is also a case of demand and supply for the same product, y, except that now demand depends on income, x, and supply depends on rainfall, z. In addition to these variables, there are error terms that influence both the demand and the supply curves. The market-clearing situation gives equilibrium values for the commodity sold, y, and for the price paid, p.

In this model, however, the values of x and z are not determined by equilibrium conditions for the commodity, y. The values of x and z can change independently of the market situation. Since these variables do not depend on the simultaneous satisfaction of the two equations specified by the model, they are called *exogenous* variables. These variables need not depend in any systematic way on error terms in the regression equation; hence, we shall assume that exogenous variables and error terms in the model are independently distributed.

The variables y and p, however, are determined by equilibrium conditions; as the error terms or the exogenous variables change, the values of those variables change as well. Since their values depend on the simultaneous satisfaction of the model, they are called *endogenous*. We cannot assume that endogenous variables are independent of error terms, because as the values of the error terms change the equilibrium values of y and p also change.

Unlike the previous exercise, only some of the independent variables of the estimated regression equation are now systematically related to the error terms. Suppose that the researcher tries to estimate the demand curve (8.35) by using direct least squares; he obtains the estimate $\hat{\beta}$ as

$$\hat{\beta} = \frac{\sum x^2 \sum py - \sum xp \sum xy}{\sum p^2 \sum x^2 - \sum xp \sum xp}. \tag{8.38}$$

8.5   Bias of Direct Least Squares Estimates

By substituting the true value of y given by equation (8.35) and using the approximation $\sum xu = 0$ for reasonably large samples, we may write equation (8.38) as

$$\hat{\beta} \simeq \beta + \frac{\sum x^2 \sum pu}{\sum p^2 \sum x^2 - \sum xp \sum xp}. \tag{8.39}$$

Since the equilibrium value of p is determined by the simultaneous satisfaction of the two equations (8.35) and (8.36),

$$\beta p + \gamma x + u = \alpha p + \delta z + v. \tag{8.40}$$

Factoring out p,

$$p = (u - v + \gamma x - \delta z)/(\alpha - \beta). \tag{8.41}$$

For reasonably large samples we use the approximations

$$\sum uv \simeq \sum xu \simeq \sum xv \simeq \sum zu \simeq \sum zv \simeq 0. \qquad (8.42)$$

Squaring and summing (8.41) and then using (8.42), we obtain

$$\sum p^2 \simeq \left(\sum u^2 + \sum v^2 + \gamma^2 \sum x^2 + \delta^2 \sum z^2 - 2\gamma\delta \sum xz \right)/(\alpha - \beta)^2. \qquad (8.43)$$

Multiplying through by u and summing (8.41) and then using (8.42), we obtain

$$\sum pu \simeq \sum u^2/(\alpha - \beta). \qquad (8.44)$$

Multiplying through by x and summing (8.41) and then using (8.42), we obtain

$$\sum px \simeq \left(\gamma \sum x^2 - \delta \sum xz \right)/(\alpha - \beta). \qquad (8.45)$$

Substituting equations (8.43), (8.44), and (8.45), into equation (8.39), we obtain

$$\hat{\beta} \simeq \beta + (\alpha - \beta) \frac{\sum u^2}{\sum u^2 + \sum v^2 + \delta^2 \sum z^2(1 - r_{xz}^2)}. \qquad (8.46)$$

Realizing that the mean of the exact distribution of $\hat{\beta}$ is not sensitive to the increase in sample size, we may approximate the mean of $\hat{\beta}$ to its asymptotic mean as

$$E(\hat{\beta}) \simeq \beta + (\alpha - \beta) \frac{\sigma_u^2}{\sigma_u^2 + \sigma_v^2 + \delta^2 \sigma_z^2(1 - r_{xz}^2)}, \qquad (8.47)$$

which may be written as

$$E(\hat{\beta}) \simeq \beta + (\alpha - \beta)\lambda', \tag{8.48}$$

where

$$\lambda' = \frac{\sigma_u^2}{\sigma_u^2 + \sigma_v^2 + \delta^2\sigma_z^2(1 - r_{xz}^2)}. \tag{8.49}$$

The direct least squares estimate of β is biased even in the case with exogenous variables. The bias depends on the coefficient of the endogenous variable in the other equation, namely α.

Note that in this model the supply curve resembles neither the demand curve nor any linear combination of both. In the vocabulary of the simultaneous-equations models, the demand curve is *identified*. Yet the bias in the estimate is present and depends on the parameters of the other equation. The variable z in the supply curve distinguishes it from the demand curve in which there is no variable z. Hence the variable z is "identifying" the demand curve.

When the identifying variable (z) is highly correlated with the exogenous variable of the estimated equation (x) then the bias of the estimate $\hat{\beta}$ is not much reduced by the presence of the exogenous variables in the model. As the correlation between x and z decreases, so does the bias. The researcher should note that trying to identify a simultaneous-equations model by including the appropriate number of exogenous variables does not necessarily "buy" anything in the estimation. When these exogenous variables are highly correlated, the statistical properties of the estimates remain unaltered by their presence.

The direct least squares estimation of (8.35) also yields a biased estimate of γ. The estimate γ is obtained as

$$\hat{\gamma} = \frac{\sum p^2 \sum xy - \sum xp \sum py}{\sum p^2 \sum x^2 - \sum xp \sum xp}. \tag{8.50}$$

Substituting for the true value of y as given by (8.35) and using the approximation that $\sum xu = 0$, we have

$$\hat{\gamma} \simeq \gamma - \frac{\sum xp \sum pu}{\sum p^2 \sum x^2 - \sum xp \sum xp}. \tag{8.51}$$

Substitution of equations (8.43), (8.44), and (8.45) into (8.51) yields

$$\hat{\gamma} \simeq \gamma - (\gamma - \delta b_{zx}) \frac{\sum u^2}{\sum u^2 + \sum v^2 + \delta^2 \sum z^2(1 - r_{xz}^2)}. \tag{8.52}$$

For reasonably large samples we may express equation (8.52) as

$$E(\hat{\gamma}) \simeq \gamma - (\gamma - \delta b_{zx}) \frac{\sigma_u^2}{\sigma_u^2 + \sigma_v^2 + \delta^2 \sigma_z^2(1 - r_{xz}^2)}. \tag{8.53}$$

$$E(\hat{\gamma}) \simeq \gamma - (\gamma - \delta b_{zx})\lambda' \tag{8.54}$$

where λ' is defined as in (8.49).

$\hat{\gamma}$ is a biased estimate of γ, the bias depending on the values of the two parameters γ, δ, and also on λ' and b_{zx}. The conclusions to be reached about the extent and direction of this bias are similar to those already discussed. For a given value of b_{zx}, the smaller the variance of u relative to that of v, the smaller the bias in $\hat{\gamma}$. Thus, the more stable the equation being estimated by direct least squares relative to the other equation in the simultaneous model, the less biased will be the estimates of that equation.

8.6 Variance of the Direct Least Squares Estimate

For reasonably large samples the variance of the estimate from (8.38) is approximately

$$V(\hat{\beta}) \simeq \frac{V(e)}{T \cdot \sigma_p^2(1 - r_{xp}^2)}, \tag{8.55}$$

where e is defined analogous to ε of equation (3.39) as

$$e_t = y_t - E(\hat{\beta})p_t - E(\hat{\gamma})x_t. \tag{8.56}$$

By using equations (8.48) through (8.54), we can write the residuals as

$$e_t = u_t - (\alpha - \beta)\lambda'p_t + (\gamma - \delta b_{zx})\lambda'x_t. \tag{8.57}$$

Taking the variance of e in (8.57) and substituting equations (8.43), (8.44), and (8.45) into the result, we may write the variance (8.55) of the estimate as

$$V(\hat{\beta}) \simeq \frac{(\alpha - \beta)^2\lambda'(1 - \lambda')}{T}, \tag{8.58}$$

where λ' is defined as in (8.49).

The introduction of exogenous variables into the estimated regression equation gives a similar expression for variance as before in (8.26) except that the definition of λ' differs from that of λ.

The presence of the exogenous variable z in the supply curve reduces the bias and the variance of the estimate of the parameter $\hat{\beta}$. The extent of each reduction depends on the variance of the variable z and also on the correlation between the two exogenous variables, x and z. The larger the variance of z, *ceteris paribus*, the smaller the bias and the variance. The smaller the correlation between the exogenous variables in the supply and the demand equation, *ceteris paribus*, the smaller the bias and the variance of the direct least squares estimate of β.

The simultaneous-equation bias is a consequence of the presence of correlation between the error term and some of the independent variables caused by the simultaneous satisfaction of all the equations of the model. When the error terms and the independent variables of a regression equation have no correlation then, of course, there is no simultaneity bias even though the equation may be part of a simultaneous-equations model. Therefore, estimating a single equation from a simultaneous-equations model does not necessarily imply that the estimates have simultaneity bias. Consider the following economic model in which the supply of the commodity, y^s, is determined by the price in the previous time period p_{t-1}, and in which the price in current time period p_t is determined by the equilibrium conditions:

$$y_t^s = \alpha p_{t-1} + \delta z_t + v_t, \tag{8.59}$$

$$p_t = \beta y_t^d + \gamma x_t + u_t, \tag{8.60}$$

$$y_t^s = y_t^d, \tag{8.61}$$

where all variables are expressed as deviations from the means. In equation (8.59) or (8.60) the independent variables do not depend on the error terms of the regression equation. The price in the previous time period p_{t-1} does not depend on the current error terms in supply curve v_t. The supply in the current time period, y_t^s, is not influenced by the presence of error terms in the demand curve u_t.

The estimation of equations (8.59) and (8.60) separately as though they were single-equation specifications does not introduce any simultaneity bias into the regression estimates. Since the independent variables in each equation are uncorrelated with the error terms, the ordinary least squares estimates are the minimum variance unbiased estimates.

8.7 Indirect Least Squares

Since the direct least squares estimates are biased and inconsistent, an alternative estimation procedure has been developed, called *indirect least squares*. This procedure estimates the parameters indirectly by estimating the *reduced-form equations*, in which endogenous variables are expressed only as functions of the exogenous variables and of the error terms.

As stated before, the equilibrium values of y and p are given by the intersection of the supply and the demand curve. We have already expressed price as a function of the exogenous variables and of the error terms in equation (8.41). Since the amount sold is also determined by the same equilibrium mechanism (8.37), we can express y as a function of exogenous variables and error terms by substituting (8.36) (solved for p) into (8.41):

$$y = \frac{\beta(y - \delta z - v)}{\alpha} + \gamma x + u. \tag{8.62}$$

By rearrangement of terms, (8.62) becomes

$$y = \left(\frac{\alpha\gamma}{\alpha - \beta}\right)x - \left(\frac{\beta\delta}{\alpha - \beta}\right)z + \frac{\alpha u - \beta v}{\alpha - \beta}, \tag{8.63}$$

which may be rewritten as

$$y = \pi_{11}x + \pi_{12}z + \varepsilon_1, \tag{8.64}$$

where

$$\pi_{11} = \left(\frac{\alpha\gamma}{\alpha - \beta}\right), \tag{8.65}$$

$$\pi_{12} = \left(\frac{-\beta\delta}{\alpha - \beta}\right), \tag{8.66}$$

and

$$\varepsilon_1 = \frac{\alpha u - \beta v}{\alpha - \beta}. \tag{8.67}$$

Equation (8.63) is called the *reduced-form equation* of y. Notice that the endogenous variable p has been eliminated by substitution and that the endogenous variable y is now expressed completely as a function of the two exogenous variables, x and z, and of the error terms, u and v. Similarly, it is possible to obtain the reduced-forme quation corresponding to the endogenous variable p as

$$p = \frac{\gamma}{\alpha - \beta} x - \frac{\delta}{\alpha - \beta} z + \frac{u - v}{\alpha - \beta}, \tag{8.68}$$

which may also be written as

$$p = \pi_{21} x + \pi_{22} z + \varepsilon_2, \tag{8.69}$$

where

$$\pi_{21} = \left(\frac{\gamma}{\alpha - \beta}\right), \tag{8.70}$$

$$\pi_{22} = \left(\frac{-\delta}{\alpha - \beta}\right), \tag{8.71}$$

and

$$\varepsilon_2 = \frac{u - v}{\alpha - \beta}. \tag{8.72}$$

Hence, the two reduced-form equations corresponding to the model are

$$y = \pi_{11}x + \pi_{12}z + \varepsilon_1, \tag{8.64}$$

$$p = \pi_{21}x + \pi_{22}z + \varepsilon_2. \tag{8.69}$$

These equations do not include endogenous variables as independent variables, therefore ordinary least squares estimation of the reduced-form equations yields unbiased estimates of the parameters (π's) in (8.64) and (8.69).

But the researcher is not usually interested in the π's. He is interested in the original structural parameters of the model, (8.35) and (8.36). Since the π's are functions of these parameters, he can estimate them indirectly from the $\hat{\pi}$'s, which are the least squares estimates of the π's from the reduced-form equations. For example, the researcher may obtain an estimate of β as

this cAN't Be correct. BC. $E\left(\frac{1}{x}\right) \neq \frac{1}{E(x)}$

$$\tilde{\beta} = \hat{\pi}_{12}/\hat{\pi}_{22}, \tag{8.73}$$

where $\hat{\pi}_{12}$ and $\hat{\pi}_{22}$ are the ordinary least squares estimates from the reduced-form equations (8.64) and (8.69).

8.8 Bias of Indirect Least Squares Estimates

Even though $\hat{\pi}_{12}$ and $\hat{\pi}_{22}$ are unbiased estimates of π_{12} and π_{22} respectively, $\tilde{\beta}$ is not an unbiased estimate of β because

$$E(\tilde{\beta}) \neq E(\hat{\pi}_{12})/E(\hat{\pi}_{22}). \tag{8.74}$$

We may, however, evaluate the bias up to the order of (T^{-1}) under the assumption that the error terms, u and v, in the original model are normally and independently distributed.

To obtain the small sample bias and variance of the indirect least squares estimates we shall use the following property of the ratio of two normal variables.

Let a and b be two normal variables from a bivariate normal population with means μ_a and μ_b respectively. Let the correlation between the two variables be ρ and the variances of a and b be σ_a^2 and σ_b^2 respectively. The ratio of the two variables (a/b) has the following mean and variance up to the order of (T^{-1})

$$E(a/b) = (\mu_a/\mu_b)[1 + (\sigma_b/\mu_b)^2 - \rho(\sigma_a/\mu_a)(\sigma_b/\mu_b)] \tag{8.75}$$

$$V(a/b) = (\mu_a/\mu_b)^2[(\sigma_b/\mu_b)^2 - 2\rho(\sigma_b/\mu_b)(\sigma_a/\mu_a) + (\sigma_a/\mu_a)^2]. \tag{8.76}$$

These results, due to Merrill,[2] were obtained by using a binomial expansion which is valid only when

$$\left| \frac{b - \mu_b}{\mu_b} \right| < 1. \tag{8.77}$$

For these results to be applicable, the variable b should be within the limits

$$0 < |b| < |2\mu_b|. \tag{8.78}$$

In most applied econometric problems the researcher does not find error terms large enough to violate (8.77), although the probability of such an occurrence is, of course, not zero. Thus, by assuming that the variable b has a truncated distribution we can take advantage of the results expressed in (8.75) and (8.76). As the sample size increases, the variance of b decreases, reducing the probability of b violating the limits set by equation (8.77).

Since $\hat{\pi}_{12}$ and $\hat{\pi}_{22}$ are estimated by the least squares procedure

$$\hat{\pi}_{12} = \frac{\sum x^2 \sum zy - \sum xz \sum xy}{\sum x^2 \sum z^2 - \sum xz \sum xz}, \tag{8.79}$$

[2] A. S. Merrill, "Frequency Distribution of an Index When Both the Components Follow the Normal Law," *Biometrika*, Vol. XX^A, 1928, pp. 53–63.

then

$$\hat{\pi}_{12} = \pi_{12} + \frac{\sum x^2 \sum z\varepsilon_1 - \sum xz \sum x\varepsilon_1}{\sum x^2 \sum z^2 - \sum xz \sum xz}. \tag{8.80}$$

Hence,

$$E(\hat{\pi}_{12}) = \pi_{12} \tag{8.81}$$

and

$$V(\hat{\pi}_{12}) = \frac{\sigma_{\varepsilon_1}^2}{\sum z^2(1 - r_{xz}^2)} = \frac{\alpha^2 \sigma_u^2 + \beta^2 \sigma_v^2}{(\alpha - \beta)^2} \cdot \frac{1}{\sum z^2(1 - r_{xz}^2)}. \tag{8.82}$$

Similarly,

$$\hat{\pi}_{22} = \frac{\sum x^2 \sum zp - \sum xz \sum xp}{\sum x^2 \sum z^2 - \sum xz \sum xz} \tag{8.83}$$

and

$$E(\hat{\pi}_{22}) = \pi_{22}, \tag{8.84}$$

$$V(\hat{\pi}_{22}) = \frac{\sigma_{\varepsilon_2}^2}{\sum z^2(1 - r_{xz}^2)} = \frac{\sigma_u^2 + \sigma_v^2}{(\alpha - \beta)^2} \cdot \frac{1}{\sum z^2(1 - r_{xz}^2)}. \tag{8.85}$$

Since $\hat{\pi}_{12}$ and $\hat{\pi}_{22}$ depend on the error terms u and v,

$$COV(\hat{\pi}_{12}, \hat{\pi}_{22}) = \frac{COV(\varepsilon_1, \varepsilon_2)}{\sum z^2(1 - r_{xz}^2)} = \frac{\alpha \sigma_u^2 + \beta \sigma_v^2}{(\alpha - \beta)^2} \cdot \frac{1}{\sum z^2(1 - r_{xz}^2)}. \tag{8.86}$$

The correlation between $\hat{\pi}_{12}$ and $\hat{\pi}_{22}$ may be obtained from equations (8.82), (8.85), and (8.86) as

$$\text{CORR}(\hat{\pi}_{12}, \hat{\pi}_{22}) = \frac{\alpha\sigma_u^2 + \beta\sigma_v^2}{\sqrt{(\sigma_u^2 + \sigma_v^2)(\alpha^2\sigma_u^2 + \beta^2\sigma_v^2)}}. \tag{8.87}$$

Now we have all the terms needed to find the *approximate* mean and variance of the indirect least squares estimate $\tilde{\beta}$. Let us set $a = \hat{\pi}_{12}$ and $b = \hat{\pi}_{22}$:

$$E(a) = -\beta\delta/(\alpha - \beta) \tag{8.88}$$

with

$$V(a) = \frac{\alpha^2\sigma_u^2 + \beta^2\sigma_v^2}{(\alpha - \beta)^2} \cdot \frac{1}{\sum z^2(1 - r_{xz}^2)}. \tag{8.89}$$

Also

$$E(b) = -\delta/(\alpha - \beta), \tag{8.90}$$

with

$$V(b) = \frac{\sigma_u^2 + \sigma_v^2}{(\alpha - \beta)^2} \cdot \frac{1}{\sum z^2(1 - r_{xz}^2)}. \tag{8.91}$$

Further,

$$\text{CORR}(a, b) = \frac{\alpha\sigma_u^2 + \beta\sigma_v^2}{\sqrt{(\sigma_u^2 + \sigma_v^2)(\alpha^2\sigma_u^2 + \beta^2\sigma_v^2)}}. \tag{8.92}$$

For reasonably large sample sizes and $\delta \neq 0$ we may assume that $\hat{\pi}_{22}$ always lies within the required bounds as given by (8.78). By substituting equations

(8.88) to (8.92) in equation (8.75) and realizing that $E(a/b)$ is just $E(\tilde{\beta})$ from (8.73), we obtain

$$E(\tilde{\beta}) \simeq \beta + (\beta - \alpha)\frac{\sigma_u^2}{\delta^2 \cdot \sum z^2(1 - r_{xz}^2)}. \tag{8.93}$$

To allow comparison of this expression with the bias of the single-equation estimation (8.38), let us write $\sum z^2$ as $T\sigma_z^2$, which holds approximately for reasonably large samples. Hence

$$E(\tilde{\beta}) \simeq \beta + (\beta - \alpha)\frac{\sigma_u^2}{\delta^2 T\sigma_z^2(1 - r_{xz}^2)}. \tag{8.94}$$

The approximate biases in the estimates of β by the two alternative estimation procedures (namely, the direct least squares and the indirect least squares) are

$$\text{Bias } (\hat{\beta}) \simeq \frac{(\alpha - \beta)\sigma_u^2}{\sigma_u^2 + \sigma_v^2 + \delta^2\sigma_z^2(1 - r_{xz}^2)}, \tag{8.95}$$

$$\text{Bias } (\tilde{\beta}) \simeq (\beta - \alpha)\cdot\frac{\sigma_u^2}{T\delta^2\sigma_z^2(1 - r_{xz}^2)}. \tag{8.96}$$

Bias in the indirect least squares estimate depends inversely on the sample size, whereas this is not true in the case of direct least squares. The indirect least squares estimates are consistent; the bias approaches zero as the sample size approaches infinity. The direct least squares estimates are not consistent.

Consistency is a stronger restriction than mere asymptotic unbiasedness. It requires the asymptotic variance to be zero, which is true for this estimate. The direct least squares estimates are not consistent because they are not even asymptotically unbiased.

Comparison of (8.95) with (8.96) leads to the conclusion that the bias in direct and indirect least squares is of the opposite sign. Before studying the consequences of bias in the estimation of demand and supply curves, let us first list the bias in the estimates of α from the supply function (8.36) by means of direct and indirect least squares. The estimates of α are obtained by estimating the supply curve (8.36) in the case of direct least squares and from $\hat{\pi}_{11}$ and $\hat{\pi}_{21}$ in the case of indirect least squares.

$$\text{Bias } (\hat{\alpha}) \simeq (\beta - \alpha)\frac{\sigma_v^2}{\sigma_v^2 + \sigma_u^2 + \gamma^2\sigma_x^2(1 - r_{zx}^2)}, \tag{8.97}$$

$$\text{Bias } (\tilde{\alpha}) \simeq (\alpha - \beta)\frac{\sigma_v^2}{T\gamma^2\sigma_x^2(1 - r_{zx}^2)}. \tag{8.98}$$

The reason for the opposite signs in bias may be understood by recognizing that the indirect least squares is a ratio of two unbiased estimates. Consider a fixed value of $\hat{\pi}_{12}$ in estimating $\tilde{\beta}$. The estimate $\hat{\pi}_{22}$ is an unbiased estimate. This distribution is symmetric because we assume that u and v are normally distributed. Besides, $\hat{\pi}_{22}$ is a truncated normal distribution because $\hat{\pi}_{22}$ satisfies condition (8.78). Corresponding to an estimated value $\pi_{22} + \xi$, there is another value $\pi_{22} - \xi$ with equal probability. The $\tilde{\beta}^*$ computed from $\pi_{22} + \xi$ is $\tilde{\beta}^* = \hat{\pi}_{12}/(\pi_{22} + \xi)$ and $\tilde{\beta}^{**}$ computed from $\pi_{22} - \xi$ is $\tilde{\beta}^{**} = \hat{\pi}_{12}/(\pi_{22} - \xi)$. Since $\tilde{\beta}^*$ and $\tilde{\beta}^{**}$ have equal probability, the mean of $\tilde{\beta}^*$ and $\tilde{\beta}^{**}$ is $\tilde{\beta} = \hat{\pi}_{12}[\pi_{22}/(\pi_{22}^2 - \xi^2)]$. Hence, $\tilde{\beta} > \hat{\pi}_{12}/\pi_{22}$. Since this is true for each value of $\hat{\pi}_{12}$, and since $\hat{\pi}_{12}$ is an unbiased estimate of π_{12}, it readily follows that $E(\tilde{\beta}) > \pi_{12}/\pi_{22}$. Similar results follow for the estimate $\tilde{\alpha}$.

Since the indirect least squares estimate is a ratio of two unbiased estimates, its expected value tends to be larger *in magnitude* than the value of the parameter.

The researcher should not forget that bias refers to the mean value of a distribution and not to the individual estimates. The fact that the bias is opposite in sign as between direct and indirect least squares does not mean that when one estimate is lower than the true parameter the other estimate will necessarily be higher than the parameter value for any given sample. Even though the biases are of opposite sign, the estimated values from both procedures may be on the same side of the parameter value.

The consequences of bias in direct and indirect least squares may be illustrated by Figure 8.3. In this graph the continuous lines correspond to demand and supply curves for given values of the exogenous variables x and z. In the case of direct least squares (represented by $\hat{\ }$) estimation, the demand curve tends to move in the direction of the supply curve. In the indirect least squares case, however (represented by $\tilde{\ }$), they tend to move away from one another.

In small samples the bias in the indirect least squares can be substantial. When the variance of the exogenous variable z, $(\delta^2\sigma_z^2)$, is very small or the correlation between the two exogenous variables (r_{xz}) is close to unity, the bias can be very large even though the sample size T is large. When the error term v has relatively large variance even though $\delta^2\sigma_z^2$ is very small, the bias in direct least squares will be small.

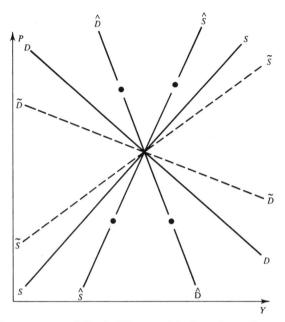

Figure 8.3. Consequence of Bias in Direct and Indirect Least Squares

As a practical matter, however, the researcher needs more information than the regression estimates from direct and indirect least squares to be able to decide which of the estimates has the smaller bias. When he can obtain a good guess about the relative variances of the error terms u and v, then he can perhaps choose the "better" estimate. In econometric studies usually the bias in the indirect least squares is small relative to that in the direct least squares, because variance of the identifying variable is usually larger than the variances of the error terms.

8.9 Variance of Indirect Least Squares Estimates

Using expression (8.76) we may derive the approximate variance of the indirect least squares estimate as

$$V(\tilde{\beta}) \simeq \beta^2 \frac{\sigma_u^2 + \sigma_v^2}{\delta^2 \sum z^2(1 - r_{xz}^2)} - 2 \cdot \frac{\alpha\sigma_u^2 + \beta\sigma_v^2}{\beta\delta^2 \sum z^2(1 - r_{xz}^2)} + \frac{\alpha^2\sigma_u^2 + \beta^2\sigma_v^2}{\beta^2\delta^2 \sum z^2(1 - r_{xz}^2)},$$

(8.99)

$$V(\tilde{\beta}) \simeq (\alpha - \beta)^2 \cdot \left[\frac{\sigma_u^2}{\delta^2 T\sigma_z^2(1 - r_{xz}^2)}\right].$$

(8.100)

The variance of this estimate $\tilde{\beta}$ depends on the sample size T, the variance of z, $(\delta^2\sigma_z^2)$, and the correlation between the two exogenous variables x and z, (r_{xz}).

The approximate variance of the direct least squares estimate $(\hat{\beta})$ is given by (8.58) which, for the sake of comparison, may be rewritten as

$$V(\hat{\beta}) \simeq (\alpha - \beta)^2 \cdot (1 - \lambda') \cdot \left[\frac{\sigma_u^2}{T\sigma_u^2 + T\sigma_v^2 + T\delta^2\sigma_z^2(1 - r_{xz}^2)} \right]. \quad (8.101)$$

Since λ' is a positive fraction and since variances of u and v are nonnegative, *the variance of $\hat{\beta}$ is smaller than the variance of the indirect least squares estimate $\tilde{\beta}$*. Of course this is an unfair comparison because as the sample size increases the bias in indirect least squares estimates approaches zero, whereas the bias of direct least squares does not. A comparison may be made by using the mean square error criterion (see p. 64). Since the square of bias of the indirect least squares estimate is of the order of $1/T^2$, let us ignore the bias in indirect least squares for this comparison. The (approximate) mean square errors of the two estimates are, therefore

$$\text{MSE}(\tilde{\beta}) \simeq (\alpha - \beta)^2 \cdot \frac{\sigma_u^2}{T\delta^2\sigma_z^2(1 - r_{xz}^2)}, \quad (8.102)$$

$$\text{MSE}(\hat{\beta}) \simeq (\alpha - \beta)^2 \left[(\lambda')^2 + \frac{\lambda'(1 - \lambda')}{T} \right]. \quad (8.103)$$

The choice of estimates now crucially depends on sample size. Even though direct least squares may show smaller mean square error in small samples, the indirect least squares estimate will have smaller mean square error provided the sample size is "sufficiently" large. In a given practical situation, however, the researcher cannot increase the sample size and has to settle for the better of the two estimates.

In addition to sample size, the variances of the errors (which are rarely known) will have a bearing on the choice between direct and indirect least squares. The researcher needs some external information on the relative magnitudes of the variances of error terms in making the choice. He has no way of inferring the appropriateness of the estimator from the computed values, since computed standard errors and regression coefficients do not necessarily reflect the true values of variances and parameters. *The researcher should resist the temptation to measure the precision of estimates from computed standard errors in making a choice between the two estimating methods.*

The comparison of direct and indirect least squares estimates is, of course, valid only when indirect least squares provide an estimate of the parameter. In some models this is not possible. Consider the case

$$y_t^d = \beta p_t + \gamma x_t + u_t,$$ (8.104)

$$y_t^s = \alpha p_t + v_t,$$ (8.105)

$$y_t^d = y_t^s.$$ (8.106)

The reduced-form equations of this model are

$$y = \frac{\alpha\gamma}{\alpha - \beta} x + \frac{\alpha u - \beta v}{\alpha - \beta},$$ (8.107)

$$p = \frac{\gamma}{\alpha - \beta} x + \frac{u - v}{\alpha - \beta}.$$ (8.108)

Estimation of the reduced-form equations (8.107) and (8.108) by ordinary least squares gives

$$\widehat{\left(\frac{\alpha\gamma}{\alpha - \beta}\right)} \quad \text{and} \quad \widehat{\left(\frac{\gamma}{\alpha - \beta}\right)}.$$

From these two estimates, the parameter β cannot be computed as was done in the previous exercise. That is, in a simultaneous-equations system it is possible that estimation by indirect least squares does not provide estimates of some parameters. When a parameter cannot be estimated by this method it is called an *underidentified parameter*. Note that this problem does not arise with direct least squares.

Sometimes the use of indirect least squares provides multiple estimates of the same parameter. In this case the researcher is in a dilemma as to which is appropriate. For an example of this, consider the following simultaneous-equations model:

$$y_t^d = \beta p_t + \gamma x_t + u_t,$$ (8.109)

$$y_t^s = \alpha p_t + \delta z_t + \theta w_t + v_t,$$ (8.110)

$$y_t^d = y_t^s.$$ (8.111)

The reduced-form equations corresponding to this model are

$$y = \frac{\alpha\gamma}{\alpha - \beta}\,x - \frac{\beta\delta}{\alpha - \beta}\,z - \frac{\beta\theta}{\alpha - \beta}\,w + \frac{\alpha u - \beta v}{\alpha - \beta}, \qquad (8.112)$$

$$p = \frac{\gamma}{\alpha - \beta}\,x - \frac{\delta}{\alpha - \beta}\,z - \frac{\theta}{\alpha - \beta}\,w + \frac{u - v}{\alpha - \beta}. \qquad (8.113)$$

When estimating the reduced-form equations by ordinary least squares the researcher can obtain two different estimates of β as

$$\tilde{\beta} = \left(\widehat{\frac{-\beta\delta}{\alpha - \beta}}\right) \Big/ \left(\widehat{\frac{-\delta}{\alpha - \beta}}\right) \qquad (8.114)$$

and

$$\tilde{\beta}' = \left(\widehat{\frac{-\beta\theta}{\alpha - \beta}}\right) \Big/ \left(\widehat{\frac{-\theta}{\alpha - \beta}}\right). \qquad (8.115)$$

When multiple estimates of a parameter are yielded by indirect least squares, the parameter is said to be *overidentified*. In a sense, this problem may be viewed as an attempt to extract too many parameters from the data. By somehow limiting the estimates it should be possible to avoid this situation, as in the use of Theil's two-stage estimation procedure.[3]

When indirect least squares provides a unique estimate of a parameter, the parameter is said to be *exactly identified*.

8.10 Two-Stage Least Squares

In estimating a single equation out of a simultaneous-equation model we obtain simultaneity bias because of correlation between the error term and the independent variables. If these independent variables can somehow be "purged" of error components, the least squares estimation of a single equation should provide "reasonable" estimates of the parameters. Since the reduced-form equations do not involve any endogenous variables as the

---

[3] H. Theil, *Economic Forecasts and Policy*, 2nd Revised Edition, North Holland Publishing Company (Amsterdam), 1965, p. 228 ff.

independent variables of a regression equation, it should be possible to estimate "purified" endogenous variables from the estimated reduced-form equations. That is exactly what two-stage least squares involves.

Let us consider the model

$$y_t^d = \beta p_t + \gamma x_t + u_t, \tag{8.116}$$

$$y_t^s = \alpha p_t + \delta z_t + v_t, \tag{8.117}$$

$$y_t^d = y_t^s, \tag{8.118}$$

with the reduced-form equations

$$y = \pi_{11} x + \pi_{12} z + \varepsilon_1, \tag{8.119}$$

$$p = \pi_{21} x + \pi_{22} z + \varepsilon_2, \tag{8.120}$$

where the π's and ε's are defined as before in (8.65), (8.66), (8.67), (8.70), (8.71), and (8.72).

These reduced-form equations may also be interpreted as follows: Each endogenous variable consists of two components, one due to exogenous variables and the other to error terms. For example, the reduced-form equation corresponding to p consists of $\pi_{21} x + \pi_{22} z$, which is due to exogenous variables, and of ε_2, which is due to error terms—namely, u and v. These two components are independent because (by assumption) the exogenous variables are independent of error terms u and v.

When the researcher knows the two parameters π_{21} and π_{22}, he can compute that part of p that depends only on the exogenous variables. Let this component be denoted as p^*, which is independent of error terms u and v.

When the researcher estimates a single equation of a simultaneous-equations model, some of the independent variables (endogenous variables of the model) are correlated with the error term. If he can purge that component of the endogenous variables which is correlated with the error terms, he makes it possible to use single-equation estimation procedures. Since p^* is nothing but p purged of the presence of error terms, the researcher may estimate the following equations by the least squares approach:

$$y_t^d = \beta p_t^* + \gamma x_t + u_t, \tag{8.121}$$

$$y_t^s = \alpha p_t^* + \delta z_t + v_t. \tag{8.122}$$

But the values of p^* cannot be obtained, because the parameters π_{21} and π_{22} are rarely known. In the absence of any information on these parameters, the researcher may use their ordinary least squares estimates instead. The purged values of p computed from the estimates of π_{21} and π_{22} are

$$\hat{p}_t = \hat{\pi}_{21} x_t + \hat{\pi}_{22} z_t. \qquad (8.123)$$

Instead of p^* the researcher may use $\hat{p}$ in estimating equations (8.121) and (8.122). The $\hat{p}$'s are also called the *predicted values* of p.

Estimation of the reduced-form equations is called the *first-stage estimation*. Having obtained the values of $\hat{p}$ from the first-stage, the researcher now can replace p^* in (8.121) and (8.122) by $\hat{p}$ and estimate the model by using single-equation estimation. This is called *second-stage estimation*.

Although estimation of (8.121) and (8.122) with p^* should yield unbiased estimates, the use of $\hat{p}$ does not yield unbiased estimates because $\hat{p}$ is based on estimates from the reduced-form equations.

When a parameter is exactly identified, the two-stage least squares and the indirect least squares procedures give identical estimates.[4] In this case the two methods have the same statistical properties. Hence, the two-stage least squares estimates are biased and consistent: the variance of the estimates is usually larger than in the use of direct least squares, but the mean square error will be smaller when the sample size is "sufficiently" large.

When a parameter is underidentified (see model (8.104) through (8.106)) two-stage least squares estimation fails; this is so because the variable $\hat{p}$ is then a linear combination of all the other independent variables in the regression by construction of the series on $\hat{p}$. When such a relationship exists, the regression cannot be estimated (see p. 49). When a parameter is underidentified, neither the indirect least squares nor the two-stage least squares approach can provide an estimate of it.

When a parameter is overidentified, the indirect least squares method provides multiple solutions to a parameter (see model (8.109)). But the two-stage least squares procedure provides a single estimate for such parameters because, through use of $\hat{p}$, it yields single values for the parameter of the estimated equation. Hence, whether the parameter is exactly identified or is overidentified, a single estimate can be obtained for it by way of two-stage least squares estimation.

When an overidentified parameter is estimated by two-stage least squares, the approximation for bias given in equation (8.96) does not hold, because in this case indirect least squares is not the same as two-stage least squares. The exact distribution of the two-stage estimate is similar to the distribution of direct least squares with different parameters.[5] *The bias in direct least*

---

[4] For an illustrative example of the equivalence, see J. Johnston, *Econometric Methods*, McGraw-Hill (New York), 1963, pp. 236–7.

[5] See T. Sawa, *op. cit.*

squares and in two-stage least squares is of the same sign when the estimate is overidentified. The bias in the two-stage estimate is usually smaller than in direct least squares, but the variance of the two-stage estimate is larger than that of direct least squares even in cases of overidentified parameters.

In comparison of two-stage least squares with direct least squares, all the properties discussed above hold whether a parameter is exactly identified or is overidentified, except for the sign of bias. In the case of overidentified parameters the bias is of the same sign in both cases, whereas in the case of exact identification they are of the opposite sign.

As a practical approach to the problem, however, the researcher may consider the choice of an estimation procedure as between direct least squares and two-stage least squares. If he applies two-stage least squares without questioning whether a parameter is identified, he will obtain all estimates of the equation if all the parameters are identified, and none of the estimates if one of the parameters is underidentified. Note that the criterion of identification is relevant only for the parameters of endogenous variables.

Direct least squares and two-stage least squares are studied under the assumption that error terms in the two equations are independently distributed. In some econometric models this may be a restrictive assumption. The three-stage least squares procedure developed by Zellner and Theil[6] incorporates information on the covariance of the equations' error terms into the estimation procedure. This is asymptotically more efficient than the direct and the two-stage least squares (TSLS) procedures. Unfortunately, little work has been directed toward the small-sample properties of this estimator. Typically, a researcher has a given sample size and wants to choose an estimator. The question of what determines the choice between two-stage and three-stage estimates in practical situations remains to be solved.

There are other estimation procedures which we have not discussed here, such as limited information single equation (LISE) estimation, ° full information maximum likelihood (FIML). Although the large-sampl. properties of these estimators have been extensively researched, little is known about their small-sample properties. Moreover, these estimators are extremely sensitive to sample size.

> ... FIML performs admirably under favorable conditions, but it loses ground when complications such as high interdependence of the jointly determined variables or structural misspecification arise. The steadiest method appears to be TSLS. LISE is so erratic in the presence of interdependence of the predetermined variables that its use seems risky.[7]

[6] A. Zellner and H. Theil, "Three-Stage Least Squares: Simultaneous Estimation of Simultaneous Relations," *Econometrika*, Vol. 30, 1962, 54–78.

[7] R. Summers, "A Capital Intensive Approach to the Small Sample Properties of Various Simultaneous Equation Estimators," *Econometrika*, Vol. 33, 1965, p. 32.

8.11   An Illustrative Example

Let us now turn to an application of the expressions for bias and variance as derived above. Consider the estimation of a Cobb-Douglas production function from data on man-hours (M) and capital (K). Let the production function be

$$Y = AM^{\beta}K^{\gamma}e^{u}, \tag{8.124}$$

where Y is the quantity of output produced.

The firm hires and fires labor (M) so as to maximize its profits, ψ:

$$\psi = P_y \cdot Y - P_m \cdot M, \tag{8.125}$$

where P_y, P_m, are the prices of output and of labor respectively. We assume for the sake of argument that the amount of capital is exogenously given to the firm.[8] The equilibrium quantity of labor required to maxmize profits of the firm is given by

$$\frac{\partial \psi}{\partial M} = P_y \cdot \beta \cdot \frac{Y}{M} - P_m = 0, \tag{8.126}$$

or the equilibrium quantity of M is

$$M^* = \beta \cdot \left(\frac{P_y}{P_m}\right) \cdot Y. \tag{8.127}$$

In the real world, however, the firm cannot instantaneously adjust to changing market conditions; hence, there may be some discrepancy between paid-for labor and desired labor. Let us assume that these errors (v) are

---

[8] A general case in which all the inputs are determined by the profit-maximization condition has been studied by I. Hock, "Simultaneous Equation Bias in the Context of a Cobb-Douglas Production Function," *Econometrika*, Vol. 26, Oct. 1958.

independent of errors in the production process and have a zero mean. The amount of M actually employed in the production process is given by

$$M = \beta\left(\frac{P_y}{P_m}\right) \cdot Y \cdot e^v. \tag{8.128}$$

The amount of Y produced and the amount of M employed in production are determined simultaneously by the production function and the profit-maximizing conditions. The model that determines the values of Y and M is

$$Y = A \cdot M^\beta K^\gamma e^u \tag{8.124}$$

and

$$M = \beta\left(\frac{P_y}{P_m}\right) Y e^v. \tag{8.128}$$

Logarithms of these equations allow the model to be written as

$$y = \beta m + \gamma k + u, \tag{8.129}$$

$$y = m + \pi - v, \tag{8.130}$$

where the small letters denote logarithms of the respective variables expressed as deviations from their means and π is the logarithm of the price of labor relative to the price of the product.

This model has two endogenous variables, y and m; two exogenous variables, k and π; and two error terms, u and v.

This model is similar to the one studied earlier, (8.35) through (8.37), except that in this model $\alpha = \delta = 1$. We may directly use the formulae for bias and variance by assigning the appropriate values for these parameters.

Suppose the researcher, unaware of the profit-maximizing condition in the model, estimates the production function by ordinary least squares. The

resulting estimates of β and γ are biased estimates of the respective parameters, and the approximate biases are (as in equations (8.95) and (8.54)):

$$\text{Bias } (\hat{\beta}) \simeq (1 - \beta)\lambda'', \tag{8.131}$$

$$\text{Bias } (\hat{\gamma}) \simeq -(\gamma - b_{k\pi})\lambda'', \tag{8.132}$$

where γ'' is

$$\lambda'' = \frac{\sigma_u^2}{\sigma_u^2 + \sigma_v^2 + \delta^2\sigma_\pi^2(1 - r_{k\pi}^2)}. \tag{8.133}$$

Since β and λ'' are positive fractions, the bias in estimate $\hat{\beta}$ is positive.
That is, the estimate $\hat{\beta}$ is biased toward 1. The bias in $\hat{\gamma}$ depends also on the
$b_{k\pi}$. We assume that k is exogenous. In a practical situation, the variables k
and π are very likely to be uncorrelated; therefore, treating the correlation
between k and π as zero, $b_{k\pi}$ is also zero. Since the parameter γ is a positive
fraction, the bias in $\hat{\gamma}$ is negative, and $\hat{\gamma}$ is biased toward zero.

Since we have ignored the information on the simultaneous nature of the
model, we have biased the estimate of the labor coefficient toward unity and
that of capital toward zero.

Suppose the researcher, interested in estimating economies of scale from
the Cobb-Douglass function, concludes that

$$\hat{\theta} = \hat{\beta} + \hat{\gamma}, \tag{8.134}$$

which is

$$\hat{\theta} = \beta + \gamma - \lambda'' (1 - \beta - \gamma). \tag{8.135}$$

When the true economies of scale ($\beta + \gamma$) are larger than 1, the estimate $\hat{\theta}$ is
negatively biased, and when they are smaller than 1, the estimate is positively
biased. That is, whether economies of scale are increasing or decreasing, least
squares estimation of this production function tends to bias their estimation
toward unity.[9]

---

[9] I. Hock, *op. cit.*

Now suppose the researcher has data on the relative price of labor with respect to the price of the product, and suppose he estimates the production function by using two-stage least squares. The approximate bias in the estimate $\tilde{\beta}$ is

$$\text{Bias } (\tilde{\beta}) \simeq (\beta - 1) \frac{\sigma_u^2}{T \cdot \sigma_\pi^2} \tag{8.136}$$

Since β is a positive fraction the bias in $\tilde{\beta}$ is negative; that is, the estimate $\tilde{\beta}$ is biased toward zero.

The approximate variances of the two estimates are

$$V(\hat{\beta}) \simeq \frac{(1 - \beta)^2}{T} \cdot \left(\frac{\sigma_u^2}{\sigma_u^2 + \sigma_v^2 + \sigma_\pi^2} \right) \left(\frac{\sigma_v^2 + \sigma_\pi^2}{\sigma_u^2 + \sigma_v^2 + \sigma_\pi^2} \right), \tag{8.137}$$

$$V(\tilde{\beta}) = \frac{(1 - \beta)^2}{T} \cdot \frac{\sigma_u^2}{\sigma_\pi^2}. \tag{8.138}$$

To discover the minimum sample size for which the mean square error of two-stage squares would be smaller than that of direct least squares, let us assume that the relative error in the profit-maximizing equation (v) is negligible, compared to error in production (u). The approximate mean square errors of the two estimates are then

$$\text{MSE}(\hat{\beta}) \simeq (1 - \beta)^2 \left(\frac{\sigma_u^2}{\sigma_u^2 + \sigma_\pi^2} \right)^2 + \frac{(1 - \beta)^2}{T} \left(\frac{\sigma_u^2}{\sigma_u^2 + \sigma_\pi^2} \right) \left(\frac{\sigma_\pi^2}{\sigma_u^2 + \sigma_\pi^2} \right), \tag{8.139}$$

$$\text{MSE}(\tilde{\beta}) \simeq V(\tilde{\beta}) \simeq \frac{(1 - \beta)^2}{T} \cdot \frac{\sigma_u^2}{\sigma_\pi^2}. \tag{8.140}$$

Let T^* be a sample size for which mean square errors of both the estimates are the same:

$$\frac{(1 - \beta)^2}{T^*} \cdot \frac{\sigma_u^2}{\sigma_\pi^2} = (1 - \beta)^2 \left(\frac{\sigma_u^2}{\sigma_u^2 + \sigma_\pi^2} \right)^2 + \frac{(1 - \beta)^2}{T^*} \left(\frac{\sigma_u^2}{\sigma_u^2 + \sigma_\pi^2} \right) \left(\frac{\sigma_\pi^2}{\sigma_u^2 + \sigma_\pi^2} \right). \tag{8.141}$$

Let $R = \sigma_u^2/\sigma_\pi^2$:

$$\frac{R}{T^*} = \left(\frac{R}{1+R}\right)^2 + \frac{R}{T^*(1+R)^2}.$$

(8.142)

By simplification:

$$T^* = R + 2.$$

(8.143)

When the sample size exceeds $(R + 2)$ the mean square error of two-stage least squares estimation of β will be smaller than that of the direct least squares estimation. R is an unknown quantity, but the researcher may have an idea of the variance of the errors of the production process (u) relative to the variance of the relative price of labor (π). By allowing for conservative margins on the variances of u and π, he may be able to choose the estimator.

When the logarithm of the relative price of labor has a very small variance relative to the variance of errors in the production process, as is typically the case in cross-section studies, the T^* will be extremely large. Unless the researcher has a minimum of T^* observations he will not gain in terms of mean square error by opting for the two-stage least squares procedure.

The value of R will typically differ for cross-sections and for time-series data. Hence, the simultaneity bias and variance for cross-section and for time-series estimates can be substantially different.

Certain procedures relevant to our discussions in this book are fully developed in textbooks devoted to econometric theory. To assist you in referring to those textbooks, we have provided here a list of those books that are often used in theoretical econometrics courses and a summary of the specific references we have made to them in this book.

Christ, Carl F., Econometric Models and Methods (*New York: John Wiley, 1966*).

Dhrymes, Phoebus J., Econometrics: Statistical Foundations and Applications (*New York: Harper & Row, Publishers, 1970*).

Kane, Edward J., Economic Statistics and Econometrics (*New York: Harper & Row, Publishers, 1968*).

Goldberger, Arthur S., Econometric Theory (*New York: John Wiley, 1964*).

Johnston, J., Econometric Methods (*New York: McGraw-Hill Book Co., 1963*).

Malinvaud, E., Statistical Methods of Econometrics (*Chicago: Rand, McNally & Co., 1966*).

Wonnacott, R. J., and T. H. Wonnacott, Econometrics (*New York: John Wiley, 1970*).

Chapter 1, page 8, footnote 1:
> *Christ, pp. 361–362*
> *Dhrymes, p. 146*
> *Goldberger, p. 158*
> *Kane, p. 221, pp. 254–254, pp. 258–262*
> *Johnston, p. 11, pp. 56–57, pp. 108–109*
> *Malinvaud, pp. 5–6*
> *Wonnacott and Wonnacott, p. 6ff, p. 57.*

Chapter 2, page 28, footnote 7:
> *Christ, p. 365ff.*
> *Goldberger, 163–164*
> *Malinvaud, p. 149ff.*
> *Wonnacott and Wonnacott, p. 49ff.*

Chapter 3, page 71, footnote 8:
> *Christ, p. 394–395*
> *Dhrymes, p. 150ff.*
> *Goldberger, p. 232ff.*
> *Johnston, p. 179ff.*
> *Wonnacott and Wonnacott, pp. 331–332*

Table 1

The Standardized Normal Distribution

$$Z = \frac{X - \mu}{\sigma}$$

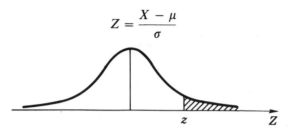

z	.00	.01	.02	.03	.04	.05	.06	.07	.08	.09
0.0	.5000	.4960	.4920	.4880	.4840	.4801	.4761	.4721	.4681	.4641
0.1	.4602	.4562	.4522	.4483	.4443	.4404	.4364	.4325	.4286	.4247
0.2	.4207	.4168	.4129	.4090	.4052	.4013	.3974	.3936	.3897	.3859
0.3	.3821	.3783	.3745	.3707	.3669	.3632	.3594	.3557	.3520	.3483
0.4	.3446	.3409	.3372	.3336	.3300	.3264	.3228	.3192	.3156	.3121
0.5	.3085	.3050	.3015	.2981	.2946	.2912	.2877	.2843	.2810	.2776
0.6	.2743	.2709	.2676	.2643	.2611	.2578	.2546	.2514	.2483	.2451
0.7	.2420	.2389	.2358	.2327	.2296	.2266	.2236	.2206	.2177	.2148
0.8	.2119	.2090	.2061	.2033	.2005	.1977	.1949	.1922	.1894	.1867
0.9	.1841	.1814	.1788	.1762	.1736	.1711	.1685	.1660	.1635	.1611
1.0	.1587	.1562	.1539	.1515	.1492	.1469	.1446	.1423	.1401	.1379
1.1	.1357	.1335	.1314	.1292	.1271	.1251	.1230	.1210	.1190	.1170
1.2	.1151	.1131	.1112	.1093	.1075	.1056	.1038	.1020	.1003	.0985
1.3	.0968	.0951	.0934	.0918	.0901	.0885	.0869	.0853	.0838	.0823
1.4	.0808	.0793	.0778	.0764	.0749	.0735	.0721	.0708	.0694	.0681
1.5	.0668	.0655	.0643	.0630	.0618	.0606	.0594	.0582	.0571	.0559
1.6	.0548	.0537	.0526	.0516	.0505	.0495	.0485	.0475	.0465	.0455
1.7	.0446	.0436	.0427	.0418	.0409	.0401	.0392	.0384	.0375	.0367
1.8	.0359	.0351	.0344	.0336	.0329	.0322	.0314	.0307	.0301	.0294
1.9	.0287	.0281	.0274	.0268	.0262	.0256	.0250	.0244	.0239	.0233
2.0	.0228	.0222	.0217	.0212	.0207	.0202	.0197	.0192	.0188	.0183
2.1	.0179	.0174	.0170	.0166	.0162	.0158	.0154	.0150	.0146	.0143
2.2	.0139	.0136	.0132	.0129	.0125	.0122	.0119	.0116	.0113	.0110
2.3	.0107	.0104	.0102	.0099	.0096	.0094	.0091	.0089	.0087	.0084
2.4	.0082	.0080	.0078	.0075	.0073	.0071	.0069	.0068	.0066	.0064
2.5	.0062	.0060	.0059	.0057	.0055	.0054	.0052	.0051	.0049	.0048
2.6	.0047	.0045	.0044	.0043	.0041	.0040	.0039	.0038	.0037	.0036
2.7	.0035	.0034	.0033	.0032	.0031	.0030	.0029	.0028	.0027	.0026
2.8	.0026	.0025	.0024	.0023	.0023	.0022	.0021	.0021	.0020	.0019
2.9	.0019	.0018	.0018	.0017	.0016	.0016	.0015	.0015	.0014	.0014
3.0	.0013	.0013	.0013	.0012	.0012	.0011	.0011	.0011	.0010	.0010

The table plots the cumulative probability $Z \geq z$.

Table 2

Student's t Distribution

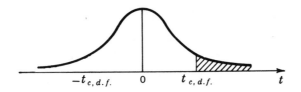

$$-t_{c,\,d.f.} \qquad 0 \qquad t_{c,\,d.f.} \qquad t$$

Degrees of Freedom	Probability of a Value Greater in Value than the Table Entry					
	0.005	0.01	0.025	0.05	0.1	0.15
1	63.657	31.821	12.706	6.314	3.078	1.963
2	9.925	6.965	4.303	2.920	1.886	1.386
3	5.841	4.541	3.182	2.353	1.638	1.250
4	4.604	3.747	2.776	2.132	1.533	1.190
5	4.032	3.365	2.571	2.015	1.476	1.156
6	3.707	3.143	2.447	1.943	1.440	1.134
7	3.499	2.998	2.365	1.895	1.415	1.119
8	3.355	2.896	2.306	1.860	1.397	1.108
9	3.250	2.821	2.262	1.833	1.383	1.100
10	3.169	2.764	2.228	1.812	1.372	1.093
11	3.106	2.718	2.201	1.796	1.363	1.088
12	3.055	2.681	2.179	1.782	1.356	1.083
13	3.012	2.650	2.160	1.771	1.350	1.079
14	2.977	2.624	2.145	1.761	1.345	1.076
15	2.947	2.602	2.131	1.753	1.341	1.074
16	2.921	2.583	2.120	1.746	1.337	1.071
17	2.898	2.567	2.110	1.740	1.333	1.069
18	2.878	2.552	2.101	1.734	1.330	1.067
19	2.861	2.539	2.093	1.729	1.328	1.066
20	2.845	2.528	2.086	1.725	1.325	1.064
21	2.831	2.518	2.080	1.721	1.323	1.063
22	2.819	2.508	2.074	1.717	1.321	1.061
23	2.807	2.500	2.069	1.714	1.319	1.060
24	2.797	2.492	2.064	1.711	1.318	1.059
25	2.787	2.485	2.060	1.708	1.316	1.058
26	2.779	2.479	2.056	1.706	1.315	1.058
27	2.771	2.473	2.052	1.703	1.314	1.057
28	2.763	2.467	2.048	1.701	1.313	1.056
29	2.756	2.462	2.045	1.699	1.311	1.055
30	2.750	2.457	2.042	1.697	1.310	1.055
∞	2.576	2.326	1.960	1.645	1.282	1.036

SOURCE: Reprinted from Table IV in Sir Ronald A. Fisher, *Statistical Methods for Research Workers*, 13th edition, Oliver & Boyd Ltd., Edinburgh, 1963, with the permission of the publisher and the late Sir Ronald Fisher's Literary Executor.

Table 3

Critical Values for the F Distribution

5% (Roman Type) and 1% (Bold Face Type) Points for the Distribution of F.

$$f(F; n_1, n_2)$$

$F_{0.05}$ $F_{0.01}$ F

n_1 degrees of freedom in the numerator

Each cell shows the 5% point (Roman) and the 1% point (bold).

n_2	1	2	3	4	5	6	7	8	9	10	11	12	14	16	20	24	30	40	50	75	100	200	500	∞
1	161 / **4,052**	200 / **4,999**	216 / **5,403**	225 / **5,625**	230 / **5,764**	234 / **5,859**	237 / **5,928**	239 / **5,981**	241 / **6,022**	242 / **6,056**	243 / **6,082**	244 / **6,106**	245 / **6,142**	246 / **6,169**	248 / **6,208**	249 / **6,234**	250 / **6,258**	251 / **6,286**	252 / **6,302**	253 / **6,323**	253 / **6,334**	254 / **6,352**	254 / **6,361**	254 / **6,366**
2	18.51 / **98.49**	19.00 / **99.00**	19.16 / **99.17**	19.25 / **99.25**	19.30 / **99.30**	19.33 / **99.33**	19.36 / **99.34**	19.37 / **99.36**	19.38 / **99.38**	19.39 / **99.40**	19.40 / **99.41**	19.41 / **99.42**	19.42 / **99.43**	19.43 / **99.44**	19.44 / **99.45**	19.45 / **99.46**	19.46 / **99.47**	19.47 / **99.48**	19.47 / **99.48**	19.48 / **99.49**	19.49 / **99.49**	19.49 / **99.49**	19.50 / **99.50**	19.50 / **99.50**
3	10.13 / **34.12**	9.55 / **30.82**	9.28 / **29.46**	9.12 / **28.71**	9.01 / **28.24**	8.94 / **27.91**	8.88 / **27.67**	8.84 / **27.49**	8.81 / **27.34**	8.78 / **27.23**	8.76 / **27.13**	8.74 / **27.05**	8.71 / **26.92**	8.69 / **26.83**	8.66 / **26.69**	8.64 / **26.60**	8.62 / **26.50**	8.60 / **26.41**	8.58 / **26.35**	8.57 / **26.27**	8.56 / **26.23**	8.54 / **26.18**	8.54 / **26.14**	8.53 / **26.12**
4	7.71 / **21.20**	6.94 / **18.00**	6.59 / **16.69**	6.39 / **15.98**	6.26 / **15.52**	6.16 / **15.21**	6.09 / **14.98**	6.04 / **14.80**	6.00 / **14.66**	5.96 / **14.54**	5.93 / **14.45**	5.91 / **14.37**	5.87 / **14.24**	5.84 / **14.15**	5.80 / **14.02**	5.77 / **13.93**	5.74 / **13.83**	5.71 / **13.74**	5.70 / **13.69**	5.68 / **13.61**	5.66 / **13.57**	5.65 / **13.52**	5.64 / **13.48**	5.63 / **13.46**
5	6.61 / **16.26**	5.79 / **13.27**	5.41 / **12.06**	5.19 / **11.39**	5.05 / **10.97**	4.95 / **10.67**	4.88 / **10.45**	4.82 / **10.27**	4.78 / **10.15**	4.74 / **10.05**	4.70 / **9.96**	4.68 / **9.89**	4.64 / **9.77**	4.60 / **9.68**	4.56 / **9.55**	4.53 / **9.47**	4.50 / **9.38**	4.46 / **9.29**	4.44 / **9.24**	4.42 / **9.17**	4.40 / **9.13**	4.38 / **9.07**	4.37 / **9.04**	4.36 / **9.02**
6	5.99 / **13.74**	5.14 / **10.92**	4.76 / **9.78**	4.53 / **9.15**	4.39 / **8.75**	4.28 / **8.47**	4.21 / **8.26**	4.15 / **8.10**	4.10 / **7.98**	4.06 / **7.87**	4.03 / **7.79**	4.00 / **7.72**	3.96 / **7.60**	3.92 / **7.52**	3.87 / **7.39**	3.84 / **7.31**	3.81 / **7.23**	3.77 / **7.14**	3.75 / **7.09**	3.72 / **7.02**	3.71 / **6.99**	3.69 / **6.94**	3.68 / **6.90**	3.67 / **6.88**
7	5.59 / **12.25**	4.74 / **9.55**	4.35 / **8.45**	4.12 / **7.85**	3.97 / **7.46**	3.87 / **7.19**	3.79 / **7.00**	3.73 / **6.84**	3.68 / **6.71**	3.63 / **6.62**	3.60 / **6.54**	3.57 / **6.47**	3.52 / **6.35**	3.49 / **6.27**	3.44 / **6.15**	3.41 / **6.07**	3.38 / **5.98**	3.34 / **5.90**	3.32 / **5.85**	3.29 / **5.78**	3.28 / **5.75**	3.25 / **5.70**	3.24 / **5.67**	3.23 / **5.65**
8	5.32 / **11.26**	4.46 / **8.65**	4.07 / **7.59**	3.84 / **7.01**	3.69 / **6.63**	3.58 / **6.37**	3.50 / **6.19**	3.44 / **6.03**	3.39 / **5.91**	3.34 / **5.82**	3.31 / **5.74**	3.28 / **5.67**	3.23 / **5.56**	3.20 / **5.48**	3.15 / **5.36**	3.12 / **5.28**	3.08 / **5.20**	3.05 / **5.11**	3.03 / **5.06**	3.00 / **5.00**	2.98 / **4.96**	2.96 / **4.91**	2.94 / **4.88**	2.93 / **4.86**
9	5.12 / **10.56**	4.26 / **8.02**	3.86 / **6.99**	3.63 / **6.42**	3.48 / **6.06**	3.37 / **5.80**	3.29 / **5.62**	3.23 / **5.47**	3.18 / **5.35**	3.13 / **5.26**	3.10 / **5.18**	3.07 / **5.11**	3.02 / **5.00**	2.98 / **4.92**	2.93 / **4.80**	2.90 / **4.73**	2.86 / **4.64**	2.82 / **4.56**	2.80 / **4.51**	2.77 / **4.45**	2.76 / **4.41**	2.73 / **4.36**	2.72 / **4.33**	2.71 / **4.31**
10	4.96 / **10.04**	4.10 / **7.56**	3.71 / **6.55**	3.48 / **5.99**	3.33 / **5.64**	3.22 / **5.39**	3.14 / **5.21**	3.07 / **5.06**	3.02 / **4.95**	2.97 / **4.85**	2.94 / **4.78**	2.91 / **4.71**	2.86 / **4.60**	2.82 / **4.52**	2.77 / **4.41**	2.74 / **4.33**	2.70 / **4.25**	2.67 / **4.17**	2.64 / **4.12**	2.61 / **4.05**	2.59 / **4.01**	2.56 / **3.96**	2.55 / **3.93**	2.54 / **3.91**
11	4.84 / **9.65**	3.98 / **7.20**	3.59 / **6.22**	3.36 / **5.67**	3.20 / **5.32**	3.09 / **5.07**	3.01 / **4.88**	2.95 / **4.74**	2.90 / **4.63**	2.86 / **4.54**	2.82 / **4.46**	2.79 / **4.40**	2.74 / **4.29**	2.70 / **4.21**	2.65 / **4.10**	2.61 / **4.02**	2.57 / **3.94**	2.53 / **3.86**	2.50 / **3.80**	2.47 / **3.74**	2.45 / **3.70**	2.42 / **3.66**	2.41 / **3.62**	2.40 / **3.60**
12	4.75 / **9.33**	3.88 / **6.93**	3.49 / **5.95**	3.26 / **5.41**	3.11 / **5.06**	3.00 / **4.82**	2.92 / **4.65**	2.85 / **4.50**	2.80 / **4.39**	2.76 / **4.30**	2.72 / **4.22**	2.69 / **4.16**	2.64 / **4.05**	2.60 / **3.98**	2.54 / **3.86**	2.50 / **3.78**	2.46 / **3.70**	2.42 / **3.61**	2.40 / **3.56**	2.36 / **3.49**	2.35 / **3.46**	2.32 / **3.41**	2.31 / **3.38**	2.30 / **3.36**
13	4.67 / **9.07**	3.80 / **6.70**	3.41 / **5.74**	3.18 / **5.20**	3.02 / **4.86**	2.92 / **4.62**	2.84 / **4.44**	2.77 / **4.30**	2.72 / **4.19**	2.67 / **4.10**	2.63 / **4.02**	2.60 / **3.96**	2.55 / **3.85**	2.51 / **3.78**	2.46 / **3.67**	2.42 / **3.59**	2.38 / **3.51**	2.34 / **3.42**	2.32 / **3.37**	2.28 / **3.30**	2.26 / **3.27**	2.24 / **3.21**	2.22 / **3.18**	2.21 / **3.16**

n_1, degrees of freedom (for greater mean square)

n_2	1	2	3	4	5	6	7	8	9	10	11	12	14	16	20	24	30	40	50	75	100	200	500	∞	n_2
14	4.60 / 8.86	3.74 / 6.51	3.34 / 5.56	3.11 / 5.03	2.96 / 4.69	2.85 / 4.46	2.77 / 4.28	2.70 / 4.14	2.65 / 4.03	2.60 / 3.94	2.56 / 3.86	2.53 / 3.80	2.48 / 3.70	2.44 / 3.62	2.39 / 3.51	2.35 / 3.43	2.31 / 3.34	2.27 / 3.26	2.24 / 3.21	2.21 / 3.14	2.19 / 3.11	2.16 / 3.06	2.14 / 3.02	2.13 / 3.00	14
15	4.54 / 8.68	3.68 / 6.36	3.29 / 5.42	3.06 / 4.89	2.90 / 4.56	2.79 / 4.32	2.70 / 4.14	2.64 / 4.00	2.59 / 3.89	2.55 / 3.80	2.51 / 3.73	2.48 / 3.67	2.43 / 3.56	2.39 / 3.48	2.33 / 3.36	2.29 / 3.29	2.25 / 3.20	2.21 / 3.12	2.18 / 3.07	2.15 / 3.00	2.12 / 2.97	2.10 / 2.92	2.08 / 2.89	2.07 / 2.87	15
16	4.49 / 8.53	3.63 / 6.23	3.24 / 5.29	3.01 / 4.77	2.85 / 4.44	2.74 / 4.20	2.66 / 4.03	2.59 / 3.89	2.54 / 3.78	2.49 / 3.69	2.45 / 3.61	2.42 / 3.55	2.37 / 3.45	2.33 / 3.37	2.28 / 3.25	2.24 / 3.18	2.20 / 3.10	2.16 / 3.01	2.13 / 2.96	2.09 / 2.89	2.07 / 2.86	2.04 / 2.80	2.02 / 2.77	2.01 / 2.75	16
17	4.45 / 8.40	3.59 / 6.11	3.20 / 5.18	2.96 / 4.67	2.81 / 4.34	2.70 / 4.10	2.62 / 3.93	2.55 / 3.79	2.50 / 3.68	2.45 / 3.59	2.41 / 3.52	2.38 / 3.45	2.33 / 3.35	2.29 / 3.27	2.23 / 3.16	2.19 / 3.08	2.15 / 3.00	2.11 / 2.92	2.08 / 2.86	2.04 / 2.79	2.02 / 2.76	1.99 / 2.70	1.97 / 2.67	1.96 / 2.65	17
18	4.41 / 8.28	3.55 / 6.01	3.16 / 5.09	2.93 / 4.58	2.77 / 4.25	2.66 / 4.01	2.58 / 3.85	2.51 / 3.71	2.46 / 3.60	2.41 / 3.51	2.37 / 3.44	2.34 / 3.37	2.29 / 3.27	2.25 / 3.19	2.19 / 3.07	2.15 / 3.00	2.11 / 2.91	2.07 / 2.83	2.04 / 2.78	2.00 / 2.71	1.98 / 2.68	1.95 / 2.62	1.93 / 2.59	1.92 / 2.57	18
19	4.38 / 8.18	3.52 / 5.93	3.13 / 5.01	2.90 / 4.50	2.74 / 4.17	2.63 / 3.94	2.55 / 3.77	2.48 / 3.63	2.43 / 3.52	2.38 / 3.43	2.34 / 3.36	2.31 / 3.30	2.26 / 3.19	2.21 / 3.12	2.15 / 3.00	2.11 / 2.92	2.07 / 2.84	2.02 / 2.76	2.00 / 2.70	1.96 / 2.63	1.94 / 2.60	1.91 / 2.54	1.90 / 2.51	1.88 / 2.49	19
20	4.35 / 8.10	3.49 / 5.85	3.10 / 4.94	2.87 / 4.43	2.71 / 4.10	2.60 / 3.87	2.52 / 3.71	2.45 / 3.56	2.40 / 3.45	2.35 / 3.37	2.31 / 3.30	2.28 / 3.23	2.23 / 3.13	2.18 / 3.05	2.12 / 2.94	2.08 / 2.86	2.04 / 2.77	1.99 / 2.69	1.96 / 2.63	1.92 / 2.56	1.90 / 2.53	1.87 / 2.47	1.85 / 2.44	1.84 / 2.42	20
21	4.32 / 8.02	3.47 / 5.78	3.07 / 4.87	2.84 / 4.37	2.68 / 4.04	2.57 / 3.81	2.49 / 3.65	2.42 / 3.51	2.37 / 3.40	2.32 / 3.31	2.28 / 3.24	2.25 / 3.17	2.20 / 3.07	2.15 / 2.99	2.09 / 2.88	2.05 / 2.80	2.00 / 2.72	1.96 / 2.63	1.93 / 2.58	1.89 / 2.51	1.87 / 2.47	1.84 / 2.42	1.82 / 2.38	1.81 / 2.36	21
22	4.30 / 7.94	3.44 / 5.72	3.05 / 4.82	2.82 / 4.31	2.66 / 3.99	2.55 / 3.76	2.47 / 3.59	2.40 / 3.45	2.35 / 3.35	2.30 / 3.26	2.26 / 3.18	2.23 / 3.12	2.18 / 3.02	2.13 / 2.94	2.07 / 2.83	2.03 / 2.75	1.98 / 2.67	1.93 / 2.58	1.91 / 2.53	1.87 / 2.46	1.84 / 2.42	1.81 / 2.37	1.80 / 2.33	1.78 / 2.31	22
23	4.28 / 7.88	3.42 / 5.66	3.03 / 4.76	2.80 / 4.26	2.64 / 3.94	2.53 / 3.71	2.45 / 3.54	2.38 / 3.41	2.32 / 3.30	2.28 / 3.21	2.24 / 3.14	2.20 / 3.07	2.14 / 2.97	2.10 / 2.89	2.04 / 2.78	2.00 / 2.70	1.96 / 2.62	1.91 / 2.53	1.88 / 2.48	1.84 / 2.41	1.82 / 2.37	1.79 / 2.32	1.77 / 2.28	1.76 / 2.26	23
24	4.26 / 7.82	3.40 / 5.61	3.01 / 4.72	2.78 / 4.22	2.62 / 3.90	2.51 / 3.67	2.43 / 3.50	2.36 / 3.36	2.30 / 3.25	2.26 / 3.17	2.22 / 3.09	2.18 / 3.03	2.13 / 2.93	2.09 / 2.85	2.02 / 2.74	1.98 / 2.66	1.94 / 2.58	1.89 / 2.49	1.86 / 2.44	1.82 / 2.36	1.80 / 2.33	1.76 / 2.27	1.74 / 2.23	1.73 / 2.21	24
25	4.24 / 7.77	3.38 / 5.57	2.99 / 4.68	2.76 / 4.18	2.60 / 3.86	2.49 / 3.63	2.41 / 3.46	2.34 / 3.32	2.28 / 3.21	2.24 / 3.13	2.20 / 3.05	2.16 / 2.99	2.11 / 2.89	2.06 / 2.81	2.00 / 2.70	1.96 / 2.62	1.92 / 2.54	1.87 / 2.45	1.84 / 2.40	1.80 / 2.32	1.77 / 2.29	1.74 / 2.23	1.72 / 2.19	1.71 / 2.17	25
26	4.22 / 7.72	3.37 / 5.53	2.98 / 4.64	2.74 / 4.14	2.59 / 3.82	2.47 / 3.59	2.39 / 3.42	2.32 / 3.29	2.27 / 3.17	2.22 / 3.09	2.18 / 3.02	2.15 / 2.96	2.10 / 2.86	2.05 / 2.77	1.99 / 2.66	1.95 / 2.58	1.90 / 2.50	1.85 / 2.41	1.82 / 2.36	1.78 / 2.28	1.76 / 2.25	1.72 / 2.19	1.70 / 2.15	1.69 / 2.13	26

n_1 degrees of freedom (for greater mean square)

n_2	1	2	3	4	5	6	7	8	9	10	11	12	14	16	20	24	30	40	50	75	100	200	500	∞	n_2
27	4.21 **7.68**	3.35 **5.49**	2.96 **4.60**	2.73 **4.11**	2.57 **3.79**	2.46 **3.56**	2.37 **3.39**	2.30 **3.26**	2.25 **3.14**	2.20 **3.06**	2.16 **2.98**	2.13 **2.93**	2.08 **2.83**	2.03 **2.74**	1.97 **2.63**	1.93 **2.55**	1.88 **2.47**	1.84 **2.38**	1.80 **2.33**	1.76 **2.25**	1.74 **2.21**	1.71 **2.16**	1.68 **2.12**	1.67 **2.10**	27
28	4.20 **7.64**	3.34 **5.45**	2.95 **4.57**	2.71 **4.07**	2.56 **3.76**	2.44 **3.53**	2.36 **3.36**	2.29 **3.23**	2.24 **3.11**	2.19 **3.03**	2.15 **2.95**	2.12 **2.90**	2.06 **2.80**	2.02 **2.71**	1.96 **2.60**	1.91 **2.52**	1.87 **2.44**	1.81 **2.35**	1.78 **2.30**	1.75 **2.22**	1.72 **2.18**	1.69 **2.13**	1.67 **2.09**	1.65 **2.06**	28
29	4.18 **7.60**	3.33 **5.42**	2.93 **4.54**	2.70 **4.04**	2.54 **3.73**	2.43 **3.50**	2.35 **3.33**	2.28 **3.20**	2.22 **3.08**	2.18 **3.00**	2.14 **2.92**	2.10 **2.87**	2.05 **2.77**	2.00 **2.68**	1.94 **2.57**	1.90 **2.49**	1.85 **2.41**	1.80 **2.32**	1.77 **2.27**	1.73 **2.19**	1.71 **2.15**	1.68 **2.10**	1.65 **2.06**	1.64 **2.03**	29
30	4.17 **7.56**	3.32 **5.39**	2.92 **4.51**	2.69 **4.02**	2.53 **3.70**	2.42 **3.47**	2.34 **3.30**	2.27 **3.17**	2.21 **3.06**	2.16 **2.98**	2.12 **2.90**	2.09 **2.84**	2.04 **2.74**	1.99 **2.66**	1.93 **2.55**	1.89 **2.47**	1.84 **2.38**	1.79 **2.29**	1.76 **2.24**	1.72 **2.16**	1.69 **2.13**	1.66 **2.07**	1.64 **2.03**	1.62 **2.01**	30
32	4.15 **7.50**	3.30 **5.34**	2.90 **4.46**	2.67 **3.97**	2.51 **3.66**	2.40 **3.42**	2.32 **3.25**	2.25 **3.12**	2.19 **3.01**	2.14 **2.94**	2.10 **2.86**	2.07 **2.80**	2.02 **2.70**	1.97 **2.62**	1.91 **2.51**	1.86 **2.42**	1.82 **2.34**	1.76 **2.25**	1.74 **2.20**	1.69 **2.12**	1.67 **2.08**	1.64 **2.02**	1.61 **1.98**	1.59 **1.96**	32
34	4.13 **7.44**	3.28 **5.29**	2.88 **4.42**	2.65 **3.93**	2.49 **3.61**	2.38 **3.38**	2.30 **3.21**	2.23 **3.08**	2.17 **2.97**	2.12 **2.89**	2.08 **2.82**	2.05 **2.76**	2.00 **2.66**	1.95 **2.58**	1.89 **2.47**	1.84 **2.38**	1.80 **2.30**	1.74 **2.21**	1.71 **2.15**	1.67 **2.08**	1.64 **2.04**	1.61 **1.98**	1.59 **1.94**	1.57 **1.91**	34
36	4.11 **7.39**	3.26 **5.25**	2.86 **4.38**	2.63 **3.89**	2.48 **3.58**	2.36 **3.35**	2.28 **3.18**	2.21 **3.04**	2.15 **2.94**	2.10 **2.86**	2.06 **2.78**	2.03 **2.72**	1.98 **2.62**	1.93 **2.54**	1.87 **2.43**	1.82 **2.35**	1.78 **2.26**	1.72 **2.17**	1.69 **2.12**	1.65 **2.04**	1.62 **2.00**	1.59 **1.94**	1.56 **1.90**	1.55 **1.87**	36
38	4.10 **7.35**	3.25 **5.21**	2.85 **4.34**	2.62 **3.86**	2.46 **3.54**	2.35 **3.32**	2.26 **3.15**	2.19 **3.02**	2.14 **2.91**	2.09 **2.82**	2.05 **2.75**	2.02 **2.69**	1.96 **2.59**	1.92 **2.51**	1.85 **2.40**	1.80 **2.32**	1.76 **2.22**	1.71 **2.14**	1.67 **2.08**	1.63 **2.00**	1.60 **1.97**	1.57 **1.90**	1.54 **1.86**	1.53 **1.84**	38
40	4.08 **7.31**	3.23 **5.18**	2.84 **4.31**	2.61 **3.83**	2.45 **3.51**	2.34 **3.29**	2.25 **3.12**	2.18 **2.99**	2.12 **2.88**	2.07 **2.80**	2.04 **2.73**	2.00 **2.66**	1.95 **2.56**	1.90 **2.49**	1.84 **2.37**	1.79 **2.29**	1.74 **2.20**	1.69 **2.11**	1.66 **2.05**	1.61 **1.97**	1.59 **1.94**	1.55 **1.88**	1.53 **1.84**	1.51 **1.81**	40
42	4.07 **7.27**	3.22 **5.15**	2.83 **4.29**	2.59 **3.80**	2.44 **3.49**	2.32 **3.26**	2.24 **3.10**	2.17 **2.96**	2.11 **2.86**	2.06 **2.77**	2.02 **2.70**	1.99 **2.64**	1.94 **2.54**	1.89 **2.46**	1.82 **2.35**	1.78 **2.26**	1.73 **2.17**	1.68 **2.08**	1.64 **2.02**	1.60 **1.94**	1.57 **1.91**	1.54 **1.85**	1.51 **1.80**	1.49 **1.78**	42
44	4.06 **7.24**	3.21 **5.12**	2.82 **4.26**	2.58 **3.78**	2.43 **3.46**	2.31 **3.24**	2.23 **3.07**	2.16 **2.94**	2.10 **2.84**	2.05 **2.75**	2.01 **2.68**	1.98 **2.62**	1.92 **2.52**	1.88 **2.44**	1.81 **2.32**	1.76 **2.24**	1.72 **2.15**	1.66 **2.06**	1.63 **2.00**	1.58 **1.92**	1.56 **1.88**	1.52 **1.82**	1.50 **1.78**	1.48 **1.75**	44
46	4.05 **7.21**	3.20 **5.10**	2.81 **4.24**	2.57 **3.76**	2.42 **3.44**	2.30 **3.22**	2.22 **3.05**	2.14 **2.92**	2.09 **2.82**	2.04 **2.73**	2.00 **2.66**	1.97 **2.60**	1.91 **2.50**	1.87 **2.42**	1.80 **2.30**	1.75 **2.22**	1.71 **2.13**	1.65 **2.04**	1.62 **1.98**	1.57 **1.90**	1.54 **1.86**	1.51 **1.80**	1.48 **1.76**	1.46 **1.72**	46
48	4.04 **7.19**	3.19 **5.08**	2.80 **4.22**	2.56 **3.74**	2.41 **3.42**	2.30 **3.20**	2.21 **3.04**	2.14 **2.90**	2.08 **2.80**	2.03 **2.71**	1.99 **2.64**	1.96 **2.58**	1.90 **2.48**	1.86 **2.40**	1.79 **2.28**	1.74 **2.20**	1.70 **2.11**	1.64 **2.02**	1.61 **1.96**	1.56 **1.88**	1.53 **1.84**	1.50 **1.78**	1.47 **1.73**	1.45 **1.70**	48

n_1 degrees of freedom (for greater mean square)

n_2	1	2	3	4	5	6	7	8	9	10	11	12	14	16	20	24	30	40	50	75	100	200	500	∞	n_2
50	4.03 / 7.17	3.18 / 5.06	2.79 / 4.20	2.56 / 3.72	2.40 / 3.41	2.29 / 3.18	2.20 / 3.02	2.13 / 2.88	2.07 / 2.78	2.02 / 2.70	1.98 / 2.62	1.95 / 2.56	1.90 / 2.46	1.85 / 2.39	1.78 / 2.26	1.74 / 2.18	1.69 / 2.10	1.63 / 2.00	1.60 / 1.94	1.55 / 1.86	1.52 / 1.82	1.48 / 1.76	1.46 / 1.71	1.44 / 1.68	50
55	4.02 / 7.12	3.17 / 5.01	2.78 / 4.16	2.54 / 3.68	2.38 / 3.37	2.27 / 3.15	2.18 / 2.98	2.11 / 2.85	2.05 / 2.75	2.00 / 2.66	1.97 / 2.59	1.93 / 2.53	1.88 / 2.43	1.83 / 2.35	1.76 / 2.23	1.72 / 2.15	1.67 / 2.06	1.61 / 1.96	1.58 / 1.90	1.52 / 1.82	1.50 / 1.78	1.46 / 1.71	1.43 / 1.66	1.41 / 1.64	55
60	4.00 / 7.08	3.15 / 4.98	2.76 / 4.13	2.52 / 3.65	2.37 / 3.34	2.25 / 3.12	2.17 / 2.95	2.10 / 2.82	2.04 / 2.72	1.99 / 2.63	1.95 / 2.56	1.92 / 2.50	1.86 / 2.40	1.81 / 2.32	1.75 / 2.20	1.70 / 2.12	1.65 / 2.03	1.59 / 1.93	1.56 / 1.87	1.50 / 1.79	1.48 / 1.74	1.44 / 1.68	1.41 / 1.63	1.39 / 1.60	60
65	3.99 / 7.04	3.14 / 4.95	2.75 / 4.10	2.51 / 3.62	2.36 / 3.31	2.24 / 3.09	2.15 / 2.93	2.08 / 2.79	2.02 / 2.70	1.98 / 2.61	1.94 / 2.54	1.90 / 2.47	1.85 / 2.37	1.80 / 2.30	1.73 / 2.18	1.68 / 2.09	1.63 / 2.00	1.57 / 1.90	1.54 / 1.84	1.49 / 1.76	1.46 / 1.71	1.42 / 1.64	1.39 / 1.60	1.37 / 1.56	65
70	3.98 / 7.01	3.13 / 4.92	2.74 / 4.08	2.50 / 3.60	2.35 / 3.29	2.23 / 3.07	2.14 / 2.91	2.07 / 2.77	2.01 / 2.67	1.97 / 2.59	1.93 / 2.51	1.89 / 2.45	1.84 / 2.35	1.79 / 2.28	1.72 / 2.15	1.67 / 2.07	1.62 / 1.98	1.56 / 1.88	1.53 / 1.82	1.47 / 1.74	1.45 / 1.69	1.40 / 1.62	1.37 / 1.56	1.35 / 1.53	70
80	3.96 / 6.96	3.11 / 4.88	2.72 / 4.04	2.48 / 3.56	2.33 / 3.25	2.21 / 3.04	2.12 / 2.87	2.05 / 2.74	1.99 / 2.64	1.95 / 2.55	1.91 / 2.48	1.88 / 2.41	1.82 / 2.32	1.77 / 2.24	1.70 / 2.11	1.65 / 2.03	1.60 / 1.94	1.54 / 1.84	1.51 / 1.78	1.45 / 1.70	1.42 / 1.65	1.38 / 1.57	1.35 / 1.52	1.32 / 1.49	80
100	3.94 / 6.90	3.09 / 4.82	2.70 / 3.98	2.46 / 3.51	2.30 / 3.20	2.19 / 2.99	2.10 / 2.82	2.03 / 2.69	1.97 / 2.59	1.92 / 2.51	1.88 / 2.43	1.85 / 2.36	1.79 / 2.26	1.75 / 2.19	1.68 / 2.06	1.63 / 1.98	1.57 / 1.89	1.51 / 1.79	1.48 / 1.73	1.42 / 1.64	1.39 / 1.59	1.34 / 1.51	1.30 / 1.46	1.28 / 1.43	100
125	3.92 / 6.84	3.07 / 4.78	2.68 / 3.94	2.44 / 3.47	2.29 / 3.17	2.17 / 2.95	2.08 / 2.79	2.01 / 2.65	1.95 / 2.56	1.90 / 2.47	1.86 / 2.40	1.83 / 2.33	1.77 / 2.23	1.72 / 2.15	1.65 / 2.03	1.60 / 1.94	1.55 / 1.85	1.49 / 1.75	1.45 / 1.68	1.39 / 1.59	1.36 / 1.54	1.31 / 1.46	1.27 / 1.40	1.25 / 1.37	125
150	3.91 / 6.81	3.06 / 4.75	2.67 / 3.91	2.43 / 3.44	2.27 / 3.14	2.16 / 2.92	2.07 / 2.76	2.00 / 2.62	1.94 / 2.53	1.89 / 2.44	1.85 / 2.37	1.82 / 2.30	1.76 / 2.20	1.71 / 2.12	1.64 / 2.00	1.59 / 1.91	1.54 / 1.83	1.47 / 1.72	1.44 / 1.66	1.37 / 1.56	1.34 / 1.51	1.29 / 1.43	1.25 / 1.37	1.22 / 1.33	150
200	3.89 / 6.76	3.04 / 4.71	2.65 / 3.88	2.41 / 3.41	2.26 / 3.11	2.14 / 2.90	2.05 / 2.73	1.98 / 2.60	1.92 / 2.50	1.87 / 2.41	1.83 / 2.34	1.80 / 2.28	1.74 / 2.17	1.69 / 2.09	1.62 / 1.97	1.57 / 1.88	1.52 / 1.79	1.45 / 1.69	1.42 / 1.62	1.35 / 1.53	1.32 / 1.48	1.26 / 1.39	1.22 / 1.33	1.19 / 1.28	200
400	3.86 / 6.70	3.02 / 4.66	2.62 / 3.83	2.39 / 3.36	2.23 / 3.06	2.12 / 2.85	2.03 / 2.69	1.96 / 2.55	1.90 / 2.46	1.85 / 2.37	1.81 / 2.29	1.78 / 2.23	1.72 / 2.12	1.67 / 2.04	1.60 / 1.92	1.54 / 1.84	1.49 / 1.74	1.42 / 1.64	1.38 / 1.57	1.32 / 1.47	1.28 / 1.42	1.22 / 1.32	1.16 / 1.24	1.13 / 1.19	400
1000	3.85 / 6.66	3.00 / 4.62	2.61 / 3.80	2.38 / 3.34	2.22 / 3.04	2.10 / 2.82	2.02 / 2.66	1.95 / 2.53	1.89 / 2.43	1.84 / 2.34	1.80 / 2.26	1.76 / 2.20	1.70 / 2.09	1.65 / 2.01	1.58 / 1.89	1.53 / 1.81	1.47 / 1.71	1.41 / 1.61	1.36 / 1.54	1.30 / 1.44	1.26 / 1.38	1.19 / 1.28	1.13 / 1.19	1.08 / 1.11	1000
∞	3.84 / 6.64	2.99 / 4.60	2.60 / 3.78	2.37 / 3.32	2.21 / 3.02	2.09 / 2.80	2.01 / 2.64	1.94 / 2.51	1.88 / 2.41	1.83 / 2.32	1.79 / 2.24	1.75 / 2.18	1.69 / 2.07	1.64 / 1.99	1.57 / 1.87	1.52 / 1.79	1.46 / 1.69	1.40 / 1.59	1.35 / 1.52	1.28 / 1.41	1.24 / 1.36	1.17 / 1.25	1.11 / 1.15	1.00 / 1.00	∞

SOURCE: George W. Snedecor, *Statistical Methods*, Ames, Iowa: The Iowa State University Press, 5th edition, 1956, pp. 246–249. Copyright © 1956 by the Iowa State University Press: reprinted by permission. The function $F = e$ with exponent $2z$, is computed in part from Fisher's table VI(7). Additional entries are by interpolation, mostly graphical.

Table 4

Critical Values for the Durbin-Watson Test
5 Percent Significance Points of d_l and d_u in Two-Tailed Tests

n	k' = 1		k' = 2		k' = 3		k' = 4		k' = 5	
	d_l	d_u	d_l	d_u	d_l	d_u	d_l	d_u	d_l	d_u
15	0.95	1.23	0.83	1.40	0.71	1.61	0.59	1.84	0.48	2.09
16	0.98	1.24	0.86	1.40	0.75	1.59	0.64	1.80	0.53	2.03
17	1.01	1.25	0.90	1.40	0.79	1.58	0.68	1.77	0.57	1.98
18	1.03	1.26	0.93	1.40	0.82	1.56	0.72	1.74	0.62	1.93
19	1.06	1.28	0.96	1.41	0.86	1.55	0.76	1.72	0.66	1.90
20	1.08	1.28	0.99	1.41	0.89	1.55	0.79	1.70	0.70	1.87
21	1.10	1.30	1.01	1.41	0.92	1.54	0.83	1.69	0.73	1.84
22	1.12	1.31	1.04	1.42	0.95	1.54	0.86	1.68	0.77	1.82
23	1.14	1.32	1.06	1.42	0.97	1.54	0.89	1.67	0.80	1.80
24	1.16	1.33	1.08	1.43	1.00	1.54	0.91	1.66	0.83	1.79
25	1.18	1.34	1.10	1.43	1.02	1.54	0.94	1.65	0.86	1.77
26	1.19	1.35	1.12	1.44	1.04	1.54	0.96	1.65	0.88	1.76
27	1.21	1.36	1.13	1.44	1.06	1.54	0.99	1.64	0.91	1.75
28	1.22	1.37	1.15	1.45	1.08	1.54	1.01	1.64	0.93	1.74
29	1.24	1.38	1.17	1.45	1.10	1.54	1.03	1.63	0.96	1.73
30	1.25	1.38	1.18	1.46	1.12	1.54	1.05	1.63	0.98	1.73
31	1.26	1.39	1.20	1.47	1.13	1.55	1.07	1.63	1.00	1.72
32	1.27	1.40	1.21	1.47	1.15	1.55	1.08	1.63	1.02	1.71
33	1.28	1.41	1.22	1.48	1.16	1.55	1.10	1.63	1.04	1.71
34	1.29	1.41	1.24	1.48	1.17	1.55	1.12	1.63	1.06	1.70
35	1.30	1.42	1.25	1.48	1.19	1.55	1.13	1.63	1.07	1.70
36	1.31	1.43	1.26	1.49	1.20	1.56	1.15	1.63	1.09	1.70
37	1.32	1.43	1.27	1.49	1.21	1.56	1.16	1.62	1.10	1.70
38	1.33	1.44	1.28	1.50	1.23	1.56	1.17	1.62	1.12	1.70
39	1.34	1.44	1.29	1.50	1.24	1.56	1.19	1.63	1.13	1.69
40	1.35	1.45	1.30	1.51	1.25	1.57	1.20	1.63	1.15	1.69
45	1.39	1.48	1.34	1.53	1.30	1.58	1.25	1.63	1.21	1.69
50	1.42	1.50	1.38	1.54	1.34	1.59	1.30	1.64	1.26	1.69
55	1.45	1.52	1.41	1.56	1.37	1.60	1.33	1.64	1.30	1.69
60	1.47	1.54	1.44	1.57	1.40	1.61	1.37	1.65	1.33	1.69
65	1.49	1.55	1.46	1.59	1.43	1.62	1.40	1.66	1.36	1.69
70	1.51	1.57	1.48	1.60	1.45	1.63	1.42	1.66	1.39	1.70
75	1.53	1.58	1.50	1.61	1.47	1.64	1.45	1.67	1.42	1.70
80	1.54	1.59	1.52	1.62	1.49	1.65	1.47	1.67	1.44	1.70
85	1.56	1.60	1.53	1.63	1.51	1.65	1.49	1.68	1.46	1.71
90	1.57	1.61	1.55	1.64	1.53	1.66	1.50	1.69	1.48	1.71
95	1.58	1.62	1.56	1.65	1.54	1.67	1.52	1.69	1.50	1.71
100	1.59	1.63	1.57	1.65	1.55	1.67	1.53	1.70	1.51	1.72

SOURCE: J. Durbin and G. S. Watson, "Testing for Serial Correlation in Least Squares Regression," *Biometrika*, vol. 38 (1951), pp. 159–177. Reprinted with the permission of the authors and the Trustees of Biometrika.

Table 5

Critical Values for the Chi-Square Distribution

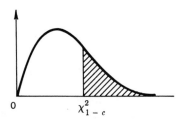

$$\chi^2_{1-c}$$

Degrees of Freedom	Significance Level					
	0.50	0.30	0.20	0.10	0.05	0.01
1	0.455	1.074	1.642	2.706	3.841	6.635
2	1.386	2.408	3.219	4.605	5.991	9.210
3	2.366	3.665	4.642	6.251	7.815	11.341
4	3.357	4.878	5.989	7.779	9.488	13.277
5	4.351	6.064	7.289	9.236	11.070	15.086
6	5.348	7.231	8.558	10.645	12.592	16.812
7	6.346	8.383	9.803	12.017	14.067	18.475
8	7.344	9.524	11.030	13.362	15.507	20.090
9	8.343	10.656	12.242	14.684	16.919	21.666
10	9.342	11.781	13.442	15.987	18.307	23.209
11	10.341	12.899	14.631	17.272	19.675	24.725
12	11.340	14.011	15.812	18.549	21.026	26.217
13	12.340	15.119	16.985	19.812	22.362	27.688
14	13.339	16.222	18.151	21.064	23.685	29.141
15	14.339	17.322	19.311	22.307	24.996	30.578
16	15.338	18.418	20.465	23.542	26.296	32.000
17	16.338	19.511	21.615	24.769	27.587	33.409
18	17.338	20.601	22.760	25.989	28.869	34.805
19	18.338	21.689	23.900	27.204	30.144	36.191
20	19.337	22.775	25.038	28.412	31.410	37.566
21	20.337	23.858	26.171	29.615	32.671	38.932
22	21.337	24.939	27.301	30.813	33.924	40.289
23	22.337	26.018	28.429	32.007	35.172	41.638
24	23.337	27.096	29.553	33.196	36.415	42.980
25	24.337	28.172	30.675	34.382	37.652	44.314
26	25.336	29.246	31.795	35.563	38.885	45.642
27	26.336	30.319	32.912	36.741	40.113	46.963
28	27.336	31.391	34.027	37.916	41.337	48.278
29	28.336	32.461	35.139	39.087	42.557	49.558
30	29.336	33.530	36.250	40.256	43.773	50.892

SOURCE: Reprinted from Table III in Sir Ronald A. Fisher, *Statistical Methods for Research Workers*, 13th edition, Oliver & Boyd Ltd., Edinburgh, 1963, with the permission of the publisher and the late Sir Ronald Fisher's Literary Executor.
For degrees of freedom greater than 30, the expression $\sqrt{2\chi^2} - \sqrt{2N' - 1}$ may be used as a standard normal variable, where N' is the number of degrees of freedom.

Table 6

Fisher's z Transformation
Values of r for Values of z

z	.00	.01	.02	.03	.04	.05	.06	.07	.08	.09
.0	.0000	.0100	.0200	.0300	.0400	.0500	.0599	.0699	.0798	.0898
.1	.0997	.1096	.1194	.1293	.1391	.1489	.1587	.1684	.1781	.1878
.2	.1974	.2070	.2165	.2260	.2355	.2449	.2543	.2636	.2729	.2821
.3	.2913	.3004	.3095	.3185	.3275	.3364	.3452	.3540	.3627	.3714
.4	.3800	.3885	.3969	.4053	.4136	.4219	.4301	.4382	.4462	.4542
.5	.4621	.4700	.4777	.4854	.4930	.5005	.5080	.5154	.5227	.5299
.6	.5370	.5441	.5511	.5581	.5649	.5717	.5784	.5850	.5915	.5980
.7	.6044	.6107	.6169	.6231	.6291	.6352	.6411	.6469	.6527	.6584
.8	.6640	.6696	.6751	.6805	.6858	.6911	.6963	.7014	.7064	.7114
.9	.7163	.7211	.7259	.7306	.7352	.7398	.7443	.7487	.7531	.7574
1.0	.7616	.7658	.7699	.7739	.7779	.7818	.7857	.7895	.7932	.7969
1.1	.8005	.8041	.8076	.8110	.8144	.8178	.8210	.8243	.8275	.8306
1.2	.8337	.8367	.8397	.8426	.8455	.8483	.8511	.8538	.8565	.8591
1.3	.8617	.8643	.8668	.8693	.8717	.8741	.8764	.8787	.8810	.8832
1.4	.8854	.8875	.8896	.8917	.8937	.8957	.8977	.8996	.9015	.9033
1.5	.9052	.9069	.9087	.9104	.9121	.9138	.9154	.9170	.9186	.9202
1.6	.9217	.9232	.9246	.9261	.9275	.9289	.9302	.9316	.9329	.9342
1.7	.9354	.9367	.9379	.9391	.9402	.9414	.9425	.9436	.9447	.9458
1.8	.9468	.9478	.9498	.9488	.9508	.9518	.9527	.9536	.9545	.9554
1.9	.9562	.9571	.9579	.9587	.9595	.9603	.9611	.9619	.9626	.9633
2.0	.9640	.9647	.9654	.9661	.9668	.9674	.9680	.9687	.9693	.9699
2.1	.9705	.9710	.9716	.9722	.9727	.9732	.9738	.9743	.9748	.9753
2.2	.9757	.9762	.9767	.9771	.9776	.9780	.9785	.9789	.9793	.9797
2.3	.9801	.9805	.9809	.9812	.9816	.9820	.9823	.9827	.9830	.9834
2.4	.9837	.9840	.9843	.9846	.9849	.9852	.9856	.9858	.9861	.9863
2.5	.9866	.9869	.9871	.9874	.9876	.9879	.9881	.9884	.9886	.9888
2.6	.9890	.9892	.9895	.9897	.9899	.9901	.9903	.9905	.9906	.9908
2.7	.9910	.9912	.9914	.9915	.9917	.9919	.9920	.9922	.9923	.9925
2.8	.9926	.9928	.9929	.9931	.9932	.9933	.9935	.9936	.9937	.9938
2.9	.9940	.9941	.9942	.9943	.9944	.9945	.9946	.9947	.9949	.9950
3.0	.9951									
4.0	.9993									
5.0	.9999									

SOURCE: Reprinted from Table V–B in Sir Ronald A. Fisher, *Statistical Methods for Research Workers*, 13th edition, Oliver & Boyd Ltd., Edinburgh, 1963, with the permission of the publisher and the late Sir Ronald Fisher's Literary Executor.

Index

Aitken's estimation of generalized least squares, 71
Alternative hypothesis, 128
Arrow, K. J., 182n
Association, hypothesis testing for, 152–156
Autocorrelation (*see* Serial correlation)

Best linear unbiased estimates, 28–29
Bias:
in direct least squares estimates, 187–192, 196–199, 214–215
example of, 32–34
of indirect least squares estimate, 203–209
in irrelevant variables, 35, 56–57
in left-out variables, 29
with proxy variables, 85–88
in regression estimates, 26–28, 53–80
simultaneity, 186

Bias (continued)
simultaneity in Cobb–Douglas production function, 216–220
in two-stage least squares, 215
Biased estimates:
of coefficient variance, 135–138
and hypothesis testing, 133–135
Box, G. E. P., 108n, 109n
Brown, Murray, 41n

Chaudhri, D. P., 154
Chenery, H. B., 182n
Chi-squared test, 155
Clustered residuals, 114–115
Constant term, 5–6
and errors in the variables, 182–183
Consumption function, 9–12, 14, 16, 184
Contamination of residuals, 112–126
Correlation coefficient, 156–158